McGRAW-HILL
INDUSTRIAL ORGANIZATION AND MANAGEMENT SERIES
L. C. MORROW, *Consulting Editor*

HUMAN BEHAVIOR IN INDUSTRY

McGRAW-HILL

INDUSTRIAL ORGANIZATION AND MANAGEMENT SERIES

L. C. MORROW, *Consulting Editor*

BETHEL, ATWATER, SMITH, AND STACKMAN—*Industrial Organization and Management*

BETHEL, ATWATER, SMITH, AND STACKMAN—*Essentials of Industrial Management*

CARROLL—*How to Chart Timestudy Data*

CARROLL—*How to Control Production Costs*

FEIGENBAUM—*Quality Control: Principles, Practice, and Administration*

FINLAY, SARTAIN, AND TATE—*Human Behavior in Industry*

GARDNER—*Profit Management and Control*

GRANT—*Statistical Quality Control*

HANNAFORD—*Conference Leadership in Business and Industry*

HEIDE—*Industrial Process Control by Statistical Methods*

HYDE—*Fundamentals of Successful Manufacturing*

IMMER—*Layout Planning Techniques*

JURAN—*Quality-control Handbook*

KALSEM—*Practical Supervision*

KIMBALL AND KIMBALL—*Principles of Industrial Organization*

LANDY—*Production Planning and Control*

LAWSHE—*Principles of Personnel Testing*

MAYNARD, STEGEMERTEN, AND SCHWAB—*Methods-Time Measurement*

MICHAEL—*Wage and Salary Fundamentals and Procedures*

NEUSCHEL—*Streamlining Business Procedures*

SMYTH AND MURPHY—*Job Evaluation and Employee Rating*

STANIAR—*Plant Engineering Handbook*

TOOTLE—*Employees Are People*

YOUNG—*Personnel Manual for Executives*

HUMAN BEHAVIOR IN INDUSTRY

William W. Finlay
Director, Business Institute
Antioch College, Yellow Springs, Ohio

A. Q. Sartain
Professor of Personnel Administration, and Psychology,
Southern Methodist University

Willis M. Tate
President of Southern Methodist University,
Formerly Assistant Professor of Sociology,
Southern Methodist University

1955

MCGRAW-HILL BOOK COMPANY, INC.

NEW YORK   TORONTO   LONDON

Library of Congress Catalog Card Number: 53-12428

IV

TO
Anita Schneider Finlay
Thelma Wylie Sartain
Joel Estes Tate

PREFACE

This book was written to assist men in industry—executives, supervisors, and foremen—in meeting and solving the personnel and human-relations problems which constantly confront them on the job. The responsibility for the development of the book belongs largely to industry, for it began as part of a growing recognition by industrial leaders for a sound approach to the problem of getting good personnel relations in industry.

The Texas Manufacturers Association recognized the need and sponsored the Institute of Management at Southern Methodist University. The Institute decided to try to do something for the firing-line executives of its industrial sponsors. It settled on a one-week course, "Human Relations for Foremen and Supervisors."

We three professors gave most of this course from the time it was started in June, 1948. During the 1952–1953 college year we took stock of what the Institute had been doing and of our own part in it. It appeared to us that our course on "Human Relations" had produced a book.

Industry is responsible for more than helping to get the course started. It has helped evolve the subjects discussed and much of their treatment by criticism and constructive suggestion from those attending and also from their bosses. It has endorsed what we have done—many times in oral or written statements, but more importantly by continuing to send its supervisory executives to take the course. There are now 1,500 alumni.

We didn't start with a lot of prepared material. Things just evolved as we went along. When the three of us compared notes, we found we were emphasizing the same principles and values, each one interpreting them in accordance with his own special field and his experience. Finlay is the engineer, Sartain the psychologist, Tate the sociologist.

So we developed our notes, which were the product of evolution, into lessons, or lectures, or parts of a course, and those parts became our book chapters. Brand marks of the three authors are on the chapters, if you can see them. Perhaps the reader can have some fun trying to decide who wrote which chapters. All three helped put the final touches to all chapters, and of course endorse everything that is said.

What has been so good for the foremen and supervisors of Southwest industry (they say it has and so do their bosses) should, it seemed to us, be equally good for the foremen and executives of industry anywhere and everywhere. Nor do we believe the value of the book should end there. We are dealing with the fundamentals, the principles, of human relations.

They are the same fundamentals, the same principles, that have to be used by management at all levels. We believe, and we have the temerity to state, that the book should be a worthwhile guide wherever management of people is practiced or studied. We have tried to make our book easy to read, and critics who ought to know tell us we have done so.

Wherever industrial people gather together to talk about their problems—be they personnel people, or production people, or sales people, or people with other kinds of responsibilities—they sooner or later (and more frequently sooner than later) get around to talking about their problems in human relations. The problems are universal, and wherever they occur they must be solved, if they are to be solved, by making use of the same fundamentals, the same principles. We hope our book can help in finding solutions.

We are indebted to many people, especially for the ideas we present. There has been little acknowledgment in the pages of the book, but we want the reader to know that we feel the indebtedness. Footnotes and acknowledgments are held to a minimum because most of the ideas, while not original, have been stated so many times, and held by us so long, that we do not know where we first learned of them. Also, we did not want to confuse the reader or send him on side excursions by the use of footnotes. What we wanted to say we said usually in the text. And we expect our readers to accept or reject what we have to say, not because

someone else—or many people—have already said it, but because
it fits the facts in the light of the reader's experience.

We owe an especial debt of gratitude to Prof. C. H. Shumaker,
Director of the Institute of Management of Southern Methodist
University, for his constant encouragement and the wise direction
he has given the Institute and the Human Relations course; and
to Mrs. Ruth Munnell, whose diligent and efficient work has made
possible the completion of the manuscript.

Our thanks and appreciation to Mrs. Caroline Warren for her
patience and invaluable help in the reading of proof and com-
piling the index.

WILLIAM W. FINLAY

A. Q. SARTAIN

WILLIS M. TATE

Note: At Southern Methodist University, Professor Finlay was Professor of Management Engineering. He left Southern Methodist at the end of the 1951–1952 college year to become Director of the Business Institute at Antioch College, Yellow
Springs, Ohio.

CONTENTS

Preface   vii

1. A Manager and His Problems   1
2. The Queer Things We Do   7
3. Some Basic Motives of Workers   20
4. Working with Others   33
5. The Mid-Century American Scene   45
6. The Changing Scene in Labor Relations   59
7. Human Relations and Organization   71
8. Authority, Responsibility, and People   81
9. Communication, a Major Function of Management   93
10. The Use and Misuse of Authority   105
11. Wages and Incentives   118
12. Dealing with the Union   130
13. Selection and Evaluation of Employees   146
14. Employee Counseling   163
15. Problems of Discipline   177
16. Making Work Attractive and Significant   192
17. Gaining the Interest and Cooperation of People   201
18. The Manager and the Public   213
19. Attitudes and Morale   223
20. Ten Years After   234

Index   243

CHAPTER 1

A MANAGER AND HIS PROBLEMS

"Thank God, that's another day!" muttered George to himself. George was tired. The noise of the plant had just died down, and the last men were leaving the factory.

George McGowan, the plant manager, was seated at his desk and was thinking of all the things that the day had brought. He felt a sense of relief that the pressure was off for another day. He was troubled and concerned but couldn't put his finger on the reason. He wasn't in the doghouse. As a matter of fact, he felt that he was doing a good job, and yet the many, many problems of his position crowded in on him. Incident after incident left him with a feeling that there was a great deal he didn't know and couldn't define, much less account for.

Most of these troublesome things had started about a month ago. It was four weeks ago today that the executive vice-president, who was also general manager of the company, had sent for George McGowan and told him that he wanted him to take over the new job of plant manager.

"George," said the vice-president, "we've been looking over our situation. We've decided it's about time we had somebody head up all the factory operations. Now, by that I mean all the production, all the inventories, planning, and maintenance. You know— the whole factory. I don't need to tell you that we've got a lot of new problems. We've got to expand our facilities. We've got these new products coming into the picture. And you know that the union brings on a lot of other problems that have to be taken care of. George, we think you're the man to handle the job."

In thinking back upon this interview, George realized that he hadn't been taken entirely by surprise. He knew he had been doing

1

a good job as a general foreman of one of the larger production departments. After all, he had put in fifteen years with the company, starting as an instrument man. He remembered well the first day he was a foreman. Man, that was a big day! Yes, when George looked back to that time, he felt that it was the biggest single step he had ever taken. Even now he remembered how scared he was. As he looked back on it, there wasn't much to have been scared about. Anyway, he had worked his way up through the various supervisory ranks, and while he was a little taken aback when he received this latest promotion, he had to admit to himself that he would have been disappointed if they had passed him by.

"Now I want you to report directly to me," said the vice-president, "and we'll get you fixed up with another office. And, George, I want you to know this: I am holding you responsible for all of our manufacturing operations. I'll send out a memo to everybody, telling them of your new authority."

George mumbled a few words of appreciation and started to leave. As he reached the door, the vice-president looked up from his desk and said, "Of course, George, there will be quite a difference in your pay envelope from now on."

George remembered that his feelings were somewhat mixed as he drove home that night. He felt proud, almost elated, that he had been chosen. There was the zest for a brand new job, with new responsibilities. But at the same time, there was a sort of fear, a kind of fluttering of butterflies in the stomach. It was a strange mixture of feelings.

When George arrived home and told his wife about the promotion, she, of course, was proud too. He remembered that she did ask if it meant an advance in salary. He had told her yes, and that they could get some of the things they'd been wanting a long time. But later on that night, after they had talked a long time about this new milestone in their lives, George remembered that there seemed to creep into their conversation a little worry about their old circle of friends, most of whom were fellow supervisors of George's down at the plant.

Quite a number of things since that time had reminded him of that particular fear. For example, just the first Tuesday evening after his promotion, when he went out to his regular poker game

His friends of lower rank

with the boys, there was naturally a lot of kidding. One of them said, "We'll have to watch our step from now on, boys. We're playing poker with the boss." And George wondered if there wasn't something more than just a joke, more than just a little kidding in that remark. And then recently, Mary, his wife, had told him that she felt she was not quite so welcome among some of the old groups, particularly some of her closer women friends.

About three weeks ago, at a meeting with the production group, Joe Reynolds, the production-planning supervisor, had come out with a remark something like this: "Well, now you're the boss around here, George, maybe some of us fellows can get a little authority to do our jobs." George recalled that he passed this off with a pleasant word or two, but the incident had come back to his mind several times, and particularly when he happened to be down in Department D a few days later and the foreman down there said with some heat:

"If those smart guys up in the office would keep their noses out of other people's business, maybe we could get some production out of this place that would really mean something."

George was feeling more uncomfortable as he thought of his problems. Right now he had the difficult job of promoting a man to foreman down in Department F. There were one or two likely candidates, but it was a big move, an important step, and a lot depended on it. George wondered just how he'd come up with an answer to that one. And thinking about the business of promotion turned his thoughts to the selection of people for special jobs. How do you pick people for jobs? You watch a man for a time; he seems all right. Then you put him in the job, and he just blows up or falls flat. Something seems to go wrong some place. George heaved a big sigh . . . just another one of those things!

He squirmed in his chair when his rather disturbed thoughts brought back to his mind the incident of a few mornings ago. Mike, the chief steward, stamped into his office claiming, "It's about time the foremen around here learned to respect the contract!" When George had calmed Mike down a little bit, it appeared that Sam Lewis, who was foreman down in Department H, had shifted a man from his regular job to work for a few hours on a job that was in a higher classification. And not only had Sam failed to arrange for the man to get the higher pay rate, but he just plain ignored the seniority rule. George got Mike out of the office by promising to do something about it and then called Sam on the telephone. Sam didn't answer the phone, so George went down to the department, right out on to the floor, and told Sam he'd better move the man back to his own job and watch his step in the future, before he got them all in trouble.

Now George wasn't sure he'd handled that just as he should have. He had a feeling that he was wrong, but he couldn't say why. He argued with himself: "You've just got to use your authority sometimes, if you're going to get anything done, and what's more, you can't pussyfoot around when you're faced with an emergency." Why had Sam done a thing like that? After all, he should know better. In fact, George remembered, Sam is a pretty good man, a good foreman. And George himself had written a memorandum of instruction on this point. He had explained just what to do under the contract in the matter of seniority and in the case of a temporary removal into a job of a different classification, and here—well, maybe Sam hadn't read it, or maybe he hadn't understood it. Now there's a thought! Perhaps he hadn't understood it.

As these and other incidents chased each other through George McGowan's mind, he found himself beset with some more very uncomfortable thoughts. Why had Mr. Frazer, the vice-president, his boss, passed George in the hall that morning without saying his usual "Hello"? "Perhaps he thinks I am not working out too well—maybe that's the reason they haven't put my name on the office door as they did with the sales manager and other executives. Why haven't they given me the conference room I asked for, so I can meet with my supervisors? Are they stalling?

"Maybe he's sore because I turned down that invitation to serve on the Chamber of Commerce industrial committee. I don't know why I'm expected to do those things. I've plenty to keep me busy here, and then some. Why doesn't the Public Relations Department handle it? It's their job. And yet, maybe . . . ?" George heaved a deep and troubled sigh.

And there are a lot of other things that have disturbed him lately, things that never occurred to him before. For example, why wasn't the bonus plan for the production group working out as well as they thought it would? He always thought it worked all right, but he had been looking over figures recently and realized that costs have gone up and that there is constant bickering about standards and allowances. And now George sometimes feels that the foremen are siding with the men and not with the management.

Then there is this problem of housekeeping. Ever since he brought the floor sweepers and machine cleaners under the maintenance department "to reduce cost and improve efficiency," there seems to be nothing but excuses whenever he points out to a foreman any untidiness and lack of good housekeeping. What he usually gets is, "Well, I can't order the sweeper around—he doesn't work for me. I can only *ask* him to do it."

George wonders, "Why can't people cooperate? That's all it needs—just some cooperation!"

After all, how *do* you catch the interest of people? How do you get them to do things? You pay them more money, and that seems all right at the time. But somehow, it just doesn't always work. Take that case he had recently. He remembered it very clearly because it upset him at the time. There was a man working out in the yard gang, and the foreman recommended him for a promotion—wanted to put him in the shop on a better paying job. So they moved him out of the old gang into the shop. Everything seemed to be all right. But no more than a week had passed when it was reported to George: "That fellow doesn't get on around here. He can't get along with people. I don't know what he wants. He's got a better job and yet he's disgruntled."

George ponders, "What does it take? What's wrong with people? Give them an opportunity, and it doesn't seem to satisfy them. Pay them more money, and that doesn't seem to satisfy them either. People are queer. Or am I queer? Maybe I'm the one that's wrong.

"Anyway, how times have changed! The old world has speeded up. I remember when I started, I did as I was told, and was plenty glad to get the job. In those days it didn't matter whether workers liked the company or not. In fact, it didn't matter whether anyone liked the company or not."

It was strange, George thought, the things that come to your mind when you get into a brown study like this. For example, there is the stenographer who has been doing quite a lot of work for George recently. He noticed that she seemed to be very keen and enthusiastic at the beginning but something's gone wrong. Being a man, George feels that "Oh, maybe she wouldn't want to talk to me." He knows that somebody ought to talk to her, or perhaps she should be able to go to somebody that she could talk to. Yet they don't have any setup that he knows of to take care of it. Maybe it doesn't mean anything anyway.

"Oh well, perhaps I'm worrying about something that doesn't make any difference, but on the other hand some of these 'little' things can become mighty important and upsetting."

Only today, Jack, one of the men from the shop, came into George's office and said he was going to quit. When George asked him what was wrong, Jack told him he wasn't "getting anywhere around here." He had been around for twelve years, and he couldn't "see any future in the place." Jack did promise to think things over, but George is afraid he is going to quit. Yet he is a good man, a skilled craftsman, and has a lot of ability.

"I wonder why he has such an attitude toward the company and toward his job. Why does he want to quit?"

George wonders about a lot of things. Perhaps the brightest part of the whole thing is that George McGowan is at least trying to think about it.

.   .   .   .

In the chapters that follow, it is hoped that most of the reasons for George's problems and many of the signposts toward their solution will be found. Most of our industrial problems are in our dealings with people—as individuals, as groups, as managers, as workers. No one can solve these problems for us, but perhaps this book will help in developing a better knowledge of people and provide a basis for *thinking* as the essential to the most effective way of arriving at the answers to problems.

CHAPTER 2

THE QUEER THINGS WE DO

> *"What's wrong with people? Give them an opportunity, and it doesn't seem to satisfy them. Pay them more money, and that doesn't seem to satisfy them either. People are queer."*

What causes George McGowan and all the rest of us to wonder are the silly, or even foolish things we see people do. Sometimes they drink to excess or fail to work hard when they'd profit a lot by doing it. Sometimes they vote for candidates who promise them the world with a fence around it, when anyone who stops to think knows the promises are absurd. Often they work their hearts out for things that don't really make any difference, but pass by important things without notice. We have all been reminded of what the old Quaker said to his wife: "Everyone is queer but me and thee, and even thou are a bit queer at times."

The truth is that these queer things that people do are more important to us than we ordinarily think. This is especially true if we have responsibility for supervising them in some way. No leader of a work group—executive or supervisor—can afford to pass them by as of no consequence. Let's look a little more closely at some of them.

THE THINGS THAT ARE OURS HAVE SPECIAL ATTRACTION

One of the best examples of this sort of thing is the way we all respond to things that are *ours*. Here we are referring not necessarily to the things we own, but to the things that we have made a part of ourselves—*our* children, *our* church, *our* union, *our* company, *our* city, *our* baseball team, and the like. The truth is that the things that are *ours* have a special attraction.

Let's take *our* city, for example. What really is the finest city in the United States? Why, *our* city, of course! We find it hard to believe that other people don't agree with us. And isn't it silly that people in an adjoining, rival city actually seem to believe that *their* city really is the finest. This makes us think of a member of that very modest "race" of people, the Texan, who said to his son, "Son, don't ever ask a man where he was born. If he's from Texas, he'll tell you, and if he's not, you don't want to embarrass him!"

Here's another illustration of the same point: Sometimes I go out to the ball park to see *my* team play a double-header with the league leaders. Isn't it amazing how many mistakes the umpires make in such games? Here's one of our players trying to beat out an infield roller, and he's safe by at least a step or two, but the umpire calls him out! And here's one of the rival batsmen who gets to first base a full second or two *after* the ball gets there and that umpire calls him safe. We know umpires are going to make mistakes because they are only human. But it's hard to understand why they make nearly all of their mistakes in favor of the rival team.

Or suppose the company has a special message to get across to its employees. Let's say it's something obviously good and really important, like some of the facts about how the American business system operates. We often call this "basic economics." Sometimes the company spends a lot of good money and effort in trying to get the message across. They get visual aids, they arrange for fine conference leaders, they get a comfortable conference room, and then hold the sessions on company time. Later, they may learn to their amazement that the workers resented the whole thing and that they show no evidence at all of profiting from the sessions. After all, it wasn't *their* program.

And our children furnish us with another example. We have all known parents who spend nearly all their spare time telling people how cute their kids are. Deep down inside, we know they think their kids are smarter than any others, cuter than any others, and the best looking kids in the world. We've been bored by these people, and probably made up our minds before our children were born that we weren't going to bore our friends the same way after ours came along. But after they've arrived, we can't help it if we happened to be favored by nature. We started out to be unprej-udiced about the whole thing, but if they really are smarter and cuter and better looking, we have to admit it!

Now it is very easy at this point to make a fatal mistake, the mis-take of thinking this applies only to the other person—to women or union members or Democrats or Yankees, for example. The truth is that it applies to all of us, regardless of rank, sex, age, I.Q., education, or anything else. The educated and the uneducated alike feel that "the things that are *ours* have a special attraction."

Here is a point that should be stressed. It is very easy to get the impression that it's the other fellow who does this "emotional" type of thinking, and that we are free of it or almost so. It is espe-cially easy to accuse people we disagree with of this sort of think-ing. Thus, we say that "country people are easily led," or that "union members are easily led," that they act from "feeling" or "prejudice" or "ignorance." But if we live in the country, we're inclined to think that it's the "city slickers" who really don't know much, or if we belong to a labor union we think it's the manage-ment representative who really doesn't use his head.

Now, in truth we're all right to a degree and all wrong to a degree. One point must be stressed: We are all strongly inclined to come to the conclusions that we really *want* to come to. We can spend a lifetime trying to be more objective, to decide on the basis of the facts—and we can improve. But none of us ever gets to be perfect—or close to perfect.

So if you want to understand what another person does, you have to understand how he *feels*. It's important, of course, also to know how and what he thinks. But if you *really* want to understand him and deal with him effectively, you have to know his feelings and emotions and attitudes and beliefs and values. And you must always keep these in mind as you try to lead him.

THE EFFECTIVENESS OF EMOTIONAL APPEALS

But let's look at some other instances of the influence of desire on reasoning and action. There are many of them.

Advertising is a case in point. We'll buy a toothpaste because it contains *irium* or a cigarette because it contains *apple-honey*, in spite of the fact that we haven't the remotest idea what either of these ingredients really is. Anybody who believes he is thoroughly rational and influenced only by facts is in for a rude shock if he ever studies his buying habits carefully. If he does make such a study, he will find that advertisers have been more clever—and more effective—than he has given them credit for being.

Politics makes another good example. Almost every candidate comes out foursquare for "Mother, Home, and Country," and also remembers to praise very highly the city or state in which he is speaking and the group that most of his listeners belong to. Besides, he doesn't always neglect the "scare" appeal. If he can find something that nearly everybody is against, and then be one hundred per cent against it, he often gets more votes. Wasn't it "Big Bill" Thompson who ran for mayor of Chicago, in the 1920s, on the platform that he was absolutely against any interference in the internal affairs of the city of Chicago by King George of England? That must have put Mr. Thompson's opponents on the spot, for the best they could say was, "Me too!"

Perhaps the best proof of how effective such appeals can be was given us by Adolf Hitler. Let's look at what he did.

In the first place, he told the German people that they were the finest people on the face of the earth, indeed that they were supermen, destined to think for and rule over inferior peoples. Do you remember how we resented it when we heard what Hitler was saying? Why did we resent it so? That's easy, of course. Who *really* are the finest people on earth? Obviously, *we* are. And we don't want anybody else getting any mistaken ideas about how good *they* are.

Hitler did a second thing: He told the Germans that the extremely bad plight in which they found themselves was not their fault, but the fault of the Jews. Now the charges against the Jews were false—in fact, obviously false. But Hitler furnished the Germans with a scapegoat, and a frustrated person who doesn't know how to get out of his difficulties needs a scapegoat. At least he feels a lot better after he has "taken it out" on one. And we must not ever suppose that only the Germans have had scapegoats. All of us—Gentile or Jew, white or black, old or young—look for scapegoats, especially when we are frustrated for a long time and don't see any way out.

Of course Hitler did something else: He called the German people to a life of service and sacrifice. He said in effect: "The way I'm asking you to go is a hard way. You'll get guns instead of butter. It may cost you your life. But," he shouted, "the Fatherland is greater than any German!" And, as we know now, people followed him by the millions.

And so again we have been saying: Don't make the mistake of thinking that you understand people when you know *how* they reason. *Why* they reason as they do is as important as how, and the *why* very often involves the attitudes and sentiments and desires and values we spoke of earlier.

Maybe we ought to bring this down a little closer to the everyday work situation. There, as elsewhere, you have to understand what people say by knowing what their desires and needs are. Here's an employee who is unhappy because he has been passed by for promotion. Maybe he lacks seniority and experience, and besides he isn't very alert. But that may not keep him from saying a lot of unkind things about the management that failed to promote him, even though everybody else knows that it would have been a serious mistake to move him up.

And then there's the grapevine. Isn't it amazing what wild and unfounded rumors get started and spread through it? Sometimes, of course, the rumors are true, but often they aren't. There are stories about a reduction in work force or a general pay increase or a change in the daily starting hour—all without the least basis in fact. Some of these stories arise through simple misunderstanding of something that is said or done, but some of them come largely from the needs or fears of employees.

Another example is the ease with which people who don't like the company sell the workers a completely incorrect account of what management has done and is doing and why it is done. Management may be accused of planning to cut wages or discriminate against union workers or lay off a work crew when there is no truth in the charges. But in spite of that, a lot of employees may "fall for" the stories and do some unwise and unfair things as a result.

Finally, there's the situation in which the union and management find themselves in disagreement and even bitter controversy.

In such a situation, one party or the other is often seriously at fault. The tragedy is that sometimes neither is acting in bad faith. There is a disagreement, feelings become strained, one thing leads to another, until two groups of fine people find themselves in a position of virtually hopeless disagreement and conflict.

It is evident, then, that we human beings are not nearly so rational as we think we are. Sometimes we reason objectively and complain about what really makes us unhappy. But a lot of times, if we *need* badly enough to reach a certain conclusion, we will, even if the facts are against us.

Let's take some other examples. Here is an office building where the partitions were solid up to about four feet from the floor and clear glass above that. The company had a rule that when a person reached a certain level in the organization he could have the glass in his office painted so that people outside could not see in. A lot of people thought that the men wanted the glass painted so that they could do something they ought not to do—kill time and not work very hard. But of course that wasn't the real reason. Getting your glass painted was a mark of status or prestige, and a boss had really "arrived" when he got the paint put on. You can imagine what a problem was created when a supervisor who wasn't high enough in the organization to have his glass painted still got it done anyway. That created a situation that baffled top management until it saw that there really wasn't much *reasoning* behind the objections. But there was plenty of *feeling*—a need for status, a need to have as much prestige as anyone else at one's own level in the organization.

There are many things like this. In this same company it meant a lot to have your name in the company telephone directory. In fact, that was another mark of having "arrived." And many a man who really could have gotten along just as well without it did everything he could to get in that directory. Of course, that doesn't make sense in terms of *reason;* but it certainly makes sense in terms of desire or emotion or need.

HOW RATIONAL ARE HUMAN BEINGS?

Maybe we'd better bring all this to a close with just a few more comments. As we have said, one of the strongest beliefs of people in the Western world is in the essentially rational nature of human beings. You know how it is: Any time we face a difficult social problem, we call upon education ("filling the student's head full of facts") for the answer. Suppose we believe that we ought to have better office-holders in local, state, or national positions. How shall we bring that about? The answer is clear to many people: Educate folks, especially the young ones, so they'll know how to vote better. Tell them about the basic facts of American history and of government and even economics, and they'll do the job. But actually, is the problem that simple?

Or take the problem of the excessive use of alcohol. It is a real problem, as everyone knows. How shall we cope with it? By filling people's heads full of facts about the evils of drink? Well, that probably helps, but one must never forget that many who *really* know the evils of excessive drinking still drink to excess. Evidently, merely knowing the evils of drink does not solve the problem.

Nothing said here is designed in any way to discourage attempts to inform people. Certainly people who vote—or act—in ignorance are not likely to accomplish much that is good, and they may do a lot of harm. But the point is that the industrial or business leader can't afford to be interested in facts alone. He must be just as interested in *how* workers are told something as he is in *what* they are told. And it is sometimes even more important *who* tells them.

Here is where some of the training that we referred to above— training in basic economics or the working of the free enterprise system—misses the real point. The material presented may be accurate and reasonably complete, and it may be given to the employees in a most attractive form. But if the workers don't trust the *source* of the material, the total effect of the program may be bad rather than good. If most of the employees are asking, "What's the pitch now?" or "How are they trying to get to us this time?" the chances are that the training will do more harm than good.

How such a program can do real harm is not hard to see. If the hearers don't trust the source of the material they will tend to distrust the material too. Thus, in their reaction against the management that presents the material, they will tend to react against the material and be less willing than they were to study our system. Certainly no management wants that result.

And so we are forced to give up the idea that human beings—including our associates and ourselves—are primarily creatures of reason, acting on the basis of thinking, and thinking on the basis of facts. Rather, we have to see them as partly rational and partly emotional; and to understand them, individually or in groups, we must understand their moods, sentiments, desires, wishes, beliefs, attitudes, and values—and the effect of all these often greatly exceeds the influence of reason as such.

HOW DO WE LEARN THESE THINGS?

One question which a supervisor or executive must face is how his people come to be what they are. They do queer things, as we have said, but they also do expected or even heroic things. They change as the years go by, but sometimes they get their minds made up and they can't be changed. We sometimes see wonderful instances of change and improvement, even in old people, but then again we find people who are so set in their ways that no argument or persuasion—sometimes not even force—has any effect. How do people learn these ways of reacting?

Learning by Thinking. Undoubtedly a good deal of learning is done by what we often call "using our heads." We get the facts and reflect upon them, and a conclusion to the facts becomes quite clear. Often these insights come all at once, and then we talk about the "click" or "flash" of insight.

Let's illustrate what we have in mind. We've all had the experience of working in or supervising a work group when something goes wrong. For an hour or two, perhaps, we try to figure out what the trouble is. And then it comes to us all at once that the rumor we heard early this morning has gone the rounds and is causing the trouble.

Or suppose there is some difficulty with the product we are making. We call the supervisors together and talk the matter over. Or maybe we carry on the investigation ourselves. Presently, the trouble has been located—an instance of insight, or perhaps several insights—and then somebody suggests a good solution without delay—another example of the same sort of thing.

By now it's clear, of course, that examples of learning by thinking, or insight, are found everywhere. Whenever we have a problem and we solve it by thinking, we say that we see through the problem, or have insight into it.

Now there has been a tendency for people to think that learning by thinking is the only kind of learning, or at least the only important kind. In line with the idea that human beings are fundamentally rational goes the notion that they learn rationally also; that is, by putting two and two together and seeing that the answer is four.

Nobody, of course, would have any reason to deny that this sort of learning is important. It is what makes our industrial organizations possible, and all other kinds of organizations too. It enables us to solve many problems that would otherwise go unsolved. But it is not the only kind of learning nor even the only important kind of learning. What is this other important sort of learning?

Learning by Conditioning. Some years ago a scientist by the name of Pavlov did an experiment that proved to have more consequence than at first glance it would appear to have. Pavlov arranged to feed a dog only when the dog was hungry and only in an experimental room. He would give the dog small bits of food, and every time he did this he rang a bell. Pretty soon, as you would guess, Pavlov was able to get the dog's mouth to water in response to the *sound of the bell alone.* That is, no food was given, but the bell was rung, and the dog salivated anyway. We say that the dog had become *conditioned* to the sound of the bell.

Just as there seems to be no limit to the examples of insight, so we could go on for a very long time with instances of conditioning. Let's look at some of them.

One of the best is a simple act like tying a tie. You can probably still remember how hard that was at first, especially if it was a bow tie. The ends just wouldn't go together the right way and the knot looked pretty terrible. But things finally changed. You developed skill, and now you can tie a tie without even thinking about what you are doing. Indeed, it's often better if you don't think about it.

Or there's riding a bicycle. Suppose a friend said to you, "I know what a bicycle is, the pedals, the handlebars, etc., but I don't know how to ride one. Won't you just write down the instructions so I can memorize them and ride the bicycle without all this waste of time and unnecessary falls?" That's a very reasonable request, but how would you answer it? Your friend knows what a bicycle is and how it operates. He even knows that you're to turn the front wheel to the right when you start to fall to the right, and to the left when you start to fall that way. But what he wants to know is, among other things, *when* and *how much* to turn that wheel. And what can we say, even if we're experts, to that sort of question?

The truth is that we don't *know* how to ride a bicycle. We've been *conditioned* to the situations that bicycle riding involves, and we *can do* what is necessary. But we don't do most of what we do in bicycle riding by thinking and insight.

Here's another example: A man was the station agent—with no helpers—in a small railroad depot. He signed bills of lading, sold tickets, collected money, handled train orders, and was the local telegrapher for Western Union and the railroad. Many's the time he was busily engaged in some of the details of his job when he'd notice that his station was being called by a telegraph operator at a distant point. Very leisurely he'd slide over to his typewriter and slip in a sheet of paper. Perhaps a full minute had passed by the time he was ready to write, and all the while the telegraph instrument had been clicking merrily away. Without any haste he started pecking away at his typewriter, and continued to peck away for another minute or more after the instrument stopped clicking.

This may not seem remarkable, but actually it is to anyone who believes that we learn only by thinking. That man didn't have to *think*, " 'a' plus 'n' plus 'd'—Oh, that's 'and'!"—far from it! He simply wrote "and" when he heard it because he had been conditioned—after months or years of practice—to respond that way.

Another interesting part is the way the man "copied behind." That is, he put the words down several seconds or even minutes after they had been sent. And if he had been forced to put them down the instant they came, he would have been very inefficient and inaccurate. The truth is that he had to "copy behind."

It's the same way when we are talking. While our tongue and vocal chords and lips are forming one word, we're planning what to say next. And thought always stays ahead of effective speech that way. We "talk behind" just as we "copy behind." We have to decide what to say and, in general, how to say it, and then let the saying take care of itself—or we'll fumble and hesitate and speak very poorly.

The truth of the matter is that all acts of manual skill are like this. We practice and practice and practice, and if we're lucky we improve a little from time to time—without knowing exactly when we improve or how. But after a while we may get to be real crafts-men—but never through reading, study, or reflective thinking alone. Most—though, of course, not all—of the skills of a craftsman come through conditioning, not through insight.

This happens to be just about as true for our attitudes and feel-ings as it is for our acts of motor skill. Most of our attitudes—toward other races or union labor or management or the government—are contagious; we "catch" them by conditioning rather than by figur-ing them out, and we adopt them because they are reasonable or indicated by the facts.

It would be hard to find a better illustration than in our attitudes toward races or groups of people. Young children simply do not show the racial and group prejudices of their parents and other adults. They have to learn these attitudes, sometimes rather quickly but often quite slowly and with difficulty. And the funny thing is the way they learn them. Sometimes, perhaps, they are influenced by what the parents say the attitudes should be, although every parent knows that such advice is not likely to have much effect. Mainly, the children "catch" their attitudes from the people they associate with; they become conditioned to certain ways of feeling and believing and acting about the group in question. And they learn these things without realizing what they have learned or even that they have learned at all. After our attitudes have been "caught," we can and often do convince ourselves that they were adopted on logical grounds, on the basis of facts, but actually that is probably not true.

Here is the case, for example, of a man who, during the 1930s, was strongly sympathetic with the New Deal. His associates then were people who shared his views. But he has since taken a respon-sible position in industry, and in a ten-year period his views have changed very much. He now tells himself that he has learned "the facts of life" and that his views were changed by these facts. Per-haps "the facts of life" had an influence, as they certainly might have. But the fundamental reason for the change is most likely his associates and their attitudes. He admired these people, and little by little his own attitudes shifted, chiefly as a result of conditioning.

This process certainly helps us to understand the "queer ideas" that many people have—on labor unions or promotion or political questions or matters of religion. By and large, we get our feelings and beliefs in these matters through conditioning, and reasoning doesn't have much influence in most cases. Thus, people who disagree with us may not necessarily be stupid or ignorant. Maybe they're just conditioned differently from the way we are.

There is at least one other aspect of conditioning that we need to notice. It concerns the various ways in which we satisfy our needs and desires, and it amounts simply to this: The more often we satisfy a need in a certain way, the more satisfying that way tends to become. In other words, there may be at first a dozen ways of satisfying some particular need of mine. But if by accident, design, or force of circumstances, I satisfy it usually or always in a certain way, that certain way is likely to become by all means the most satisfying of all the ways available.

For example, if a child is hungry there are usually many foods that would satisfy his hunger. But if a certain food—let's say cornbread—is furnished him regularly, the chances are that he will develop a definite taste for cornbread. True, this does not always work. Most of the time, however, he'll like cornbread better and better and never lose his taste for it as long as he lives. He may, through practice, come to like other breads better, but the chances are that he'll always like cornbread.

The same thing is true of many other things that we do. Thus, we may canalize upon a certain type of dress—and persist in wearing it long after it has gone out of style. Or an older and outmoded type of furniture or architecture may look good to some of us long after it has ceased to be popular.

This process lies at the basis of some of the problems we have in getting workers—or bosses—to change their ways of doing certain things. Perhaps a new and better way of doing a job has been worked out, and is being explained to the workers. To any outsider it may be clearly and obviously better, but to the worker who has canalized upon another way of doing the job, it certainly may not *seem* better. And the workers may thus resist something that would help not only them but the company as well. This becomes even more serious if the worker has made his way of doing the job a real part of himself. Then it will be difficult indeed to sell him the new method.

CONCLUSION

In this chapter we have pointed out that human beings are complex and complicated in their ways of behaving, and that any *simple* theory of why they behave as they do is bound to be too simple. One of the attractive theories that is obviously too simple is the belief that human beings are to be understood in terms of what they think and what they learn by thinking. On the contrary, we are also creatures of emotion, need, desire, wish, sentiment, mood, attitude, belief, and the like, and are probably more influenced by a combination of these things than we are by reason. And we learn not only by thinking and planning, but by practice, by doing the same thing over and over, until we are changed—often unconsciously—in skills and habits and beliefs and attitudes.

CHAPTER 3

SOME BASIC MOTIVES OF WORKERS

"That fellow doesn't get on around here. He can't get along with people. I don't know what he wants. He's got a better job and yet he's disgruntled."

Like George McGowan, everybody is interested in why people act as they do. As we said earlier, the behavior of other people is a constant source of interest and even amazement to us. There are probably no more important questions anywhere than, "What makes people tick? What does the worker really want from his job?"

Certainly these questions are of great interest to a supervisor or executive. If he could really understand why his employees act as they do, he could answer questions he has asked himself many times. And of course, much more important, he could make some good guesses about what they might do, and might even influence what they do do.

IMPORTANCE OF A LEADER'S VIEWS ABOUT HIS WORKERS

We have long recognized that what George thinks and what his motives are will have a lot of influence on what he does. But we have not recognized as fully as we should the importance of one particular aspect of George's thinking and feeling: namely, what George thinks and feels about the *motives* of his subordinates. He may, for instance, believe that people in general and his workers in particular are a pretty fine lot, willing to work hard for something that they believe in, and not too hard to arouse to enthusiasm. Or he may believe that they are grasping and selfish, and out to get as much as they can for as little as they can put out. Now, either of these sets of attitudes is likely to have two different effects.

First, it will have a good deal to do with how George treats his workers. And second, it may very well have as much—or even more —influence on how the workers treat him.

Undoubtedly, what we believe about people has a lot to do with how we treat them. If a supervisor believes that people are out to get as much as they can for as little as they can put out, he will certainly treat them differently from the way he will if he believes that people generally are respectable, sincere, and basically honest. In a certain company there was an executive who didn't trust those who reported to him. It wasn't that he thought them dishonest. It was just that he didn't believe they were really capable of doing their jobs. The result was that he didn't delegate very much authority. A lot of unimportant matters came to his attention, and he spent time on them when he should have been planning for the future. His life would have been much easier if he could have trusted his subordinates—and so would theirs.

By contrast, there are leaders who *do* trust their people. These leaders gladly delegate authority to meet responsibility—and they are often much more effective, for they really have time to be executives. And needless to say, the subordinates are happier and more effective also.

But this is only the beginning. One of the fundamental facts of human relations is that people usually give us just about what we give them. If we treat them kindly, we are *likely* to get kind treatment in return. If we are generous with them, they will probably be at least somewhat generous with us. But if we don't trust them, they probably won't trust us. And if we fight them, they are very likely to fight back. One of the major difficulties facing management and the union in a certain plant is that each believes that the other is not to be trusted, that it is selfish and either ignorant or dishonest. Somehow, what people think about us we tend to think about them. And let's not forget that it works both ways. When management thinks the union is not to be trusted, the union usually thinks the same of management. And when the union believes that management is trying to cut corners or deal from the bottom of the deck, management soon gets the same ideas about the union. Needless to say, these beliefs on the part of each have a lot to do with what happens in the plant or store or office involved.

This point can be overdone, of course. But generally speaking, if you really think that your workers will try to put something over on you and do as little as possible for their wages, you will show the feeling in spite of all that you can do. And when workers know you feel that way, they resent it and are very likely to show it by what *they* do.

And it is just as true that sincerity and confidence toward others lead to similar attitudes and actions on their part. If you trust your workers (or your boss or wife or children), they will probably trust you, and everybody will be helped.

Now we shouldn't leave the impression that this is the whole story, for it isn't. There are a lot of things that influence how we treat our subordinates or our bosses, and we have mentioned only one. It is a plain fact of experience that you can't afford to trust some people—or some groups—very far, and the leader who doesn't recognize that fact is not being very smart. All we're saying is that we must trust people as much as their conduct will let us. We must have as much confidence in them as their actions will permit. Maybe we'll have to start slowly with some groups, for perhaps they haven't learned to shoulder responsibility and do their jobs without being watched. But with wise leadership we *ought* to be able to lead them to improve, until after a while we *can* trust them, because they are responsible.

Let's emphasize the point: In many, many cases *the attitudes that work groups show toward the boss are a reflection of the attitudes that he shows toward them.*

SOME THEORIES ABOUT WHY PEOPLE WORK

The Economic Man. One of the popular theories as to why men work is that they work almost entirely for money. The idea here is that work is unpleasant and that people would not work unless they had to. The theory stresses the importance of money (including good working conditions, pensions, and other things costing money) in all negotiations and labor disputes. In effect, it says that the only important considerations in work are economic ones.

This theory covers more territory than we might think at first. There is a view, known as the materialistic theory of history, which holds that all important events and movements of the past can and should be explained in economic terms. Thus, wars are fought, according to this view, so that nations may secure economic advantages; laws are sponsored and passed for the economic gain they bring to certain people or groups of people; and even social institutions are set up and used for the same purpose. If we accept this theory, man is thus an "economic animal."

Now, we have to agree that there is a lot of truth in the theory. Most of us would resign from our jobs if the company should stop our pay. And certainly most people have to work in order to buy the necessities of life.

There can be no serious doubt, also, about the fact that the economic plays a large part in the national and international affairs of any country. Surely wars *have* been fought chiefly for economic gain, and social institutions used for the same purpose. But our question is: Is this the *whole* story? Does it take important facts and make them *all-important,* and thus neglect other important facts?

Actually, that is exactly what it does. Surely, men work for money, but they work for many other things besides. Surely, wars have been fought to gain territory or trade rights or raw materials, but wars have been fought over religious beliefs and ethical ideals, too. Legislation has sometimes had an economic basis, but it has sometimes been aimed at the protection of children or the aged or the working man. The trouble with the theory of "the economic man" is that it takes a half-truth and makes it the whole truth.

Specifically, the theory is only partly the true reason why men work. Many of us work primarily because we love our work. The only holiday some people know, or at least enjoy, is the "postman's holiday." When on vacation we give all sorts of excuses about why we should go to the office—to answer some correspondence or "check on some things"—but oftentimes we go to the office because we love to be there.

And certainly we work for prestige and position. These are undoubtedly more important to some people than additional income. And we sometimes work in order to accomplish something we have planned. Surely there are few rewards greater than that of "a good day's work well done."

The trouble, then, with the theory that men work for money is its failure to recognize that they do not work for money *alone*. One of the most important mistakes we have made in dealing with labor disputes is to give the desire for money more importance than it deserves. We have often assumed that if workers are unhappy, they want more money. If they don't work efficiently, they will have to have more money. If we are to keep them out of unions, we must give them more money. But all the while the workers may really be unhappy because they are not treated with proper respect and dignity, or because they get no real satisfaction from their work and work situation, or because they believe the bosses are dishonest or not to be trusted. More wages may help many labor disputes, but money won't cure grievances having to do with a man's sense of his worth or concerning his moral values. In every labor dispute we must ask ourselves, "What is this dispute *really* about?"

The Hedonistic Man. Another theory of why people do what they do is that they always pursue their happiness or pleasure. The theory does not say that they *should* do it; it says that that is what they *have to* do by nature. Thus, if you can find out what a worker thinks will bring him the most pleasure (or cause him the least pain), you can predict what he will do. He never intentionally does otherwise, if the theory is correct.

In trying to decide how much truth there is in this theory, one point should be made clear right at first: You *can* explain all of human behavior in terms of it. Every act of generosity *can* be said to be planned to increase our happiness or to decrease our pain. Thus, if a mother gives up things for her child, you can say that she did it for the pleasure she gets from seeing her child grow and develop, or because she thinks that to do otherwise would cause her pain in the future. Or if a man gives a large gift to charity you can say that he did it for the advertising it brings him, or to keep his conscience from hurting, or to escape eternal punishment after death. We *can* explain all acts of all human beings in terms of the theory, but the real question is, "*Should* we explain them that way?" Are such explanations really the correct ones?

Frankly, they are not. Theories of this sort have been widely accepted chiefly because people have failed to recognize (or at least failed to recognize the importance of) a process known as *identification.* It is a fact of human experience that we do identify at times with other people, including strangers, or our pets, or some great cause. Now, when we identify with these things we make them literally *a part of ourselves.* And when we make a thing a part of us, we may sacrifice the pleasures of the body—and even give up life itself—to preserve that thing.

Here is an illustration that is well known to everyone who grew up in the country where a boy and his dog were almost constant companions. There are at least two ways to start a fight with such a boy. One way is to kick the boy, and the other is to kick the dog. And if you want to start a real fight, you kick the dog. The boy will let you do things to him that he won't let you do to that dog. And he'll often make some very real sacrifices for that dog without counting the cost.

There is every reason to believe that men may likewise identify with their country or their branch of the service or their buddies— and then run great risks, risks which no amount of *money* would persuade them to take. Everyone knows stories like that of the young captain in World War II whose company was ordered to take a small village in northern France. As the attack began, he was wounded, not too seriously but enough to have turned back for medical aid without being thought of as "yellow." Indeed his men urged him to do just that, but he refused. A short time later he was wounded again, more seriously, and again refused to turn back. Finally he was wounded a third time, and fatally.

Similar things have happened in industry. "The mail must go through" and "The show must go on" represent attitudes we have all seen in some workers, unskilled, skilled, clerical, managerial. Indeed, these attitudes may appear anywhere in a business.

Any true friendship has something of this in it. Suppose it could be proved that the person who is in your opinion your very best friend is in actuality just "using" you. That is, he is a friend of yours only so long as he thinks he will gain by it—in terms of money, convenience, pleasure, or something. If you really accept this account of his motives, he is no longer your best friend, but rather an acquaintance of convenience. (It should be added that there is nothing wrong with having "acquaintances of convenience," but they are not true *friends*.) We believe that the person who is our

best friend would help us if the chips were down, without counting the cost. And we would be willing to measure the depth of his
friendship by how much of a *net* sacrifice he would be willing to
make. A little sacrifice, only a little friendship; great sacrifice, great
friendship.

The point we are trying to make is just this: It is not correct to
believe that everyone is looking out for himself at all times, and
that he has no interest in other people except as he can get something from them. Of course, we are interested in our own desires
at times—and there is no reason why that is necessarily bad. But
there are other times when we have *identified* with something outside of ourselves—and we *may* make real sacrifices for the things
with which we identify.

Along this line, there is one question which every leader of
workers should ask himself constantly: Am I assuming that the
only way to motivate my workers is to *give* them something, to see
that they get more and more for less and less? On the other hand,
am I helping them to identify with the department or the plant or
the company? They need to identify with these things. How good
a leader am I?

WORKER'S NEEDS THAT ARE OFTEN OVERLOOKED

To ask the question "What do workers want from their jobs?" is
to start a list of needs that could become very long. Workers want
many things: security, good pay, opportunity to advance, good
working conditions, good tools, good methods of work, good houses,
good fellow-workers—the list could go on and on. So we are not
trying to make a list of all the things they want, but we would like
to discuss the things that may easily be overlooked, that is, those
desires of workers that ordinarily do not receive enough emphasis.

One important precaution before we begin: Human beings often
have desires or motives that they know nothing about, or are aware
of only vaguely. This has been a hard doctrine for many people to
accept. They are willing to believe that certain processes go on
unconsciously in the body (for instance, digestion). But to ask
them to believe in unconscious *mental* processes is to ask too much.
The fact remains, however: Everyone has unconscious motives,
desires that sometimes he would not recognize if they were de-

scribed to him, even desires that would embarrass him if he had to admit that they were his. There is really no longer any way to deny successfully the existence of motives that are unconscious. Incidentally, it is because the needs that we are going to list are usually unconscious, or at best only vaguely conscious, that they are so easy to overlook.

What we are actually saying, then, is that other people may know more about some of our motives than we know ourselves. We may be unaware of them but other people may be able to see their effects quite clearly. Sometimes, indeed, we may fight against them and swear that they are not our motives, but other people may recognize them beyond doubt.

The Need to Be Needed. This phrase, the need to be needed, describes a very significant fact about people. Everyone wants to feel that what he does makes a difference to someone else—indeed, he wants to feel that *he* makes a difference. He has a genuine need to believe that, in addition to earning a living for himself and his family, he is making a worthwhile contribution to a worthwhile endeavor.

It is hard to imagine anything connected with the work situation that is more discouraging than to realize that all you are doing is just making a living. Making a living is fine and necessary. But we all want to feel that we are doing more than that, that we are doing something that to some extent "really counts."

One of the tragedies of modern industry is that so many workers do not have this sense of making a genuine contribution. The craftsman of an earlier period had it, and also the farmer, the professional man, and others. But today many jobs have been broken down into small parts, and each part is given to a worker as his whole job. The result is that many people have little idea of what they are doing from the standpoint of real relation to the finished product or to the social order as a whole. Under these circumstances, of course, many people work almost entirely for money —and are unhappy no matter how much they get—because they see nothing else to work for.

This is a situation which we allow to continue, at great risk to our whole society—political, economic, and social. People desire —yes, they definitely *need*—something important to work for, something with which they can genuinely and proudly identify, something that satisfies the need to be needed. And a wise management will do all in its power to help satisfy this need.

Another comment before leaving this particular need. The need to be needed is not, as some might suppose, the same as the need for recognition. Everyone wants recognition too; there is no doubt of that. But recognition sometimes comes by chance or for achievement that merely glitters without having any real substance. Recognition is satisfying, of course; but often more satisfying and more desirable is the knowledge that one really *has* contributed. The recognition of a contribution makes it more satisfying. But recognition can never take the place of a sense of having done something truly worthwhile.

This need also goes beyond a need to belong, to be fully accepted as a member of a group, important as that desire is. We want to be accepted, that is true; we want to feel that we are a genuine part of the lodge or club or work crew. But recognition and belonging can often be bought with a price or may come about through chance. However, when we know that we are needed—even if our importance is not recognized by others—there comes a feeling of satisfaction that is difficult to equal.

Fortunately, we do not usually have to give up one of these needs to secure the others. There is no reason why one should not be doing an important job, a job recognized by everyone as important, and at the same time be a real member of the work group. As in most human affairs, this is not a question of *either* this *or* that, but of *both* this *and* that.

Every leader of workers should constantly ask himself these questions, then: "Do my workers really know the meaning of their jobs and the combined results of all the jobs in the business? Do they understand, and do they accept emotionally, the real importance of their jobs? Have I made the mistake of supposing that they want to put into their jobs just as little as they can and get out of them all they can? Have I ever challenged them with a difficult task and enlisted their cooperation in a job truly worth doing?" Effective leadership affords people an opportunity to *give* as well as to *get*.

The Need to Be Treated with Dignity and Respect.   Another need that people seldom think about or talk about is the need to be treated as a human being having value in and of himself, and not simply as a means to an end. Nobody wants to be just a cog in a machine or a number on a payroll. We all want to be treated as persons having a worth over and beyond what we can do. We demand treatment that is due a human being, a creature who is more than his body and more than his productive labor. The fact is that the individual worker will always see himself as more than a "handful of clay" and will never respect or do his best for a management that sees him only as a means of getting the goods out the door.

A very peculiar situation arises from all this. Management can never get superior performance from workers if it is interested only in performance. It must be interested in workers as ends in themselves and not merely as means to an end. In a word, if management is to get the best from workers, it must respect them as individuals, it must have genuine affection for them. It is not enough to be interested only in what they can do, even if one pays very well for their work.

The fact with which we are dealing here is not a simple one, and we have made serious errors in attempting to deal with it. One thing we have told our foremen is that they must treat their workers as individuals—that they must show an interest in them. Now, that is well and good, provided the foreman—and the rest of management too—really has that interest. But the foreman who pretends an interest which he does not feel is in for trouble. And the foreman whose only interest in workers is for what they can do is in for trouble too. If the foreman does not respect and even love his workers, he had better not pretend to do so, for they will find him out, and the results are always unhappy ones.

A similar conclusion can be drawn about many popular personnel devices. If a welfare program is instituted out of respect for workers and as a genuine contribution to their health and happiness, it may very well end in increased production. But if it is put in as a trick to make workers believe the company has a genuine interest in them, when in reality the company is interested only in the work they do, the program is almost sure to do more harm than good.

It is here, of course, that we find the greatest of the dangers of paternalism. The "great white father" does many things for his workers, things that they use and enjoy. But suppose he does all this in a patronizing way (or what is the same as far as results are concerned, in a way that the workers take to be patronizing). Suppose he asserts his superiority to his workers and moves them about like chessmen on a chessboard. American workers will not permit that; they demand treatment with dignity, respect, and intrinsic equality. Woe be unto the management that forgets and resorts to tricks or to its own assumed superiority to workers!

Need to Enhance and Defend the Self. One of the most meaningful facts about any individual is his feelings and thoughts about *who* he is, *where* he is, *what* he is, *why* he is, and the like. Everyone of us carries around inside of himself a picture of himself, including just these thoughts and feelings. And we go to great extremes to keep that self-picture satisfactory and to make it more so.

An illustration: If you tell me I cannot play football as well as "Red" Grange once did, that does not bother me at all, for I do not picture myself as a football player. But tell me I am not a good father to my children or am not a decent citizen, and I will almost certainly reject that. These things are a part of my self-picture, and only rarely will I allow anything to detract from it. On the contrary, I try to defend it and build it up.

Let's look again at the question of introducing a better method of doing a certain task. We have learned that workers (and their bosses) often do not want to change to a better method because they have canalized upon the old one. But there is an even more significant reason for their not wanting to change: The work method has become a part of the self-picture. It is *my* work method, and giving it up is to give up a part of myself. And that is never easy to do.

Or suppose a foreman has made a serious mistake in judgment. The department head calls him in and confronts him with the facts. The foreman may very well say at this point, "Yes, I did it, *but—.*" And then he proceeds to show why anyone under his circumstances would have done what he did. He must defend his self-picture. He cannot admit that he is a stupid foreman. Often, indeed, he cannot even admit to himself that he is just an ordinary foreman. In his self-picture he is most likely at least a better-than-average foreman. And he defends that self-picture.

A very important distinction needs to be made here: There is a lot of difference between telling a story for its effect on other people and telling it to influence ourselves. Sometimes we tell a falsehood deliberately, in order to escape punishment. That is one thing, but a very different one from telling a story to convince oneself. Self-defense is illustrated best by convincing ourselves of our own worth and dignity even when we are not very worthy. At times we will go to almost any length to defend and enhance the self.

Here is where the so-called "defense mechanisms" come in. We hear a lot these days about rationalization, repression, regression, and the like. These are often simply names for ways in which the self-picture is defended.

Finally, it must never be forgotten that what we identify with is thereby made a part of the self. Certainly we attempt to preserve life and the pleasures of life, and we often do whatever we can to increase the joys of living. But when I identify with one of my children, when I make that child a part of me, then I will work hard to improve that child or to make him happier. And the history of the human race is full of instances of parents who made genuine sacrifices for their children, even sometimes to the extent of giving up life itself.

The same thing is true about the groups with which we identify. The union is an example for many workers. It has been made a part of the self, an important feature of the self-picture. And when that happens, the worker will often sacrifice for the union beyond any likely gains in money or recognition or security. Indeed, it is a serious mistake to try to understand the appeal of a union to its members if one asks only this question, "What do they gain personally by belonging to it?" It is often necessary to ask, "Why have they *identified* with it?" If they have done so, they will strive to uphold and strengthen it, regardless of the fact that to do so may cost the particular member heavily in terms of personal gain. The self, in other words, is not the same as the body. It is the body and all other things with which we identify. And it must never be forgotten that one of the basic desires of practically everyone is to defend and enhance the whole self.

SUMMARY AND CONCLUSION

In this chapter we have made the point that the motives of workers are many and varied. Workers work, we have said, for a variety of things. Among them is their desire for a feeling of the significance of what they are doing, a feeling that they are respected for what they *are* and not merely for what they *can do,* and a feeling that the self-picture is sound and worthy.

We have emphasized the fact that a human being may serve and sacrifice for things with which he identifies, and that he certainly does not always seek an easy job or more and more for less and less. Finally, we have insisted that sound human relations in the work situation cannot be achieved on a basis of trickery or cleverness but must rest on *mutual trust and confidence.*

CHAPTER 4

WORKING WITH OTHERS

. . . There seemed to creep into their conversation a little worry about their old circle of friends. . . . Just the first Tuesday evening after his promotion, when he went out to his regular poker game with the boys, there was naturally a lot of kidding. One of them said, "We'll have to watch our step from now on, boys. We're playing poker with the boss."

ON BECOMING A HUMAN BEING

A twelve-year-old boy was found locked up in a back room of an out-of-the-way house. It was discovered that this little boy had never been out of this room and had never seen another person outside of his immediate family. He was an illegitimate child, and his presence in the home was a successfully guarded secret for these many years. The little fellow was more like an animal than a human child. He had no abilities other than to eat what was put before him. His utter helplessness was pathetic. The boy in his isolation had not developed into a human being, and he was without nearly all of the characteristics that we think of in a child.

Of course, he was placed in a foster home and slowly began to learn the things that a normal little baby learns. But he never became really normal in any respect. The scars of his isolation were so deeply intrenched that he could never successfully cope with the outside world.

This illustration makes us realize that all of the life of each of us is tied up with other people. Everything we do is a contact with some other person or group of people. No one can live unto himself. Even the cave dwellers needed one another to survive. Our very complex society leaves us absolutely dependent upon others. We are even dependent upon many people we never see. We take

33

for granted the South American who raises the coffee we drink, and the dairy farmer who milks the cow for the cream we use in it. We seldom consider what we would have to give up if we lived the life of a hermit, since someone prepares all our food and others buy our services or the materials we produce. The money we receive we deposit for someone else to guard, or we spend it with somebody in a transaction. We cannot cut our own hair or even tie a good knot without the help of an extra finger.

We take all of this for granted. We get used to dealing with all sorts and kinds of people, and we know this is the normal way of life. Our greatest task is getting others to help and understand us. Our earliest cry is for a mother to come and meet our needs, and the most important lessons we learn are the techniques we employ for securing and giving assistance.

We have developed many tricks. We know how to smile, how to plead, how to command, how to give in. Fortunately we are made very pliable, so that our adjustments to others may be easy. The people we like the best are those who are skilled in getting along with us. Through contact they seem to bring out the best in us. The successful boss is the one who can inspire loyalty and enthusiastic work from those who work with him. It is important for us to examine these skills and abilities to work with other people.

Since we are born into a world of groups, we begin at once to pick up the human way of doing things by the experiences we have in our contacts with other people. In our family group we learn how to act. We pick up the attitudes and values of our parents. Through imitation and other types of conditioning, we learn the knack of being a human being. Throughout our lifetime we are learning from others. Every other person has his influence on us. It is through all these relationships that we learn the system of the past and *the* way to act and think and feel. The sum total of all of these experiences and lessons is what we really are. No one can be understood without taking into account all of his experiences and various associations in his background.

Take the example of little Pete. He could not get along at school. He spent more time in the principal's office than the principal. He did everything that a boy wasn't supposed to do in school. He whispered and daydreamed, he fought on the playgrounds and "sassed" the teacher. He didn't study and he was always tardy. Nothing his teacher said would do any good, and punishment only seemed to make him worse. One day the principal requested that he bring his mother to school. For the first time the boy became excited and made all sorts of promises to avoid having to tell his mother. The principal, thinking he had at last found the sensitive spot that he could use to make the boy comply, insisted that the mother come to school. Early the next morning the mother came to school. She not only was very hard of hearing, but very drunk. In a loud, shrill voice she berated the principal and all the teachers, insisting that the boy had been mistreated and urging him to quit school and go to work. Of course the little boy did not have a father. He had deserted years ago, because of his inability to live with the mother. She was Pete's only pattern, and she had never wanted him in school. The teachers began to see that Pete was not a mean or bad boy. In fact, they were amazed that he had done as well as he had when they considered all of the handicaps in his background. Nearly everyone has shortcomings, and many times these weaknesses can be explained and understood in terms of the human contacts of the individual.

It is misleading, of course, to think that we *always* imitate those with whom we have contact. Sometimes a relationship produces quite the opposite effect. The boy from a bad home is not always a problem child. A man raised in a minority group is not always antisocial. We have many cases of outstanding people coming from the worst possible environment, and all of us are able to overthrow some of the bad influences around us. A boy raised in the family with an alcoholic may be so conditioned against strong drink that it will never be a problem to him. A worker can have such a poor foreman that he profits by this experience and develops techniques of leadership so that he can avoid such pitfalls. The important lesson is that we are affected by our experiences with others. We must realize the effect we have on all the people we contact, and the effect that others have on us. A close self-examination will reveal that what we are is pretty largely a matter of the influences that have been thrown around us.

Perhaps the most crucial crisis of our age is the fact that we have developed so much scientific "know-how" in the fields of produc-

tion and mechanical skills, while at the same time we have un-
covered very few facts to guide us in breaking down barriers between men. We can manufacture on a production line nearly
everything that man can imagine. New powers and new imple-
ments are being discovered every minute. Weapons that will destroy cities in an instant are now available. But the tragedy is that
we have so little knowledge in this field of human relations.

The physical scientist has had an advantage over the people
who study human behavior. The chemist or physicist can put his
substances into test tubes and experiment with all sorts of pressures and devices. We cannot treat human beings as we do physical forces or guinea pigs. No one will submit his baby at the
instant of birth for complete isolation for twenty-five years to see
what effect isolation will have under controlled conditions. No one
will volunteer to be placed under sufficient pressures to find out
at what instant personality will disintegrate. The social scientist
must be content with slow, deliberate observations of human beings in their everyday life. Out of this slow process must come the
knowledge that will allow men to live together peaceably on earth
without war or malice. It is important for each of us that we discover the best means possible to work comfortably and successfully with other people in a relationship that will bring out the best
in all.

WHAT IS A GROUP?

Group activity is such a common thing that we are prone to take
it for granted. It has a very simple definition. Individuals meet and
act and work together no matter how casual their relationship.
This is group activity. Practically all of our endeavor takes place
in groups. It may be a casual meeting on the street, or a formal
committee meeting with its chairman and a sergeant at arms. Both
of these experiences are group experiences. In other words, when
any sort of activity takes place where there is a feeling of "we,"
there is group experience. Groups may range from the intimate
face-to-face relationship which is found in a close-knit family to the
relationship of those who work together in an office or on a certain machine in a factory. It includes the impersonal association
like that of belonging to the Democratic Party, or the white race,

or even Western Civilization. Because we belong to these groups, we find ourselves discussing them or talking about their activities as the things that "we" do. It can be a very casual crowd standing on a corner watching a dog fight, or it can be a mob intent upon a lynching, or even the boys involved in George's poker game.

In every group there seems to be a division of labor. There are different members of the group who take different parts and play different roles. There is the group leader, and there are those who follow him. Each person in the group finds the part he is to play and attempts to live up to the expectation that the group defines for him. To a certain degree, the individual seems to lose his own identity and his own individuality in the group activity. It becomes a collective matter, and while we all feel that we have a part, we realize that the group itself takes action together. This has some effect on us and what we do and think.

To watch a group is a very fascinating experience. Sometimes we see examples of mass hysteria and panic. We find the leaders "whipping up" the emotions of the members to such high pitch that they will follow with utter disregard of their own welfare. They are led into activities and actions that no one of them would ever attempt alone. We have all seen instances of deep contagious resentment sweep over a group of workers when the standards of achievement are set too high, or when the boss has been unreasonable. Each of us has had the experience of walking into a room and feeling the spirit of the crowd. We can tell immediately whether the group is happy or despondent, whether it is excited or downcast, whether it is elated or angry. While group activity is responsible for some of the things that we do of which we are not too proud, it is not evil in itself. There is a warm, comfortable feeling when we know we are not alone.

We must not lose sight of the fact that a group is a whole. It acts like a unit and sometimes takes on a personality of its own. It is more than a sum of all its parts. It cannot be understood merely by looking at or studying the individuals who compose it, because the group has an agreement or a unity of its own. This unity is different from just adding up all of the individuals that are found in the group. We can know every single member of a group and not fully know the group. This is true because people act and feel dif-

ferently when in a crowd or in an intimate association than when they are alone.

A machine is made up of wheels, shafts, switches, and wires; but it has a function and an ability to produce over and above the consideration of any of its parts. Its ability and value are to be considered in the machine as a whole. So it is that the group can produce and can act in a way that the individuals who compose it cannot. It can have its own unrest and fear. It can give approval and disapproval. It can collect sentiment and values and experiences. The individual becomes a part of this group mind and group will. In turn he adds his part and influence to the stimulation of others within the group.

Great leaders understand this group unity. They know that to please all the individual members is not necessarily the same as pleasing the group. The boss can satisfy the gripes of every member of his work staff, and still there may be a deep resentment on the part of the group who works for him. It is not necessary to know every member of the group to understand it. John L. Lewis, one of the most effective labor leaders of our time, does not know every single miner. He understands well, however, what miners want and he knows his limitations and his opportunities in leading them to these group needs and desires.

All of our knowledge comes from our group experiences. Even our attitudes and our values are transferred to us through the groups to which we belong. Our likes and dislikes, our political party affiliations, our taste in music, and even the way we pray or make love, are all products of the groups we have known. We can never completely understand or deal with the individual and his needs unless we understand his group life and what this life with others does to and for the person. Every problem person can be explained in part by looking into his background and seeing the effect of his past associations.

A person cannot be understood in terms of one group alone. We are all a different "person" for each group to which we belong. We are not the same entertaining individuals at the office that we were at the club the night before. We have a different role to play on Saturday night from what we have in church on Sunday morning. A brave combat general may be henpecked at home. To see the

whole self we must see the many associations both past and present which have gone into making the individual person.

WE LIKE TO BELONG

The words, "in group," have been coined to describe the awareness of belonging, or the feeling of "we." There seems to be a
strong consciousness of who is "in" and who is "out" of the group.
The old expression, "blood is thicker than water," is merely an
expression to show that we have a closeness to those we consider
in the family, and that this loyalty is different from that for those
who are on the outside. One of the most cruel and damaging experiences in life is living outside a group solidarity to which we would
like to belong. If George McGowan in his new position is invited
to come to a meeting of the top executives of his company and arrives to find them clannish and indifferent, he has a strange feeling of hostility and of being left out. Everyone knows the experience of the first day on a new job. Here we see new faces and new
routines. We have a helpless frustration because we are not accepted. We are the new man. We have to prove ourselves. The only
thing that keeps us going is the hope that we soon can be on the
"in." No one likes the feeling of being left out.

When we do "belong," we have a feeling of intimacy and closeness. We share common experiences and build up common memo-
ries and traditions. We like to tell how we weathered the crisis together. We insist that we have a good way to do things around
here. This is called "esprit de corps." It fosters enthusiasm. It is
found in the cheering section at a football game and the common
worship at a religious ceremony. Sometimes this sense of being
identified as "together" is made even stronger by attacking some
outsider or enemy. Our patriotism is strongest and our national
unity most obvious while we are at war with a common enemy.
A company is solidified by competition. Unions are sometimes
strengthened by a strike. When we think something threatens
our group, we have a tendency to pull together. Sometimes, when
this collective will becomes so strong, the welfare and significance
of the individual are less important than the welfare of the group.
We have then what we call "high morale." Good morale is best
illustrated by heroism in war, when a man will give up his life

so that his buddies may have a chance or may achieve an objective. This spirit gives determination to a group and creates the power to act together.

To understand why we act as we do, it is most important to consider how our group acts and expects us to act. We learn to defend our group's way as *the* way. These ways of acting and thinking common to the members of a group are called *folkways*.

Some of the folkways have a *must* about them. We are compelled to comply with them. These folkways have the element of "truth" or "right" about them. They are called the *mores*. When we do not observe the mores we are considered bad or wicked instead of peculiar. We *must* show respect to the flag when we are in the presence of others. We can marry only one wife at a time. These are *musts* of our society. They are the folkways that have a compulsion about them and have turned into mores. These mores are different in other societies or groups. Nevertheless, we must comply with them in order to preserve a feeling of belonging within the group. You see, the definition of what is right and wrong by the group is always more powerful than the written rules or statutes. Laws cannot be enforced if they are not consistent with the mores of the group. One of the popular magazines runs a column each month telling about laws that are no longer enforcible because they now seem ridiculous. In Texas, there is still a law on the books making it illegal to carry pliers. It was passed in the early cattle-rustling days. It has never been repealed but of course it cannot be enforced. The mores have changed, and to carry pliers is no longer wicked.

Many difficulties come when the mores change in a group. These mores are dynamic and will not stand still. We have seen our ideas change about Sunday observance and women smoking. These changes cause conflict between generations over what is respectable in a bathing suit and what time a young person should come home at night. It is even more disastrous when an individual is identified with two groups which sometimes have conflicting mores, such as the adolescent who belongs to the family and also to the neighborhood gang that calls him "sissy" for conforming to the family expectation. Consider the worker who identifies himself with his employer and likes his company, but at the same time is a member of a union which is in conflict with the company. This inner conflict causes unhappiness and unrest. It has a tendency to break down "esprit de corps" and morale.

GROUP POWER

More and more we have come to realize the extreme pressure of group expectation on human behavior. One writer once philosophized that we are born into slavery. The minute we enter the world we have the chains of social convention thrown on us, and we act in accordance with what the people expect us to do. There is a little boy in our neighborhood who is always fighting. He has a square jaw and a pug nose. Almost from infancy, people were telling him that he looked pretty tough and that they knew he could scrap. Everyone was always urging him to show that he was as ferocious as the face he owned. He is now merely living up to their expectation of him. It is no wonder that redheads are temperamental. They are told all their lives that they should be.

A recent experiment in the treatment of habitual criminals was performed by giving plastic surgery to the faces of these criminals. With a new set of ears or a straight nose they were "new persons." For the first time they felt that society expected them to be different. Before the operation they were merely fulfilling, as criminals, the role that they felt had been delegated to them. Our adjustments with others and our own self-esteem are made by the responses we receive from the group around us.

Why is it that we do conform to group expectation? There are some who feel that obeying the group will comes only from fear of punishment or fear of ridicule. It is true that we do have a dread of being ignored or ostracized. But a more positive explanation is that a person pleases the group because he wants to comply. Most conformity is spontaneous, and it is not done necessarily to curry favors or avoid serious consequences. A person is merely more comfortable when he pleases others. We all like being liked. We do what the group wants us to do because we have accepted the group's ideas as our own.

The worker can identify himself so closely with the union that the union's ideals and purposes become his very own. He does not join a picket line or solicit membership for the union simply because he is afraid of punishment. He may do it because he has a feeling that the union's way are his ways, and the union's ideas and activities are his own. Nevertheless, his behavior must be explained in terms of the pressure of the group on the way he acts and thinks and feels.

But what about the nonconformist—the one who is different? How are we to understand the person who will not cooperate and is constantly throwing sand into the machinery of human accord? One reason that some people will not buckle under the will of the group and are constantly acting different is an attempt to meet their needs for attention and recognition by means of rebellion. None of us can stand to be ignored totally. We will go to great lengths, even invite group displeasure, to have somebody notice us. If you have an elementary school child who comes home to say, "Daddy, the teacher has made me the vice-president in charge of passing the wastepaper basket," or "The teacher said I could be the assistant fire chief and close the door whenever we have a fire drill," you must be sure to congratulate the little lad, but as soon as it is convenient, go to the teacher and ask about the little boy's reading ability. You see, an elementary-school teacher is smart enough to know that if a child is not excelling in his school work, he may soon resort to antisocial behavior to gain recognition. If he cannot be a good reader, then he must be a good spitball thrower, or "teacher sasser." She has merely given him some recognition that will keep him conforming to the group standards and expectations of the class. She knows that people will resort to any extreme to secure attention.

Sometimes we will find a rebel in the group, a person who has cast off the influence of the people around him because he feels that his best future cannot be served by belonging or conforming to the group. He cannot accept the folkways because they do not make sense to him. He is a nonconformist because he is in the process of pulling out of the group and forming other affiliations.

Many times nonconformity can be explained in terms of conflicting group expectation and social background. A worker who has foreign parents may have been reared to respect folkways and mores that we think are useless or even "un-American." An Italian boy now in this country may have been taught to eat certain foods and to dress in a certain manner. He is considered queer and peculiar by the people in his new environment. His new associations force him to cast off old values and attitudes. Accepting brand new ones is difficult and sometimes impossible in the span of one lifetime. This conflict and confusion causes nonconformity and reluctance to go along with the group. Take the example of the country boy who comes to the city to work. When he is taken out of his ordinary environment, he is made to look ridiculous and inadequate. He knows that on the farm he would be a much better man than his foreman, but he is forced to take advice and leadership from someone he does not respect. He feels that he is constantly being pushed into an unfavorable position. It is little wonder that there is noncooperation and conflict.

One of industry's problems is the worker who belongs to a minority group. As an example, look at the Negro who must work with a white foreman or superintendent. This boss usually generalizes about all Negroes. He thinks that all black men are thus and so. He little knows what it means to have a black skin. There is nothing in his white background that has given him the viewpoint of what it requires for a Negro to comply and achieve happy working conditions under rules that are made and administered by someone of a different background and culture. It is understandable that there is a barrier to conformity and good morale under these conditions.

We are beginning to realize, also, that class structure in America is stronger than we have believed. Most overt conflict behavior can be explained in terms of the different class values and attitudes. Most management is recruited from the middle class, so that middle-class folkways and mores are imposed on the unskilled worker, who may be in a lower class. The boss cannot understand why the lower-class worker will throw away his money and refuse to save for a rainy day. The boss does not understand that thrift is not in the folkways and mores of the lower class to the same extent that it is in his. He expects the worker to see things as he does and maintain middle-class morality and ideals. But the worker was shaped in a different mold, and nothing in his lower-class background gives him the understanding of the mind of the middle-class supervisor. Much of the industrial strife of our age can be explained in terms of class misunderstanding. We merely assume that everyone thinks and acts as we do, and that all classes have the same folkways and mores. This is not the case, and we are judging other groups by our own standards. No wonder that when we sit around the table to iron out industrial difficulties there are unseen obstacles in our way.

Fundamentally all men have the same basic needs, but we must realize that each one is the product of his own environment or group or class. If we can understand that the other fellow does not act exactly as we do because he has not had the same experiences that we have had, it will help us to see some common values and common needs in all men. It will give us an insight into the behavior of others. It will facilitate our working together.

CHAPTER 5

THE MID-CENTURY AMERICAN SCENE

*"Anyway, how times have changed! The old world has
speeded up."*

An American tourist in the far parts of the world stands out like
a sore thumb. There is something about the way he acts and the
way he thinks which stamps him as a typical American. The thing
that really makes him conspicuous is the contrast he presents to
the environment of the strange country. He is the product of a
different world. The strange, mysterious background only accentu-
ates his American characteristics.

In the preceding chapter we considered how an individual is
the product of his face-to-face group relationships. Here we will
weigh the influence of the social matrix, or this environmental climate, of the United States in the understanding of an individual
American. Every worker, as well as every boss, not only reflects
the influence of his family, his class, his education, and his other
group experiences, but he also casts back as a mirror the over-all
background of our American way of life. This American environment is like an enclosure which fences in our American ideas. It
completely surrounds our actions and gives a flavor, or climate,
to almost everything that we do.

Of course, we live so close to this American scene that we cannot feel it or see it unless we are in a strange, contrasting country.
It is something that we take for granted. It is so much a part of
us, and those with whom we deal, that we consider it "normal"
or "natural." It is so "normal" that we neglect to realize its great
influence in all our relationships and undertakings. Not only do
individuals reflect these over-all American opinions, but businesses
and industries mirror them as well. For example, the institution of

45

advertising is a phenomenon of our country. In fact, every factory or plant is permeated with the "American" way of doing things.

"I don't see why you're so backward. Why, at home we go at things differently," says the American businessman overseas.

Our way is a background for everything we do in industry. Even if he wanted to, George McGowan has little or no chance to behave outside the unique circumstances of this surrounding background or American social climate. Sometimes, George finds himself changing his opinions and attitudes. He becomes mellow about things that once irritated him. He takes for granted things that used to startle or frighten him. These changes in George's behavior are confusing and inconsistent until they are seen as a part of a larger change in this, our American way of life.

Our temptation is to consider George, or the man who works for him, only in terms of his relationship with the plant, but it is important to remember with whom he lives away from the shop. It is also pertinent to know in what year he lives. All of us recognize the difference in prewar and postwar days. A war speeds up these social changes. We are not shocked now at a woman taxi driver or a woman riveter. We have accepted new tools and machines as a part of daily life. An old-fashioned model of one of these machines is a liability, and we try to replace it; and we cannot use outmoded ideas or values either without the risk of higher costs. We cannot go back to "the good old days when men were men."

This constant change in our way of thinking and doing things stirs up many problems. The transition is from the old and outmoded, on the one hand, to the new and modern, on the other.

The philosophers are calling this the age of *anxiety* and *fear*. Certainly it is a time of rapid change and transition. Sometimes we feel that the only thing we can be certain of is uncertainty and change. Restlessness and uneasiness impose a heavy burden on the individual, of which he is not conscious. Dr. Mayo reveals that most of our industrial problems are not plant-centered at all, but are the result of disturbances in the over-all social environment in which we find ourselves today. Before listing the problems of our age, it might be well to consider the content of our American convictions.

OUR AMERICAN IDEOLOGY

The geometry teacher defines an axiom as a statement which is accepted as true without proof. Americans have fashioned their lives around certain principles which are universally received as self-evident. When these basic "truths" are under attack or are questioned, it gives us anxiety, and we feel that essential bedrock is being shaken. Let us examine some of these foundations of our American scene. Perhaps our most obvious conviction is that we know we have a superior way of life. All of our progress and attainments we attribute to this "American way." We are fundamentally idealistic, and we feel that these assets of truth and liberty are worth protecting, even if they lead to war and great personal loss and suffering. These are some of our fundamental convictions:

1. Our first axiom is *popular government*. We believe in a government controlled by a majority. We think this is the best way to insure a government for all the people. Long ago we discarded the notion of a government run for a privileged few or a particular class, whether this class be the aristocracy, the laborers, the owners, or the power-hungry. Although we will admit that the minority is sometimes the "right" group, we feel secure in a government if the majority can always rise up and overthrow it. Even when the majority is not enlightened, we still put our faith in it as being the safest power in the long run.

2. *Freedom of thought* is also important to us. Although faced with radicals and crackpots, we know that progress comes from an inspired man who has a new idea. It is a God-given right for man to use his mind. In this connection we put great store in man's creative ability, and there is a premium on any creative spirit. Every man should use his mind to determine his destiny, we believe, and the man who does is clever and sensible. There is great virtue and power in the free mind.

3. We hold to *government under the law*. In the ultimate we think the function of government is to protect the rights of the individual and to insure that he lives and grows without oppression, exploitation, or fear. Our great legal machinery is geared to

save the innocent from oppression, and we are innocent until we are tried by a fair court and held to be guilty by due process of law.

4. We worship *individual initiative*. We have a feeling that all progress has come by giving man the motivation to achieve. We fear and dread any influence or system that will stifle this eagerness of an individual to improve himself and his community. Thus, a man is entitled to the fruit of his own work, and we do not mind a man's success if we feel that it is the product of his hard work and individual initiative.

5. We have great faith in *organization*. We believe that men can create more by joining together. We belong to clubs, lodges, societies, and conventions. This has led to specialization and cooperation. We willingly and gladly join a corporation, a political party, a labor union, or a church if we feel that we shall find kindred spirits through whom we can further our own causes. This has led us recently to accept the idea of international organization. There is a growing conviction that we cannot keep the peace of the world alone and that to do so is possible only through cooperative structure.

6. We have a passion for *social justice*. For some reason we love the underdog and will make personal sacrifice willingly to see that those who have had bad breaks get a proper chance. We cannot stand by and see someone imposed upon or "used." We even have patience and tolerance for the degenerate bum in our society. We have a feeling that it might have happened to us, and we do not want anyone to take unfair advantage of misfortune.

7. We worship at the shrine of *education* and *religion*. We think that no one can have too much of either. This blind faith in education does not carry over to a blind faith in teachers any more than our respect and admiration for religion makes the church infallible in our eyes. Nevertheless, the practice of religion and education gives us respectability and social status. We encourage our children and fellow men to rely heavily on both.

These great virtues are not fixed. We all recognize that our society is changing. Many of these cherished allegiances are threatened today. Nevertheless, these basic principles explain, in part, the American mind, of which we are all a reflection.

SOME NEW DEVELOPMENTS IN AMERICA

A close objective view of our society and its treasured axioms will indicate that there are forces at work making headway in changing our values. These forces are giving new definitions to things which we hold dear. More and more these new influences are motivating our behavior. Let's look at some of them:

Materialism. No one living in America can fail to be impressed by the importance of *things.* Technology is the king of our age, and we think that anything can be fixed or improved by research or the laboratory and that all problems are just a matter of engineering. We are often judged by what we own or at least by what we spend. Our success in life is measured by our standard of living and this is gauged by the things we own or have at our disposal. We even fool ourselves into believing that our country is great because of its vast physical resources. We believe that our defense is in our physical might.

Sensualism. If we follow the current advertising in our periodicals and on the radio and television, we may become convinced that the zenith of all living is in the gratification of our appetites and in knowing the ease and comfort of idleness. Many philosophers feel that our overemphasis on the things that affect our senses are showing up in our literature, art, and religion. Every means possible is used to whet our slightest appetite, and our passions are constantly being stimulated. We have put a new virtue on ease and idleness; anything can be sold to the American if it is labeled as a labor-saving device.

Factualism. There is an overemphasis of the importance of facts. Knowledge, not wisdom, is the order of the day. Truth for truth's sake is emphasized, and research for new factual material is justified whether or not the results can be used and related to our over-all idealism. Consistent with the worship of fact is the importance of the college degree. It seems as if the purpose of going to college is to receive a degree and not necessarily to get an education. Certainly, the former seems to many more important than the latter.

Speed. Complexity and swiftness are the key words of our modern life. Everything must be done to speed up our activities. Our cars must go faster. Our airplane schedules must be shortened, and our specialization for efficiency must be redoubled. We are putting more and more premium on time. Our impatience and frustration with delay and slowness give evidence of our geared-up way of living.

Secularism.   Most people believe that there is a breakdown in our orthodoxy and a change in authority. Certainly the power of religion in controlling the lives of individuals seems to have weakened. We are also less influenced by the powerful "what-will-people-think." The responsibility and authority for our conduct seem to be gravitating away from individual conscience toward external control and law. This has led to more emphasis on government, especially the central government, and dependence on it to control those who get out of line. Conduct is often being based upon "What is the law and what can I get away with legally?" If it is legal, it is all right. This places a new burden on the function of government. The local, state, and federal legislatures are vying with each other to obtain control of the individual and his behavior.

SOCIAL PROBLEMS OF OUR DAY

We have listed some of the assets of our present idealism. We have also indicated the forces that are changing or are likely to change these basic values. Out of this matrix, or climate, and from these social conditions many great social problems come. They are all situations for which no individual or no small number of individuals is responsible, but which nonetheless threaten serious results for many persons. All of them emerged out of a common environment, and they are interrelated and interdependent. None of them is simple, and all are the result of many causes. These problems will be listed here, with little explanation or attempt at solution, in order to give merely a glimpse of our day.

Urbanization and Industrialism.   The city is the symbol of man's attempt to live and work together. It certainly illustrates the extent of our association and interdependence, and many consider it the highest achievement of our civilization. In the early history of our country we were largely a rural and agricultural people.

Our main asset was the rich farmland, and the basic industry was farming and related agriculture.

But now the pendulum has swung over to a high degree of industrialization, and this has led to a concentration and congestion of population in our great cities. Labor and capital, instead of land, are now the dominating factors of our economy. The great industrial centers have sprung up. To these, raw materials are shipped, then fabricated and refined, and shipped out to consumers.

This massing of population and the concentration of activity have given rise to many of our social problems. In large centers of population, living is geared to a high pitch. Multitudes of activities and interests overwhelm and overstimulate the urban dweller. The home is not a stable place where many generations have lived, but rather a multi-unit apartment dwelling where people live stacked on top of each other. Since the jobs are so highly specialized, no one can produce the satisfaction for his own needs.

A high degree of dependency is also created by the nature of city life. Many functions of life that were so simple in the village or on the farm have become major problems in congestion. Police protection, sanitation and public health, water supply, garbage disposal, sewerage, building codes, and utilities are all examples of the complication of city living. Things like these have caused a great deal of growth in municipal government, and our record in political graft and corruption in American city government has been one of our national shames. Many modern attempts at zoning and city planning are being put into effect. Fear of the atomic bomb is also of vital concern to the modern American city. This threat may do more than anything else to break up our metropolitan centers as we know them today.

The task of providing decent housing for the population in our cities and around our factories is one of the most troublesome problems we have today. Nearly half of our population lives in substandard homes. American slums in the big cities are still a national scandal, and many of our industrial concerns, life insurance companies, and even the federal government are providing programs for better housing projects. Until this problem can be solved, the many problems associated with it are likely to be increased.

International Tension. We are living under the constant threat of war. Twice in the memory of most adults our country has been involved in a global conflagration. Not a single family has entirely escaped its tragedy, and now we live from day to day in constant fear. The cold war becomes increasingly and alarmingly hot. The United States and Russia, representing two conflicting ideologies, maneuver and spar for advantage. Our fear of war seems only secondary to our fear of totalitarianism and particularly of communism. On the other hand, this has led us into world government and cooperation as an attempt to settle our differences. At the same time we have reason to distrust foreign notions and tactics, and we are impatient for peace and security. We want nothing to happen to our nationalism; that is, the absolute right to settle our own affairs in our own way. But at the same time we wish that there were some power of restraint over the other nations to keep them from becoming belligerent and aggressive. This constant threat has its effect on the life and behavior of every single individual in our country.

Sex and Family Life. Although there is much debate about what is happening to the modern American family, every authority agrees that it is undergoing rapid change. The traditional family founded on our former rural life and with the father as the head of the house has changed. The increasing economic independence of women and the decreasing economic function of the family have had their effect.

Since children are now more likely to be economic liabilities than assets, our birth rate has shown decline, and the size of the family is constantly being shrunk. Many of the functions formerly belonging to the family are now assumed by the church, the school, and the government. The opposition to divorce is being undermined, and divorce is increasing in all our urban centers. Much of our juvenile delinquency is attributed to the breakdown of the authority of the family over the children.

Our sex code has changed and modified so much that it is difficult to be shocked. About a third of the population of the United States is unmarried and their problems of sex life and social adjustment are apparent. The stress and strain of the broken home, and the related problems of prostitution, illegitimacy, and homosexuality are a part of our social structure.

Race Prejudice. Few problems are as loaded with emotional dynamite as the matter of race tension and conflict. Race prejudice persists, and people are classified, not on the basis of biological traits, but on the basis of emotionally conditioned notions about race and racial superiority. Although race tension is not limited to any one group, the Negro population in the United States offers the obvious example. Ever since the Civil War there have been discrimination and segregation. A migration of the Negro population to cities in the North and West has spread the problem throughout the entire United States.

A good many Negroes have come to places of prominence and achievement, and in a way this has helped to accentuate the problem and to expose its injustice. Political parties have been quick to exploit this situation, and many reforms have been promised and accomplished through the power of the Negro at the polling place. Even the casual observer will be aware of the rapid change in our folkways and mores in regard to race. The problem still remains critical, however, and the more spectacular the victories of racial understanding, the greater has been the hostility of many of the opposing forces.

Although the myth of Negro inferiority is discredited by the impressive role of the Negro in American art, music, science, sports, and literature, it will still require many years and much patience to dissipate this idea. Of course, the Negro problem is not the only prejudice of national proportions. Anti-Semitism, religious persecution, political bias, class snobbishness are all examples of generalizations that are heavy with emotional content. It is an American custom to lump all people with similar characteristics into a group and "prejudge" them with our feelings.

Statism. Our forefathers, in establishing a democratic government, fulfilled the aspirations of the people to be free. Great limitations were placed upon the state in order that nothing could dominate the liberties of the individual. Gradually, however, as man has sought to solve his problems of complex living, the state has become more central and important, until today it seems that some people look to the state to meet their every need. The government has become more and more powerful in many new fields of activity, until we tend to view the state as the controlling agency over every situation and condition that affects our rights and interests. Along with this trend has come the attempt to assure economic security to the masses by state manipulation. Direct economic security is now furthered by government in such means as workmen's compensation, unemployment insurance, pensions to veterans, assistance to the aged, and retirement payments. Health security is being dispensed by government in ever-increasing amounts. The "planned society" of modern government is costing more and more. Taxes have become enormous but not enough to balance the cost of our expenditures.

Now, in order to make this plan work, there is a resort to regimentation. Business has learned to take directions from government. Labor and capital also are coordinated by law. Farmers and miners are told what to do and how much to produce. This high power centralized in the state and national capitals tends to breed corruption and graft, a situation for which selfish private interests must carry a large share of responsibility. One of our largest problems is to perfect efficient, effective, economical government with integrity.

Old Age, Dependency, and Relief. Our society has always placed a great premium upon youth. As a result of the declining birth rate and the increase of life expectancy, more and more old persons are to be found in the population. It is a popular notion in modern industry that the magic age of 65 makes a person too old to work, and most of the retirement plans have compulsory retirement at that age. It is becoming less popular for the aged to live with sons and daughters. Freedom from parents has become an axiom of modern family life. Thus the aged are faced with the economic and psychological problems that go with not being wanted. Since the 1930s, the state and federal governments have provided social insurance plans to protect and give subsistence to the old people. As the proportion of older folks increases in the total population, the financial burden of such a pension system will continue to increase and become a responsibility of the able.

Poverty also continues to be a major social problem. The sick and the maimed, the inefficient, and the misfit remain public charges, although private relief is still in existence. The matter of dependency is administered by trained social workers in the large role of public relief. Many people feel that as long as our wealth is drained off to support a perpetual threat of war, there is little prospect that poverty can be prevented or cured.

Disease and Medical Care. Before the modern scientific miracles that we know today, illness, pestilence, and suffering were considered the normal and common lot of all men. In the last several decades this has been completely reversed, and the general public has come to feel that good health is the right of every person and that this health has tremendous cultural and economic values. Public health services, including standard housing, food inspection, recreational facilities, water supply, sewage disposal, etc., have become accepted functions of government. The great advance of our scientific research and the discovery of the miracle drugs, along with preventive measures, have lengthened the expectation of life at birth from about 35 years, in 1825, to about 65 years, in 1950. This is encouraging. The greatest gains in health have been made through the control of communicable diseases such as tuberculosis, diphtheria, malaria, typhoid, and diseases common in children. There are, however, many problems yet unsolved. Leukemia, cancer, heart disease, and many other illnesses offer a challenge to medical research.

A severe problem is the rising cost of medical care. Although there are many public and private clinics which give free medical service to the underprivileged, the person who would pay for private medical care oftens finds the financial burden overwhelming. It is estimated that less than half of the American people actually obtain adequate medical care, and many of them receive virtually no medical attention at all. There are still a large number of people who die each year who could have been saved if they had received sufficient medical attention. The physical condition of our draftees during World Wars I and II revealed a situation little, if any, short of a national scandal.

During the last half century there has been an alarming increase in mental disease, and it now constitutes one of the most serious afflictions of the American people. Statisticians tell us that about one out of every twenty persons fifteen years of age or older will require hospital treatment for some sort of mental disorder, and about half of the beds in public hopsitals are filled with mental patients. There has been progress in detecting and hospitalizing mental cases, and the attitude of the public is more realistic in its evaluation of mental disorder and its cure. The mentally diseased are no longer treated like wild animals and chained down. Although few hospitals have adequate medical staffs, the afflicted are at least treated as people who are sick and in need of care. There are approximately 4,500 medically trained psychiatrists in the country, instead of the 20,000 required to handle the burden of our age. The mental-hygiene movement seeks to prevent illness and breakdown and to improve institutions for the mentally diseased and mentally defective.

Crime and Law Enforcement. Crime rates continue to rise. This does not mean that people are necessarily more wicked than their forebears. It is an indication that more and more of human behavior is being controlled by the law. We depend on the government to police and correct those who break our social standards. The fact that the home has lost much of its control over children has led to a higher percentage of juvenile offenders than ever. The congestion of the cities seems to provide a setting for criminal behavior. Along with the great emphasis on material gain in our culture, there has been a revolution in the nature of crime, due to the wide acceptance of the "get-something-for-nothing" ideal. Organized crime became prevalent during the prohibition era and has since entered many new fields of operation. Gambling and racketeering have been the source of activity for the professional criminal. "White-collar crime," or the crime connected with the operation of a business, has certainly been given more attention recently.

The whole matter of treating effectively the majority of criminals has been poorly handled. Our penitentiary systems have been built on the theory of punishment, and legal complications have often made it almost impossible to apprehend or convict the most guilty. There is a great tragedy in the wasted manpower of our jails, prisons, and penitentiaries, with thousands of convicts having little hope and showing less sign of reformation.

Juvenile addiction has brought the drug problem to the public's attention, and public indifference and ignorance concerning the dope traffic have been jolted by the revelation of an alarming amount of addiction. Alcohol is a problem because of its high economic and social cost, its relation to accidents, and the severe problems of chronic alcoholism and alcoholic addiction. Prostitution and other forms of illegal sex exploitation are part of the total crime problem of our age.

Breakdown of Primary Controls. In early American life, the two institutions that did most to control the activities of an individual were the neighborhood and the church. The neighborhood had many eyes, and the fear of gossip and social disapproval was enough to keep the individual on the straight and narrow track. Supernatural religion provided the intellectual and moral foundations of a community. With the speeding up of our communication and transportation system, it has been possible for the individual to break away from the watchful eye of his community and to question the authority of his church. This has tended to break down the traditional American morality, already weakened for many by the absence of a meaningful faith. Although the church shows an increase in percentage of members from year to year, the power of the church as an agency for control in the life of people has been weakened. The secular and scientific influence has caused us to question every dogma. In order to be popular, a religion must be reasonable and intellectually acceptable. This breakdown in controls has caused conflicts between generations and between various groups and denominations. It has caused distrust and fear between sects. There are those who see signs of a return to a religious idealism, and they pin their hopes for the solving of many of our social problems on this trend.

Ignorance. H. G. Wells characterizes modern civilization on the whole as "a race between education and catastrophe." The great tragedy of our age is the great number of people who act through ignorance. Even those who show that they have been exposed to schooling still are woefully inadequate in the use of an intellectual approach to the solving of their individual problems. The inability of many people to act from the dictates of a trained mind is not due to the unpopularity of education. As a matter of fact, education is one of the most popular elements of our society, and great premium is placed on college degrees and high school diplomas. We seem to have a blind faith that education can cure any evil if given enough time, but we have been slow to evaluate our methods and techniques. Upon the completion of our formal education, we are woefully lacking in our training for life's many problems, Surely the demon, ignorance, has not been banished from our world, and this leaves in its wake untold misery and suffering. Perhaps if we could place a premium on wisdom instead of schooling, our race against ignorance could be won.

A SUMMARY

Every man receives a great heritage in the environment into which he is born. It encompasses him in all the things which he does and thinks and believes. It becomes a part of him, and he becomes a part of it. From its great beliefs he gets his philosophy of life and determines his guideposts of truth. To attempt to understand man without viewing this backdrop would be futile, because it is only in a person's relationship to the over-all society in which he lives that we are able to have insight into his behavior and success in living.

Our modern, mid-century America has certain cold winds blowing upon it that may change or wither some of the standards upon which we have always depended. The complexity and speed of our culture, the materialism and sensualism of our values, and the worship of scientific fact, plus the breakdown of authority make us more interdependent and take their toll of our individual liberty.

Growing out of this dilemma are the great social problems which affect us all. Even if we do not know the touch of a policeman's hand on our arm, or the tug of an alcoholic urge, or the pain of poverty, we still live tentatively exposed to these great problems everywhere. In sympathy, we become aware of and carry them with us to work, and they show up in our relationships to our boss and in the problems that George McGowan wrestles with as he contemplates his new job.

CHAPTER 6

THE CHANGING SCENE IN LABOR RELATIONS

"I remember when I started, I did as I was told, and was plenty glad to get the job."

One of the easiest things for anybody to do is to live in the midst of social change and still hardly be aware that it is going on. Somehow, after we have become accustomed to a new way of travel or of doing something else, we tend to take it for granted and to forget that there was a time when we didn't have it. And we soon become so familiar with a new product that we take it for granted too.

This is even easier to do in the realm of ideas or social habits than it is for material things. For one thing, ideas and values probably do not change as rapidly as material things do. But, more importantly, they usually change so gradually that we literally do not know that the changes are really taking place. We'll have some examples of this on the next page or so.

LIMITATIONS OF THE "HUMAN NATURE" APPROACH

A popular way of looking upon human beings is to ask what they are like by nature. We are inclined to look for their basic motives—all of them, or at least all of the important ones—and to assume that what is true for one is true for another, that basically the American and the German, the Yankee and the Southerner, the Britisher and the Polynesian are all alike "under the skin."

Now, it must be confessed that all people do have some things in common. But if there is anything that is outstandingly true in this field it is that the social environment makes a tremendous difference. As has already been pointed out, in one sense we grow into being a human (that is, grow into our human habits, values, and ideals) rather than being born so. And certainly the American worker of today is no exception. If we wish to deal effectively with him we have to become familiar with some of the social movements that have made him what he is. It is not enough, in other words, to know human nature in general. It is necessary, at times, to try to understand *American* human nature and the nature of the American worker in particular. And this means looking at some of the recent changes in the employer–employee relationships in America.

THE CRISIS IN LABOR RELATIONS

The truth of the matter is that we are living in rather critical days so far as employer–employee relationships are concerned. Here, among others, two social movements have taken place, each going along largely independent of the other, until they now come together in this area and furnish us with some of our most pressing problems. These two movements are (1) a loss in job significance on the part of many American workers and (2) an increasing freedom for the worker. Let's look at each of these.

Loss in Job Significance. There seems to be no doubt that many workers in the United States have lost a great deal in the way of job significance. As will be made clear later in this book, our methods of mass production have had a lot to do with this. For millions of workers little initiative or opportunity to exercise judgment is left. What they are to do is carefully determined in advance. How they are to do it, when they are to do it, and where it is to be done—all these are definitely planned beforehand. Furthermore, many jobs involve doing the same relatively simple operation over and over. These developments certainly do not increase the thrill of working.

It might be objected, of course, that these jobs actually have as much significance as jobs did fifty years ago, and indeed a good deal more. Certainly we work to closer tolerances these days, and an operation correctly performed can have everything to do with the success of the finished product. Likewise, a mistake by today's worker may actually be much more harmful than the same mistake was in 1900.

But our point here is not that today's jobs are unimportant.

It is rather that they *do not feel important*. They are important, indeed they are vital to the success of the business. But doing the same thing over and over, especially if no particular judgment is required, is not the most thrilling thing possible.

Before we leave the point, one more observation: We are not suggesting that we "turn back the clock" and do away with mass production. We couldn't do that if we wanted to, and we don't want to. Maybe we could do something to make jobs more thrilling and less deadening, but actually we probably can't do a lot about the jobs. Our real problem is to help workers get a sense of significance from the jobs they are doing rather than to remake thousands of jobs. Much of the rest of this book is an attempt to say how that might be done.

So far we have talked about one thing that has caused a loss in job significance to the workers, and that is mass production and its effect on jobs. We want to mention two more, centralization of authority and the commodity conception of labor.

We all know that the present is an age of centralization. Maybe the trend has been slowed up a little recently, but certainly it has been carried pretty far. Now a certain amount of centralization probably just naturally goes with bigness. But sometimes we've carried it beyond what is necessary. Things that should have been decided "down the line," or actually in the work area itself, have gone "up the line," or to a staff function. The first-line supervisor has probably suffered most as a result of these changes, but the worker has suffered also. Indeed, if the foreman suffers, so does the worker—usually indirectly, if not directly.

The final point in the loss in job significance is the commodity conception of labor. This is a conception which holds that the only interest that the owners or managers of a business have in workers is the profit that can be made from their services. It holds that we are never interested in workers primarily for what they *are* but only for what they can *do*. Thus, if an owner employs ten people to work in his drug store, he is never really interested in them—or never should be—but only in the money they can make for him. In other words, according to the commodity conception of labor, our workers are simply a means to an end and never an end in themselves.

Now, it must not be thought that this theory necessarily means harsh and unreasonable treatment of workers. Indeed the exact opposite might be true. For example, if it can be shown that to pay workers well and express an interest in their work leads them to work harder and produce more, the commodity conception of labor would insist that we pay them well and express an interest in them. But under these circumstances we never give high wages and praise to workers because we have regard for them, or love them, but rather because we want more from them for ourselves. In other words, there is always a "pitch" or an "angle" to any apparently generous act of any management that accepts and follows the theory.

Before we attempt to evaluate the commodity conception of labor, a couple of points should be made clear. One is that management must certainly be concerned, and usually seriously concerned, about labor costs. Unquestionably, labor must be used efficiently and an attempt made to keep labor costs down. We do not want to be understood as suggesting anything else.

And it is also a fact that labor is a means to an end. If there were no work to be done, we would hire no workers. And if our need for workers should vanish, we would have no alternative except to suggest that they get jobs elsewhere. But our question here is, "Is labor *just* a means to an end?" Have we no concern for our employees *except* what they can do for us? Or, on the other hand, do we see workers as ends in themselves as well as a means to an end?

The answer to these questions is clear. We cannot treat workers as *just* a means to an end, but must have regard for them as also having value in and of themselves. Here the Judeo–Christian tradition and the fundamental principles of the American way of life combine to give the same answer: Every human being has value for what he *is* first and then for what he can *do*. Management must have and show an interest in workers because if it does, workers will work harder and more efficiently. But management must also have and show an interest in workers for another reason that is just as important: because it has genuine affection and regard for them.

The lack of this affection and regard—or what workers interpret as a lack of it—has been the basis of much misunderstanding in employer–employee relationships in America. Nobody works well for a boss he does not respect or for one who does not respect him. We really "put out" only for the boss who believes in us and loves us. The tragedy is that some bosses seem not to have learned this simple lesson.

So far we have made just one point: Millions of workers work because they have to, primarily, and not for any fun they get out of working. Agricultural workers, clerical workers, and even factory workers of a generation ago got more of a "kick" or thrill from their work than their descendants do today. The questions facing us all are, "What can we do about this? How can we restore some part of this loss in job significance?"

Increasing Freedom of the Worker. A second development in this area of boss–worker relationships has been the fact that in the last fifty years workers have gained a great deal in freedom and the right to be self-determining. Thus, workers now protest openly and publicly if they disapprove of a management decision, and even strike if their unhappiness is great enough. They often talk back to the boss, at least through the grievance procedure. And they frequently insist on having a voice in determining things that affect them.

All this is a great change in a short time. Fifty years ago most people—including most bosses and most workers—believed that the boss owned the jobs, in the sense that he could give them to anyone he chose, at any pay rate that could be agreed upon. Furthermore, the worker was to do as he was told—that's what he was hired for. And the boss kept him as long as he wanted him and then let him go, for any reason or for no reason at all. What did it matter if the worker lost his job because of the color of his hair or the shape of his head or the color of his skin? Wasn't the job the possession of the boss, and couldn't he do with it whatever he wanted to?

All this, of course, has changed decidedly. A number of states and the federal government have adopted antidiscrimination provisions and have gone on record to say that there are circumstances under which a boss may not refuse to hire a worker and circumstances under which it is illegal to separate him from the company. And regardless of what we may think about FEPC or antidiscrimi-

nation legislation, most people in the United States would agree
that it is wrong—morally if not legally—for a boss to be highly
arbitrary in his personnel decisions.

More striking and more influential on employer–employee relationships, of course, is the growth in size and power of the labor
union. Unquestionably, unions have taken from management—or
insisted on sharing with management—the right of decision in
many matters affecting workers and their bosses, and this has led
to a certain amount of independence and feeling of freedom on
the part of many workers. And when we consider that one out of
every four people gainfully employed in the United States is already a member of a labor union, it is evident that this desire for
independence is powerful and widespread.

Now it must be acknowledged that unions have grown and developed under the influence of legislation, especially federal legislation. Some people make much of this, and insist that unions
would not amount to much if they had not received the backing
of the government. What unions would do if their existence and
functions were not recognized by federal legislation might be de-
bated at great length, but one thing is sure by now: Federal legislation approves of unions because the American people do so. If
such legislation had been on the books for four years and then had
been repealed, it might with good logic be argued that the Congress misjudged the desires of the people. But legislation recognizing the basic rights of unions has been in effect *at least* since 1935
(or 1933 if one counts Section 7a of the National Industrial Re-
covery Act), and while it has been modified somewhat and no
doubt will be further modified in the future (though the direction
of such modification is not always clear), the basic provisions are
apparently safe and sound because they represent not the schemes
and plans of the politician but the convictions of the people.

All this is to say that the increasing freedom of the worker has
come about because of the convictions of the people that the
worker should have a larger freedom. This development may be
the tragedy of the ages, or, on the other hand, it may be the beginning of the millennium. The chances are, of course, that it is
somewhere in between, having, like most things human, its strong
and weak points, its advantages and disadvantages. But it is ap-

parently here to stay. Let's see if we can account for this development.

For one thing, the virtual *shutting off of immigration* following World War I was influential. Workers from the "old countries" were much more likely than the native-born to do as they were told and not question why or talk back. In the first place, they were coming in at the bottom of the social and economic order, and they knew it. Often they had barely enough money to get to America and couldn't be very particular about the jobs they'd take when they arrived. Besides, jobs at the bottom were often the only ones available, older workers having already filled the better ones. And in the second place, many of these workers came from a society in which they had been told what to do and taught to be subservient and obedient. If a nobleman drove by, they were to uncover their heads and bow before him. If the emperor issued an order, it was to be obeyed, not questioned. Certainly it was easy for one with that sort of background to fit into a factory in which the boss was to do the thinking and ordering and the worker was to do as he was told.

But, naturally, there are other reasons for this increasing freedom of the worker. Another one that we would like to discuss is the *growth of democracy.* It is easy to get the idea that democracy sprang full-grown from the Declaration of Independence on July 4, 1776, but that is not true. On the contrary, while the signers of the Declaration set forth the fundamental principles of democracy and started us moving in the right direction, we've made a lot of progress since then. Let's look at some of these developments.

For one thing, as you probably know, not all adults could vote at first. Certain property and other qualifications were required. And it was considerably later that the first elections were held with all male citizens twenty-one years and over eligible to vote in the then backwoods communities of Kentucky and Tennessee. It said that people along the Eastern seaboard threw up their hands in horror and expressed grave doubts as to "what in the world this world's coming to."

An even more striking development has been the giving of the ballot to women. It is hard to realize that considerably less than a half century ago—well within the lifetime of many people now living—women were not considered the political equals of men. (It might be remarked, incidentally, that the increasing freedom of women, in many other fields as well as in politics, has been one of the most striking developments of the last few generations. So far, however, this has not greatly affected employer–employee relationships, but certainly no one knows what the future holds along these lines.)

Another evidence of our increasing faith in the worth and good judgment of the common man (and woman) is our giving the people the right to elect directly the senators to represent them in Washington. Until the present century people did not vote directly for senators, just as today they still do not vote on candidates for the presidency. The electoral college does not function as it was supposed to, of course. Now it reflects the will of the majority in each state and is not a collection of men sufficiently wise to do what the common man is not supposed to be wise enough to do, namely, choose wisely the President of the United States.

Many other similar developments could be cited. The decisions of the courts of the land and the antidiscrimination legislation, whether wise or unwise, were probably motivated primarily by a belief that there should be no second-class citizens in the United States. There is no escaping from it: This is an age of belief in the common man, in his dignity and worth, in his integrity and ability. Inevitably this has affected labor relations, both externally, in the form of legislation, and internally, in the day-to-day relationships of the worker and his boss and of management and the union.

It may very well be that our third point has been the most influential of all in contributing to the freedom of the worker: the *growth in education and communication.* Some of the changes in this area have been simply unbelievable and may very well be unbelievably far-reaching.

The facts about education are pretty well known. Schools have increased in enrollment and length of term, to say nothing of physical plant, facilities, and teaching methods, and more people are going to school each year. As an example, in World War I the average educational attainment in the United States was the sixth grade, while in World War II it was the eighth grade. That is an increase of a third in twenty-five years! But when you consider the longer school term and the better facilities, the increase is all the more striking. And the end of this development is certainly not in sight as yet.

Important as education is, however, our increasingly rapid means of communication may well be more important in contributing to a sense of freedom and an unwillingness to "knuckle under" to an arbitrary and dictatorial boss. Let me tell you a personal experience: I grew up in a small county-seat town, about thirty miles away from the nearest other town of any size. It was in the horse-and-buggy days, and only a few of us school children had ever been to this larger town. Indeed it took a whole day to drive to it and another whole day to drive back, and people didn't go very often. But how is it today? Now people are driving that thirty miles in thirty minutes—and less—and there are very few people in the town who haven't been to the city many times.

But that is only the beginning. As a people we've traveled everywhere—and we're traveling more and more each year. Shortly we'll probably be able to go across the continent as fast as the sun, and what is more, we'll have the money and the resources with which to do it. Needless to say also, our servicemen have traveled all over the world—and probably will continue to travel in the years ahead.

It is hard to realize how much this has changed us—and our relationship to the boss. A few years ago he could tell us how they did it a thousand miles away, and we'd believe him for we'd never been there to see. But today, what he says had better be good. If he's wrong the chances are somebody's been there, and will probably let the boss—and the workers as well—know about it.

But travel is only one means of communication, and we've developed a lot of them. Take magazines and newspapers, for example. A few short years ago the daily newspaper was unknown except in the city, and most people didn't live in the city. Magazines, too, were few in number and small in circulation as compared to today. And the amazing thing is that newspapers and magazines are not the exclusive property of the rich. They are available to practically all our citizens, and practically all our citizens make some use of them. Obviously, you don't order informed people around as easily as you do uninformed ones. And you don't violate their rights or fail to respect them or treat them arbitrarily without serious risk.

And then there are radio and television. Do you remember when radio first came in? Here was a man fifty miles away, and when he'd talk, we could hear him, amidst much screeching and interference—but we could hear him even without a wire running to where he was. But if we could hear him, he could tell us what was happening there and even let us hear some of the events as they happened. The range of radio has expanded greatly, and you and I—workers and managers alike—have been present at many recent great events in history. At least we *heard* what happened *when* it happened.

But what has television done? It has *really* taken us to where things are happening. We attend a national political convention and the inauguration of a president, and we have better seats—literally we know more about what is going on—than the people sitting in the front row! We go to a World Series baseball game or a national-championship football game—and for all these purposes we never leave the easy chair in front of the television screen! The days of provincialism in the United States are numbered. So far as the events of current history are concerned, soon we're all going to know what any one of us knows.

The one thing we must never forget in all this is that radio and even television are not possessions of the rich alone, but of all of us. There is no need to cite figures on the number of sets of each now in operation, for the number is constantly increasing, at least for television. It is probably sufficient to say that shortly the great majority of our people—young and old, rich and poor, black and white or other color—will have or will have access to a television set.

Now it cannot be too strongly emphasized that all this exercises, and will continue to exercise, a tremendous influence on labor relations and employer–employee relationships generally. You just don't order the modern American around successfully for very long. He has a lot of ideas about how much he knows—about his freedom and worth—and you neglect them at your own peril. One of our biggest limitations in supervising people is to fail to take into account the great changes that the recent past has brought about in them. Thus, we try to supervise the 1945 model of American worker as though he were the 1935 model or the 1925 model or even the 1915 model! And we can easily make—and many of us have been making—the same mistake every year since 1945. You might not like this year's model of the American worker as well as you liked last year's or that of some previous year. But this year's model is the model that's out this year. And it's the model you'll have to supervise, like it or not!

By now it is obvious what the crisis is. Little by little, a great many workers have been losing in job significance, until for many of them little of the feeling of significance remains. But at the same time they have been getting more and more freedom on the job— an opportunity to influence, at least, hours, wages, and working conditions. What will be the result if these two trends continue, if workers each year feel the significance of their jobs less and less and yet each year have more and more freedom to do as they wish?

There are, of course, two possibilities, among many others. One is that the two trends will continue unchecked, with increasing worker demands of more and more for less and less. Now there is no reason why workers should not be paid increasing wages as the years pass and the economy expands and likewise no reason why human beings should not be freed from backbreaking toil. But these are benefits that must be *earned,* and not merely given. The truth is that demands of more and more for less and less of real contribution can really lead eventually only to economic bankruptcy, for there is clearly a limit along this line beyond which the economy cannot be pushed. But what is much worse, such demands will eventually mean moral and spiritual bankruptcy, and that is the sort of bankruptcy from which we cannot recover. We can pay our debts and restore our credits, but when the integrity of our citizens is gone, all is lost.

Fortunately, there is the other alternative: That employers and employees, working together, may recapture some of the thrill of working, the joy of achievement, and more and more of us come to work because we really *love to work* as well as *have to work.* If that time comes, we will set production records that we have not heretofore believed possible. And many of the pressing problems of labor relations will be solved.

WHAT DOES IT MEAN?

The authors of this book believe that the future of labor relations in this country is not unusually bright. We would like to believe that the stormy days are over, and that there is nothing but fair weather ahead. But such optimism is clearly not justified by the facts. There is little, if any, reason to believe that employer–employee relations have really improved recently or that they will do so in the immediate future. Indeed, a pessimist in this field could find a good deal to support his conclusions.

The truth of the matter is that today, as probably never before in our history, we need industrial statesmen, men and women who can see that ultimately we are all in this thing together, that the defeat of those who work means the defeat of those who lead, and that, in our society, a real defeat of management is also a defeat of labor.

 How do we lead our people to accept this simple truth? How do we bring people to get a thrill or a "kick" or a "bang" out of working, and to work not only for what they are being paid but because it is good to work? There is no easy answer to these questions, but perhaps the pages that follow will throw some light on them.

CHAPTER 7

HUMAN RELATIONS AND ORGANIZATION

> *"George,"* said the vice-president, *"we've been looking over our situation. We've decided it's about time we had somebody head up all the factory operations. Now, by that I mean all the production, all the inventories, planning, and maintenance. . . . We think you're the man to handle the job."*

OBJECTIVE AND FUNCTIONS

Organization in some form is necessary to the accomplishment of any objective. If there is no objective, there is no need to organize.

It is difficult to think of any objective, even the performance of the simplest task, which is of course an objective, without thinking of some organizing. Further, the simplest piece of work or recreation can be performed much better when good organization is applied to it.

This approach to the accomplishing of tasks, which we call organizing, takes two forms: first, the coordination of the necessary functions, and second, the coordination of the abilities and efforts of people. Perhaps these points can best be illustrated by thinking in terms of what *you* would be most likely to do.

Suppose you have decided to go into business for yourself. Also let us assume that it is a small business requiring only your own full-time effort to run it. Either at the same time as the decision is made to go into business or very shortly thereafter, you must make up your mind as to the kind of business it is to be. This is, of course, the objective. To help our discussion of functions and organization we should make another assumption. Suppose we assume that the business you are to enter is the manufacturing business, and even more definitely, it is to make and sell a household gadget, a new type of egg beater.

Having made the major decision which defines the objective of the business, you now go into action aimed toward accomplishing this objective. At just about this point, widely differing activities will occupy your attention. The problem of *finance* has to be met. This is a definite function and to some degree will be present as long as the business operates. (The idea of varying degrees in the performing of functions will be discussed later on.)

It will be necessary to establish the amount of capital that is available for your business—in personal savings or in loans from friends or possibly the bank. This is all part of the finance function, as is the allocation of these funds to the different requirements of the business. How much for equipment such as machines and other tools? How much for working capital?

Then there is the problem of what is to be made; in other words, the specification of the product. The original decision to start the business included the idea of the egg beater. And in order to obtain the materials, determine the tools, and be in a position to make thousands of these egg beaters, it is necessary that all details of the design be established. The size of the steel strip, the kind of gears, whether it should have a plastic or wooden handle, the kind of coating to prevent rusting, and scores of other definite items of design information must be arrived at before any further action can be taken. This we will call the *product-design* function. It is a basic function in any manufacturing business, and it is one of the several widely differing activities you will have to perform in your one-man factory.

Knowing exactly what material you need for the gadget, you now perform another function, namely, *buying*. You buy material in order to change its form by applying skill and effort, and then sell it in its changed condition. This is what is meant by "manufacturing."

You are now at the point of actually making the egg beaters. In doing this you perform another basic function of your business, which we will call the *fabricating* or *making* function. And having now produced some of the articles that you set out to make, the function of *sell* must be performed.

It should be noted here that while five different basic functions are necessary to the accomplishment of the business objective, there is a close relationship between them. The fabricating function cannot be performed until the specifications have been drawn up and the buying function has operated. Buying is very difficult if the finance function has not provided the cash or credit. And certainly the selling function is an empty gesture unless the egg beater can be delivered to the customer. To complete the cycle, the customer in paying for the article you sell him provides finance for the continuation of the business activity.

To summarize to this point, you have defined an objective, namely, to manufacture, for sale, a domestic egg beater. You have also determined the necessary basic functions to attain this objective, which for clarity we will list as follows: (1) financing, (2) product designing, (3) buying, (4) fabricating, and (5) selling.

COORDINATION OF FUNCTIONS

Assuming that you are capable of performing each of these functions, your big problem is one of coordinating them so that the proper emphasis is put on each function as circumstances require, and at the same time maintaining the proper interrelationship of each function to the other.

To illustrate this point, during the early stages of getting this business underway there will be a time when most of the effort will be applied to the working out of the details of the design of the product. Once this has been accomplished, the emphasis changes and there will be a concentration on the buying of materials. Once these two functions have been taken care of, again the emphasis will change to the actual business of producing the goods that you expect to sell. The obvious and natural sequence will now be to transfer the effort into getting the product into the hands of the customer, in other words, the selling function.

This is a fairly simple concept while thinking of the initial stages of establishing this simple enterprise, but it becomes a little more complex when we think of the enterprise as a dynamic, or "going," concern. Now is the time when we are concerned with the maintaining of good balance in coordinating the functions.

Each of the five basic functions suggested has to be performed to some degree while the business is in operation. The problem of balance is primarily one of acquiring and applying the art of determining the proper amount of emphasis that each function requires at any given time in the business operation. As an illustration of this, suppose there has been considerable concentration on the fabricating of your gadgets, and you have built up a large inventory. This has done two things. It has absorbed a considerable amount of your working capital, both in the form of materials used and the time (wages) employed in working on the making function, and of course, it has also depleted your available materials.This calls for a change in emphasis, or in other words, a shift in the amount of attention that must be paid to other functions. You must increase your sales, at the same time replenishing through these sales the cash or credit available, and then use a portion of this finance to buy more materials in order to complete the cycle again.

Theoretically, we are aiming toward an ideal in maintaining a balance in the operation of all of these functions. We are trying to reach a plan where we are not even conscious of any need for shift of emphasis. However, while this is an ideal to which good organization aspires, it is nevertheless very rarely attained in any business as a practical matter.

So many of the reasons that cause unbalance in the required amount of emphasis on the functions of a business are the result of circumstances not within the control of business ownership. For example, suppose your beater manufacturing has been quite successful, maintaining a steady shipment of goods to customers, with a consequent income and allowance for a smooth schedule of manufacturing, which in turn simplifies the function of buying as well as finance. But made available competitively to your customers, there appears on the market an egg beater that is better than the one you are making. This immediately creates an unbalanced condition in your business, and a decision has to be made whereby the competition is to be met. The result is probably a concentration (to the almost complete elimination of attention to the other functions) on the product-design function, an activity that has been of comparative unimportance in terms of the attention it required since the early days of organizing the business.

The important thing to note here is that there is not a fixed formula for the relationships of functions. In any organization, there is a definite need on the part of everybody engaged in organized effort to know enough about each of the necessary functions required to meet the objective successfully, in order to coordinate all of these activities; for want of a better word, this is usually referred to as "judgment." However, while this quality of judgment is very hard to define in definite language, it should be remembered that an essential, and possibly the most important, ingredient in judgment is knowledge.

The following shows the structure so far as we have discussed it.

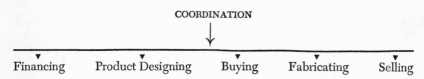

The above is obviously our "organization chart" and represents the basis of the organization of functions common to most manufacturing businesses. Naturally, different types of business will involve a different set of functions, but the one of *coordination* is common to all organization, whatever the objective.

SELF-COORDINATION

So far in this discussion of coordination, only the functions have been considered. But there is another aspect of major importance, and that is the individual involved; in other words, you as a person. Because you are an individual, different from all other people, and the product of your heredity, environment, early training, and all of the other things that make an individual what he is, there has developed in you certain preferences in the things that you like to do and the things that you prefer to avoid doing. It would be a rare person who would have equal skill and preference, for example, for each of these suggested basic functions required to carry on a manufacturing business. The chances are that as an individual you have a greater knowledge and a greater liking for one of these activities. For example, you may be a designer, the gadget inventor; if so, your natural tendency will be to pay a great deal of attention to the design aspect of the business and to avoid as much as you can the other functions.

So much of our approach to the business of organization deals with the jobs that have to be performed and with the use of charts and lines to illustrate them. While these things have their importance, it is suggested that too little attention has been given to the problem of the individual coordinating himself when in the position of supervising the performance of a variety of activities. The old copybook adage to "do the hard part of a job first and then the rest will come easily" might be an excellent precept, but it certainly does not describe normal human behavior. Assuming there is a choice in the matter, our tendency is to do that portion of any task that comes most easily and hope that the remainder of the work will be more simplified once we get started, or perhaps that the other things will take care of themselves.

An illustration might be the general manager of a company whose natural tendency, resulting from his developed personality, was to spend much of the time "out on the road" meeting the customers. Of course, while he was gone, the assumption was that the rest of the business—in other words, all the other functions— were being carried on. But it probably never occurred to him that the coordination function was almost entirely absent while he was not in his office, and that he was tending to overemphasize one of the necessary functions at the expense of the others.

To summarize this thought: In order to coordinate successfully one must know oneself and be prepared to apply a very strong and persistent discipline to one's own actions, if a condition of balance in the coordinating of all the necessary activities is to be accomplished successfully.

ORGANIZING PEOPLE

Using our illustration once more, the one-man business, we will assume it proves to be a successful enterprise and becomes too big for you to handle alone. Your next move is to hire somebody to help you. It may be that you need someone to take care of the clerical work or do the selling, or perhaps work in the shop on production to relieve more of your time for the other functions. You will most likely be influenced by two things in your decision as to the work to be performed by this additional person: first, by the particular activity in the business where the greatest work load is; and second, by the function that you like the least to perform yourself. The chances are that the second influence will dominate, and the new assistant will be employed to perform those tasks for which you have a distaste or the least liking.

Naturally, there is nothing wrong about this procedure. There is much wisdom in doing it this way, but it is important to discipline oneself by examining *why* one does things. There is always the danger of falling into the habit of rationalizing our actions. Knowing that a function is necessary to good organization and knowing that one is responsible for the performance of that function, sometimes one is ashamed of a dislike for it and will go to great lengths to justify avoiding the performance of a function by oneself. This thought will be covered more fully when we discuss delegation of authority.

In the meantime, we will assume you have hired your additional man. You now have the problem of coordinating people as well as functions; you now have a group. Any activity that requires the efforts of more than one person for its accomplishment is group activity and contains the inherent problem of the interrelationship of people, each of whom is different from all the others. When thinking of the problem of organizing groups to attain an objective, it is particularly important to keep in mind the fundamental truth that these differences are normal and natural.

We have discussed the matter of functions as necessary and definable parts of human effort aimed toward successful accomplishment. But when these functions have to be performed by different people, we are faced with the difficulty that the people available to carry out these activities do not necessarily fit exactly into the defined function. This probably represents one of the greatest single difficulties in this whole business of organizing functions and people. In other words, it is unwise to assume that we can fit people into an organization that has been planned purely in terms of the functions to be performed and expect them to adhere rigidly to the defined structure, and at the same time expect to get effective operation from the group action.

As an example of this point, an examination of the trend in military organization, particularly in the military forces of the United States, will show a tendency toward less rigidity and much greater flexibility in individual action all the way down to the private soldier. Those whose military experience goes back to the traditional European method are inclined to look upon this new technique as a form of laxness. More mature thought, however, will show that it really stems from a greater understanding on the part of military leaders of the individual nature of people, and that ultimate higher performance is obtained by providing in our organizational structure for a much greater degree of individual expression in the performance of assigned tasks.

There is another variation that must be provided for when we organize people. Not only must we recognize differences from person to person, but we must also take into account that each individual will behave differently from time to time. By this it is meant that while a person might, because of his individual personality, generally behave or respond to a set of circumstances in a peculiar fashion, nevertheless this is not a rigid condition. The state of an individual's health or sense of well-being will modify his behavior to particular circumstances.

For example, if Bill Jones, the warehouse superintendent, arrives on the job and finds that one of the men has damaged some merchandise by improperly loading it on a truck, the kind of person that Bill Jones is will give us some clue as to the probable way he will respond to the circumstances, and we might predict in general how he will act. However, if Jones did not have a good night's sleep and his breakfast did not taste good, or if he got caught in a traffic jam on his way to work, his behavior would probably not conform entirely to our prediction of the way Bill Jones would behave. On the other hand, if he felt in particularly fine fettle and had received in the mail that morning very encouraging news from his son in college, the chances are that he would take a still different approach to the problem of handling a case of carelessness on the part of one of his men.

ORGANIZING FOR GROUP ACTION

In organizing for group action, much has been said and written on the subject of cooperation and the essential nature of cooperation in group relationships. Alvin Brown, the well-known writer on organization principles, has said that sound organization cannot be built on the assumption of voluntary effort. This does not mean that one can accomplish an objective without cooperation. Obviously the word itself, if examined carefully, means operating or performing together. The danger lies in the loose meaning that has been applied to the word. What do we mean when we say, "Fred Smith is not cooperating"? It could be that Fred Smith is not doing his part, that he is not fitting into the group, that he is refusing to give any credence to the point of view of others. On the other hand, too often when we say, "Fred Smith is not cooperating," we really mean that "Fred Smith refuses to do things *my* way."

The important thing in building an organized structure is so to develop it that it will not fall apart if voluntary effort on the part of any of the people involved is not forthcoming. Further, it should be so built that a natural atmosphere can develop in which cooperative action will flourish. This involves an understanding that most human motivation stems from self-interest, a serving of self in getting the highest degree of personal satisfaction out of the work and association, the satisfaction of the needs that everyone has in varying degrees for material things, for the needs of our gregarious natures, and for our personal ego.

This is quite challenging because in the integrating of people into groups for organized effort it means that the coordinator, organizer, or leader must learn much about human motives and human needs. It also means that the members of the group, including the leader, must also expand their own knowledge of what constitutes their individual self-interest, not necessarily subordinating their own interest to the group but developing a broader vision of the relationship of the success of group operation and successful satisfaction of individual need.

While recognizing the need for flexibility to provide for individual self-expression, nevertheless there is need for definition. People like to know what is expected of them; therefore, in the combining of people and functions, it is necessary that each person know the function that he is supposed to perform and the basis upon which he is going to be judged as to the degree of his accomplishment. Again, this does not mean that the definition of the job should necessarily contain all of the detailed methodology of how that job should be performed, but rather should be expressed in terms of the objective of the job.

In the employment of an individual, whether in the capacity of vice-president or machinist, if there is an inherent expectance of skill and job knowledge brought by the individual to the job, then as much latitude as possible should remain in the carrying out of the required task, if one expects to get maximum performance out of the individual. Also, included in any definition of a function must be a clear statement of the amount of authority that the individual has in order to perform this function. The statement of the objective and the standards of performance should constitute a clear definition of the responsibility in the job. Too often in the organizing and coordinating of group activity we fail to apply a cardinal rule that the area of authority must be adequate to meet the responsibility.

SUMMARY

In summarizing these observations on the organizing of people we have pointed out the need to know one's real reasons for assigning tasks to others.

Because of natural differences between individuals, we cannot logically expect rigid conformity with every detail of a predetermined structure of task specification.

Also, while behavior in individuals might fit a pattern, specific behavior at any one time might vary considerably from the norm for that individual because of stress of circumstance.

A warning was sounded about the loose use of the word "cooperation." It should not be used in assuming that people will do things voluntarily outside the assigned defined task, but rather to build the opportunity for "self-interest," which should include "self-expression," into the group structure.

The need for definition of what is expected of people in the carrying out of assignments and the basis of judging accomplishment was urged as necessary parts of the job definition.

To philosophize a little, the ideal in the organization of functions and people is to make the serving of the interests of each individual involved coincident with the serving of the interest of the group.

CHAPTER 8

AUTHORITY, RESPONSIBILITY, AND PEOPLE

". . . I want you to report directly to me," said the vice-president. . . . "I am holding you responsible for all of our manufacturing operations. I'll send out a memo to everybody, telling them of your new authority."

RESPONSIBILITY

When the boss says he is "holding you responsible," he means he has assigned to you some of his own responsibility. He has not given it up; he has in no way lessened his own responsibility by this process.

As an example of this, let us suppose that the maintenance superintendent has assigned the job of tearing down an old boiler to one of his foremen. He tells him that he is "holding him responsible" for getting this job done during a week-end shutdown. For some reason or other, the boiler is not torn down in time to get a full start of all processes on Monday morning. True, the superintendent blames the foreman for failing to meet his responsibility, but when the works manager gets a report of the delay, he does not blame the foreman assigned to the job. Certainly not! He calls the superintendent on the carpet. The plant manager holds the superintendent responsible, not the foreman; likewise, the executive vice-president holds the plant manager responsible, not the man to whom the plant manager assigned the responsibility. None of these people in the whole chain could actually give up any of his responsibility, even if he wanted to.

AUTHORITY

The term *authority* has several meanings and uses. In its application to industry, the three more important of its meanings

81

are as follows: first, the power that comes from the right of a person to command or act by virtue of his job; second, the power that develops from knowledge; and third, the power that derives from the influence of character as manifest in the opinion, respect, and esteem of others.

Now, there is a close relationship between these definitions as they apply to our business organizations. If a company in Kansas City needs a general manager and the board of directors decides to hire a man from outside, possibly from Chicago, they will, of course, pick the man who in their opinion will most likely perform as a highly satisfactory general manager. The directors of the company are satisfied with their choice based on their knowledge of his past experience and demonstrated executive ability. But the operating organization does not know this manager, and they will accept the decision of the directors with varying degrees of reservation. To all intents and purposes the new general manager enters his new duties with only the authority delegated to him from the board of directors. This is the authority of our first definition, namely, the "power to command or act by virtue of his job."

But here is a strange thing about this sort of authority: It may very well be effective at first, but if it is the only sort of authority the new general manager has or can acquire rather quickly, it loses much of its effectiveness. And if the person having this type of authority depends entirely upon it to maintain his relationship as leader in the organization, he is almost sure to experience a sad awakening. For a time he can operate because the others in the organization will recognize his power to dispense with their services. In other words, they will "go along" with the situation largely because of the fear of the consequences of *not* going along. But this situation will not last long, because it is based on suspicion and has no sound basis in mutual respect and cooperation. Thus, our new general manager is faced with the problem of gaining the acceptance of an authority beyond that which the board of directors conferred on him.

Here is where we find use for the second definition of authority, the "power that develops from knowledge." We expect of a leader that he will have knowledge of the job, and we respect him for his knowledge when we find that he has it. By a demonstration that he does have at least considerable knowledge of his job, our new general manager can increase the degree of acceptance of himself in his position and extend the length of time of this acceptance. In other words, when the people in the organization begin to say, "The new manager knows his stuff," and "It seems like the new boss has got a lot on the ball," the newly appointed executive has authority not only of position but also of knowledge.

This is a much stronger position, but it still falls a long way short of permanence. The third definition of authority was that it is the "power that derives from the influence of character as manifest in the opinion, respect, and esteem of others." And it is in this definition of authority that we find the degree of acceptance that has the elements of long life in the leadership relationship. This is a power of authority that must be earned. It cannot be given or conferred by any superior officer or board of directors. Indeed it can only be accorded to the leader by his followers; this is the authority that the group can and will, if it is earned, give to the boss. And this is the form of authority that is of real consequence, particularly in a free, democratic society. No part of this authority can be forced by edict or the giving of orders, and there is no substitute for time in the process of earning it.

To sum up, then, our new general manager by the authoritative nature of his position has an opportunity to demonstrate his job knowledge in order to have time enough to earn his real authority. Having earned the relationship of having "authority by esteem," while the authority by "virtue of position" may still remain, the need to use the "tools" of the latter type of authority will almost disappear. Such a leader will find it no longer necessary to give orders. In fact, he will by this very process have learned that giving orders to get things done is undesirable and, in the long run, ineffective.

For the purpose of examining the organization structure of an industrial business we will use that part of the definition of authority that says, "the right of a person to command or act by virtue of his job," and call it *formal authority*. When George McGowan was made factory manager he was given formal authority in the sense of this definition. He was empowered by the vice-president to make decisions, to act, and to give orders for the purpose of getting action to carry out his decisions. George's "area of authority" was limited to the job of factory manager and was probably defined in the memorandum put out by his boss "to everybody telling them of your new authority." Actually, the vice-president had given George some of his own formal authority in order to get the job of running the manufacturing end of the business performed more effectively.

To illustrate this, let us suppose that before George's appointment the organization chart of the company looked something like this:

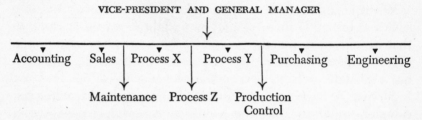

Note that the general manager has nine separate functions reporting directly to him. These nine functions represent all that is necessary to meet the objective of the business, which is the delivery of goods to the customers in return for cash payment. The general manager coordinates these functions, and they represent his area of formal authority. In other words, he has the "right to command" each of the people heading these functions.

The appointment of George to head up all the manufacturing was a reorganization of the structure and resulted in this:

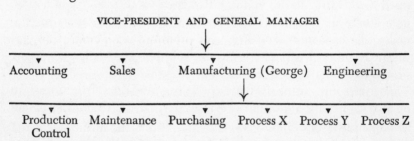

Now there are four functions reporting directly to the general manager instead of nine. The six functions that have been brought under George's direction are still the same as they were when they reported directly to the general manager, but now George in his "area of authority" has the "right to command" each of the people heading these functions. He obtained this formal authority from the general manager who *gave up his rights to command* the people heading the six functions in order that George might have this right. This means that the vice-president (George's boss) no longer has the right to give orders to the maintenance superintendent. That right, among others, he gave up to George.

THE COINCIDENCE OF AUTHORITY WITH RESPONSIBILITY

When assigning responsibility to anybody, it is essential that sufficient formal authority be delegated to the person involved so that he can carry out the responsibility. This is a cardinal rule urged by almost anyone who has studied this subject seriously, but a rule that probably is violated as often as it is followed.

No man has absolute authority, and no business executive has complete authority over the people in a business or any other organization. Perhaps the captain of a ship on the high seas at one time came very close to complete formal authority, but by now that has become much more limited. In our industrial life there are several agencies tending to lessen the formal authority of management. Of these, two are outstanding: first, the limitation imposed by the laws of the land (and administrative directives), and second, the contracts between managements and unions. Obviously, if the top executive of a company has had formal authority taken away from him by government, or if he has given up formal authority by signing a union contract, he cannot delegate the formal authority that he no longer has. For example, the government passes a law that says premium wages must be paid in the amount of fifty per cent over regular rate for all nonsupervisory work performed in excess of forty hours in any one week. This limits the authority of management. And if the company officers sign with the union a contract providing seniority rights to nonsupervisory employees, this, too, limits the authority of the management. In other words, there are external factors limiting the authority that an executive may delegate, just as there are, of course, internal factors (such as the authority of other executives) that limit delegation.

Now it is obvious that when a manager does not have what is usually considered to be essential authority he cannot delegate it. But if they understand the situation fully, the people in an organization will usually recognize the manager's position and continue to work diligently and well even under difficulties. Thus, if the government has established a policy of not permitting a certain company to increase wages, the employees will often go along without complaints against management. Needless to say, however, this is true only when the people are convinced that management is not using the government regulation as a "dodge" to keep from raising wages.

On the other hand, when the management has authority that it should delegate to those performing assigned tasks but withholds all or part of the formal authority, a natural resentment arises from a sense of injustice. For example, if the plant manager assigns the function of factory maintenance to Dave Brown but withholds from Dave the authority to say who shall be the foreman pipe-fitter, then Dave is most likely to resent such a limitation on his authority and question the justice of being held fully responsible for the quality of the pipe-fitting work in the factory. This suggests a modification of our so-called cardinal rule, to this effect: When assigning responsibility, all of the available formal authority that can be used in the most effective meeting of that responsibility should be delegated to whoever is being held responsible.

CONTROL BY WITHHOLDING

Very often the withholding of part of formal authority is done in the name of "control." This is illustrated by common rules of practice such as: "No foreman shall work any hourly-paid employee overtime without first obtaining approval by the plant manager," or "No capital expenditure shall be made by a branch manager in excess of $50 for any one item unless approved by the Budget Director." The above illustrations do not necessarily represent wrong or improper practice under all circumstances, but illustrate the kind of practice that stems from a policy of "control by withholding." It is often the result of lack of confidence in himself on the part of the boss who "withholds," a lack of confidence either in his selection of his subordinates or in his ability to control their performance or over-all accomplishment. This is a situation which usually results in an ineffective type of control, and it almost invariably leads to a gradual weakening of the people in the organization. If we never trust a boy to try to swim, he will never learn how to swim.

SOME EFFECTS OF TRADITION

The need to examine why we do things is very important in the field of organization. Most early attempts at organization for large undertakings were military in form, and much of the form and structure of our industrial organizations can be traced to the military concept. The military tradition is summed up in the lines of Tennyson's poem:

> "Theirs not to make reply,
> Theirs not to reason why,
> Theirs but to do and die."

What does this mean? Well, it means the taking away or the withholding of many human rights: the right to appeal against a decision affecting us; the right to know what is expected of us, and why; the right to participate in plans and decisions that are very important to us and our group; and the right that we have to feel that we are of consequence and of some importance. This view also means that people are expendable at the caprice of others, presumably "those in authority."

Much of human history which is concerned with doing a job involving large numbers of people will disclose the dominance of the above-described attitude toward people. This has often been true of military and political organizations, and it is not surprising when we find industrial organizations of the early modern period following a similar pattern. Thus, in the textile industry of Great Britain 150 years ago, the worker was to a large degree expendable. He was of use to the owner or manager for what he could do, and the owner or manager often had no interest in him beyond that. The worker's job was to *work*, not to think, plan, or participate. His place in the organization was not to question why but to do as he was told to do.

While we in industry are moving steadily away from the hard

and fast one-way street of traditional military organization (as also are the military themselves), nevertheless we are always subject to the conditioning of our thinking by tradition. It is not in an attempt to be peculiar or merely to be different that one important company in the steel industry draws its organization chart in the form of a circle of functions around a nucleus of administration. Thus, instead of putting the executives at the top of the organization chart and showing every person as *beneath* them (with the ordinary worker at the bottom), the executives become the axle of a wheel, and the various spokes of the wheel represent the functions present in the organization.

STAFF FUNCTIONS AND THE CONCEPT OF AUTHORITY

Modern business has grown increasingly complex, partly because of the competition for lowered costs and partly because of the growth in numerical size of our industrial plants, and this increasing complexity has brought the *staff* concept into the picture. The idea of having highly trained technical specialists available in an industrial plant was made popular by the teachings of Frederick W. Taylor, the accredited father of "scientific management."

The basic idea behind the staff specialist is that every executive, particularly in a large organization, cannot be equipped with sufficient specific knowledge to enable him to perform as well as he could if he had that knowledge. We are accustomed to having doctors of medicine, lawyers, and architects, to take some obvious examples, to whom we as individuals or groups can go for advice from their highly specialized knowledge. There is no real difference from this in the relationship between the staff personnel man in industry and the instrument-shop foreman. The foreman is not a highly trained specialist in training methods, let us say, and so he avails himself of the services of the training specialist, normally a member of the personnel department.

But there is much uncertainty among those engaged in industry as to what is "line" and what is "staff." Perhaps this can best be thought about as representing a relationship. A "line" relationship is one in which there is a chain of formal authority, of command. A "staff" relationship is one of service to help make more effective the work of others. Therefore, in many cases it is difficult to say specifically of a certain person that he is a staff man or that he is a line man.

Suppose that John is the chief time-study man, with several time-study engineers reporting to him, and that John's boss is the chief industrial engineer. The function of the time-standards department is to serve the other departments in the organization with specialized skill in work measurement and the establishment of good time standards of performance. Not all other departments use these services, but only those who feel that time measurement of jobs will aid them in doing their job in a better way. For example, the time-standards people may aid in bringing about better planning of work flow or more realistic manpower requirements or perhaps a good basis for establishing "standard costs." The important thing to note here is that we are talking of a "service." Whenever the people of the time-standards department are called upon to perform this service, they do so in a staff relationship to the person or department being served. Now on the other hand, within the industrial engineering division, of which time standards is a part, we have a "line" relationship between the chief industrial engineer, the boss of time study, and the time-study engineer. In other words, there is a line of formal authority within this division.

This example is typical of a case in which a function is purely staff; that is to say, the department exists only as a service, with no power or formal authority to compel others to use their services. (The misuse of this relationship will be discussed later.) It must be remembered, however, that there are cases within the industrial structure where a composite condition exists, where the same group perform work of a service or staff nature and at the same time have an area of responsibility specifically assigned to them. An example of this is the maintenance department. It is common practice in industry, when a breakdown occurs in the production department, to "send for the maintenance crew." Assuming that the foundry is having trouble with the overhead crane and that the electrical maintenance crew has been called in to work on it, this crew is now performing a service to the foundry, and the relationship is a staff one. The electrical gang is responsible for the good quality of their own work, even though the use of the crane in production is a responsibility of the line.

At the same time, the maintenance department is held responsible for bringing electrical power into the plant and delivering it to the various shops and departments. When this same electrical crew is working on the main distribution switchboard in the power-house, their relationship is that of working in the line; that is, they are now part of a chain of command within the maintenance department and have a direct assignment to meet a certain responsibility. Naturally, this supplying of power could be described as performing a service, but there is this difference: In connection with many of the staff services, the line has the option of accepting or rejecting the offered service. Thus, the training department may offer to help in training the supervisors of a certain department. But the line officials of that department may reject the services of the training department, and do their own supervisory training. However, when it comes to bringing power into the plant and maintaining an effective quantity, the line hardly has that privilege of rejection. And so we say again that this "line to staff" relationship is not always as simple as it is sometimes pictured to be.

A case in point is the hiring of people. A common practice is for the personnel department to handle this function for all but the upper levels of the organization. But, of course, there are two ways of handling this. The personnel department, having received a request for a draftsman from the engineering department, proceeds to hire a draftsman and send him to the engineering department. Under this method, the engineering department has given up or has had taken away from it the formal authority to say who shall work in the drafting room. The chief draftsman is presumably being held responsible to the chief engineer for the quality and quantity of work turned out by the drafting department. The kind of people employed to work there is very important to the accomplishment of the job, and therefore the right to say who shall or who shall not work in that department should be part of the formal authority of the person who is being held responsible for the results.

The other method of handling the hiring of people is to permit the personnel department to operate as a skilled service in the obtaining of candidates for work, and then requiring the boss for whom the individual is to work to make the final selection. The personnel department in this case operates in a staff relationship, recruiting, investigating, testing, interviewing, and screening applicants—using its skills and knowledge of how to do these things —and then submitting for final approval or disapproval the candidates felt to be most acceptable. Under these conditions, where the user of a staff specialist's service has the right of rejection of the service, the people performing a function in a staff relationship must keep constantly on their toes in the performance of a first-class service. They justify their very existence by the demonstration of their usefulness.

On the other hand, those who use the staff service must do so in full recognition that they (the line) are responsible for the results. If you employ the services of a lawyer to advise you on a point of law, you make the decision whether or not you use the advice. If it is bad advice and you use it, you, not the lawyer, are the one who goes to jail.

If George McGowan asks the cost department to give him a statement of unit costs for the product that is being made under process Y and, acting on that information, does several things that eventually prove to be wrong, he is responsible. When he discusses it with Mr. Frazer, the vice-president, he will no doubt explain the circumstance—how he based his judgment on the cost data he received—and probably Mr. Frazer will be sympathetic, but George's responsibility is in no way lessened. Frazer, having the accounting function as part of his responsibility, will bring the bad service on the part of the cost section to the attention of the executive in charge of accounting, and of course the cost people will be blamed for doing a bad "costing" job, but it is still George McGowan's fault for using bad services.

SUMMARY

And so we see that these matters of authority are not so simple as they might appear to be. In the last analysis, for example, a boss isn't *given* authority—he earns it. And it must also be remembered that he carries full responsibility for the use of that authority. He may delegate formal authority, but he still carries responsibility for its wise use. And he may call upon a staff specialist for advice, but again he, not the staff man, carries final responsibility for the actions he takes. The staff man may have responsibility for good *advice*, but the line cannot escape responsibility for wise and efficient *action*.

It has also been pointed out that the relationship between the line and the staff is not always as obvious as it is sometimes pictured to be. More will be said about this point in a later chapter.

CHAPTER 9

COMMUNICATION, A MAJOR
FUNCTION OF MANAGEMENT

> *George himself had written a memorandum of instruc-*
> *tion on the point in question. He had explained just what*
> *to do under the contract in the matter of seniority and in*
> *the case of a temporary removal into a job of different*
> *classification, and here—well, maybe Sam hadn't read it*
> *or maybe he hadn't understood it. Now there was a*
> *thought! Perhaps he hadn't understood it.*

Communication is a big word for a simple idea. It is the art of sharing information, ideas, and feelings. Most people think that it poses the major problem of modern industry. It is not an exact science or formula, but rather, an art or a knack. The real leader is the one who has the ability to express his ideas and feelings to others. Through his aptness people willingly receive what he means to say, and he is able to share himself in an ingenious way. Many people mistake communication for a technique and a scientific manipulation of words. This is a misconception, since fundamentally communication is the art of understanding and being understood.

The miraculous thing about communication is that the more ideas and feelings a leader shares with other people, the more he actually has for himself. This understanding of others and being understood by them is an enriching experience. It stimulates our capacities and develops our inner resources. The more we give of ourselves to others in understanding, the more we have left that is significant to ourselves.

In the plant, nothing is more important than the free, uninterrupted flow of understanding from the top boss to the lowest unskilled worker, *and* from the bottom man up to the top. Communication is always a two-way flow. It is expressing or having your ideas understood, but it is also understanding the ideas and feelings of others. In the company, communication is like a double set of pipes, with a faucet and feed valve for each person in the organization. There is a constant, uninterrupted flow of ideas and understanding from the bottom, unskilled worker, up through management to the top desk; while at the same time there is a steady flow from the top desk down through the bosses to the last employee. Each person in the plant must have access to this pipe and must have the ability to add to its content. The communication must always be a constant flow without leaks, clog, or pollution. The management has no other task so vital as the maintenance of this pipe line. When for some reason it becomes stopped up, untold personnel problems of the plant develop. George McGowan is stymied in his new manager's job unless he has the art and ability to make his ideas and influence felt. He will "fall on his face" unless he can get to the ideas and attitudes of those who work down the line. It proves to be the key to morale.

COMMUNICATION AND THE ORGANIZATION CHART

The typical organization of management in industry offers the *means* of communication even though at the same time it is apt to present the most restricting *limitations* on communications. The line of command is built-to-order to make the flow possible. Each level of authority acts as a division point in the pipe and adds a valve for inserting information and ideas. In a very large corporation, the many valves and levels sometimes reduce the pressure of the ideas that come from the top until they can barely be recognized down the line in Department A. Every person who has worked in any organization has learned early to put a filter on the ideas that come to him by saying, "Who said it?" or "Is it reliable?"

The successful executive must take pains to see that the instructions and ideas that come from his desk are kept in a pure, undefiled form all the way through the various levels of administration. He must be able to hear his ideas from the lips of the last worker in the plant and recognize them as his own. In fact, the *subordinate administrator's chief responsibility is the emphasis and clarification of the ideas of the top management.* It is the function of the line of command to confirm top management's original concepts. The boss who issues a policy on compensation for overtime work must have the support of his subordinate administrators. The supervisor and the foreman must consistently understand that the boss expects to pay for this when anyone is imposed upon beyond his regular work schedule. If this policy is muddled and the top boss is made to look unreasonable or is put in a position of seeming to exploit the worker, then the line of command has failed in its communication function. The boss must see to it, too, that the line gives him a "real" version of what is going on down in the plant. If there is dissatisfaction on overtime pay, the subordinate administrators have no right to stifle this information or keep it from the executive. It is his right to know what the accurate story is down on X machine in Department A.

The key persons to effective communications in the plant are the foremen. They are particularly the ones who directly represent management in the minds of the worker. They must always be set up as reliable and authentic sources of information. They must carry the stamp of authority as well as understanding. When the executive delegates his power to these supervisors, he is simply multiplying his own influence. The boss who thinks he can sit in the front office and keep all the authority on his desk is simply condemning himself to the all-consuming task of carrying out his own communication system by himself. When he releases some of this authority and builds up the power and dignity of his supervisors in the plant, he is freeing himself for more important planning and also extending the power of his ideas in many directions. Keeping subordinate bosses informed and backed up will bring a loyal flow of helpful information and understanding. When the distortions are removed from this flow, confidence and integrity are built up. In other words, the line produces that for which it was intended.

When the line of command is short-circuited, the trouble begins. It seems such a simple device for the superintendent to handle a situation on the floor of the factory without regard to the foreman. Is there ever an excuse for the superintendent's issuing an order directly to a worker without consulting the foreman? It is permissible only in the severest emergency. A command to a man working near an exposed wire or a worker on a faulty rig might be understandable. Even this emergency is allowable only if the superintendent covers by talking over the incident with the foreman and assuring him of the superintendent's desire to protect the foreman's men and influence. The entire line is broken down unless, in general, the executive works completely and exclusively through his subordinate managers or bosses.

Suppose a supervisor asks for a new piece of equipment. The manager says that his conversation with an operator convinces him that it isn't needed. The supervisor's usefulness is now at an end, because the manager is taking the word of the worker rather than the subordinate boss. Not only in his own eyes, but also in the eyes of the operator, the supervisor's recommendations are worthless because he was not consulted in the judgment that concerns his department. Whenever a superintendent jumps over the head of his subordinate for knowledge or advice, or whenever he gives orders directly to the workers, he has in reality relieved the subordinate of ever making decisions or giving advice again. The subordinate's wings and confidence have been clipped, and as a result the poor worker is uncertain where to get his correct communication.

One of George's problems, now he is manager, is his *new* relationship with his former fellow supervisors. He used to be on the same level with them, but now in order to give power to the flow of his ideas he must be the boss and he must maintain a distance above them. How much distance is required to keep his authority secure? Is it more important for George to be respected by the men than to be well liked by them? All of us have seen the fatality of either extreme. We know of bosses who have failed because they went all out to be "one of the fellows." They destroyed all dignity and distance and thus became ineffective as master decision-makers. Equally tragic is the leader who pulls himself so far from his subordinates that they can't reach him or feel the influence of his leadership. The men expect the boss to act like a boss. He must fulfill this role. *Fortune's* recent series on communication, "Is Anybody Listening?" closely defines the beautiful balance for the boss between eagerness and restraint, between aggressiveness and calmness, between accessibility and distance. In the end, George must be in the position where the power of his ideas and feeling are naturally accepted as coming from the top.

Cliques and cleavage within status levels can be disastrous to communication. If three of the four assistant managers are buddies, and one is left on the outside, resentment and blocks will destroy the flow. Protections will be erected and mutual trust broken. The cleverest ingenuity of the boss will be required to prevent or heal such a situation. Not only must he keep the circulation of confidence between the various levels of management, but he must break down the barriers that grow between men on the same level of authority.

NATURE OF LANGUAGE

We put too much faith in words. Language is not invincible. The written or spoken word seldom says exactly what the author intended. What is *not* said is sometimes more powerful than what is told. You remember that George was worried because the vice-president didn't speak to him in the hall. His silence was more powerful than any rebuke would be. *How* something is said is much more important than the actual words used. We have become conditioned to worship the printed word—thinking that anything in print is authoritative and reliable. And yet people can read the same passage or hear the same utterance and come away with entirely different conclusions. We have a tendency to see and hear only what we want to believe. We use quotations from others to back up what we felt was the truth originally.

As a matter of fact, language is not rational. Nearly every word is loaded with emotional content. Nice, clean words like soapsuds can mean sanitation to one, drudgery of dishwashing to another, and nausea from tasting them as a child to another. You never can tell what a seemingly innocent word will touch off in the mind of another.

We are also conditioned to read between the lines. We are never content to accept the words at face value. In reading a communique on economy from the top office, we say, "I wonder if he means that my inventories are too long," even though the word inventory was never used. The classic story to illustrate this is the one about the two workmen who were passing down the hall.

They passed the president of the company, who smiled and said, "Good morning." When the president was out of earshot, one of the workers said, "I wonder what he meant by that."

We never take words at their face value. We usually try to read something into their meaning. In our minds there is a distinction between the obvious and the underlying aspects of any statement.

An illustration of this distinction between what we say and what we mean is found in our generalizations and stereotypes. We love to "bunch up" people or ideas and brand them with a name. The word "Communist" has come to mean anyone who does not agree with us politically. The word "Mother" means something sentimental, kind, and good. "Economic Royalists" has come to mean something bad. "Dictatorship" has a very simple basic meaning, but to use it is dynamite. Even "Fair Practices" is emotion-laden to a high degree. This leads us to realize that words are tricky and that communication is essentially an exchange of feelings and not of ideas.

METHODS OF TRANSFERRING IDEAS

And now let us analyze the various methods of communication used by industry. Each of them has its strong points, but all contain certain limitations. A variety and wise use of all types must be employed.

First, we will discuss the written type of communication. This includes the written bulletin, or communique, and the formal letter. The written method insures definite and consistent treatment of a subject. There is a limit to the amount of misunderstanding if the words are put down in black type on a white piece of paper. When a bulletin goes to all the employees, it is telling a story in exactly the same words to all those who read it. It may be received differently by each reader, but at least it is consistent in its wording and presentation. The written method is usually the best way to make a clear-cut announcement, to fix responsibility or to define authority. George McGowan was not really the plant manager when the vice-president called him into the office. He became the plant manager when the vice-president sent out a memo about it to all concerned.

The written communique, however, is usually cold and rigid.

Persuasive explanation is lacking, and it is almost impossible to put the personal appeal into the written language. The written word cannot break down the emotional barriers or carry the personality of the writer. It does bring, however, the most definite type of information. When it is tucked away in the file, it offers the best possible protection and guidance to subordinates from the boss.

The oral face-to-face conference, or interview, has its function in communication. It gives the boss a chance actually to sell his point. He can utilize his personality and shade his emphasis when the material is in the spoken word. In a conference the hearer knows that he is expected to make a response, and so the situation of the interview produces a give-and-take relationship. Even if the receiver is silent, the teller can ascertain whether or not his words are accepted. The person being instructed or interviewed can be studied, and the boss can tell whether or not he is being understood.

The talking method affords a better opportunity for the use of emotion in communication. We all know the power of a harsh word said with force or a soft word said with a misty eye. Excitement, anger, sentiment, and love all can be expressed in the way the words are said. This is a powerful advantage for the spoken word in transmitting an idea and being understood.

When the boss wants to break down some resistance to his idea, it is an easier task to do it face to face than it is through written communication. An expert in the conference or "meeting" technique can call the group together and here, with the power of persuasion, break down the obstacles to his plan. If he is apt, sometimes he can turn this opposition into group acceptance and even persuade the group to help him, and through group pressure force compliance of his ideas.

Of course, the limitation to the oral method of communication is the high degree of misunderstanding and the variety of interpretations of what is being said. It seems that we take more liberty in giving interpretation to what we hear than what we read. Witnesses on the stand can give a more accurate review of what they have read than of what they have heard. One has only to hear the contrasting quotations given by people who have attended the same conference to realize the weakness of this method of communication of concrete information and policies. Many successful executives, when they have an important piece of information or a new idea to impart, will use a combination of both methods. They will type or print the bulletin giving the factual information. They will not send it, however, but call the men together and explain it sentence by sentence. Such an obvious device is sometimes considered by the worker to be a reflection on his ability and intelligence. If the boss talks down to an employee or makes it obvious that the worker has little individual ability to comprehend, the worker will build a wall and resist whatever comes to him from the source of the boss.

Visual aids have become a tremendous help in transferring ideas and communicating good understanding. Moving pictures, cartoons, bulletin boards, posters, house organs, advertisements—all of these are utilized as communication devices. By attractive presentation and repetition they can tell the story and drive home a message. There seems to be less conscious resistance to this type of propagandizing. They lose their effectiveness, however, if they are overused or forced upon a group. A clever moving picture is effective to demonstrate an idea. If the worker, however, must see a movie every time a group conference is held, he will soon build up a resistance. An effective, well-placed poster conveys an idea, but if the same poster is scattered in every direction, and everytime the worker looks up he sees the poster, he becomes immune to its message. The defensive attitude creeps in when the subordinate or worker realizes that he is being manipulated or propagandized by the visual aids. No one likes to be a pushover for a sales trick. Each of us likes to think that a new idea is partially his own, and not one that is forced down his throat.

The visual-aids method has a one-way flow and must always be recognized for this limitation. No one can answer back at a well-planned moving picture. There is no rebuttal to a barrage of posters. The best that we can give for our side is an anonymous pencil notation to a bulletin on the bulletin board. If the subject matter is in the realm of controversy, the fellows on the receiving end merely build up a wall to protect themselves from this pressure that they cannot answer or overcome.

Great use is being made of still another method of communication. These are the audio-aids, such as loud speakers, speeches, committee meetings, lectures, and "schools." These methods offer many of the same limitations that are found with visual aids. They can, however, add to the fellowship of the group and the "esprit de corps." When they are used on company time, these forms of communications give a break to the routine. They can build good will within the plant if they are well conducted. If they are always set up on a one-way flow from the boss to the worker, they may give the worker the idea that he is being pushed. This obviously does more harm than good and merely confirms tension and distrust.

DISTORTIONS TO THE FREE FLOW OF COMMUNICATION

Every work group in which there are two or more employees has what is called the "grapevine." It is the vast moving and informal type of information that spreads through a group. It has a terrific effect on the employees of a company, and no administrator can operate effectively as a leader without access to what is being said. One wise man has said that the best source of information and communication in his office is the water cooler. There, several times a day each employee will come and, while obtaining a drink, will exchange the latest choice morsels of information. These are taken back to the departments and desks and spread throughout the entire organization. The boss has to know what goes on at the water fountain as well as what is happening in his accounting department. Of course, he must not be naive enough to believe all that he hears, but it is important in administration for the executive to know what is being said.

This accumulation of "common knowledge" makes a profound impression on the plant. The wise boss knows how to discount and interpret the "scuttlebutt." He knows that no information picked up in this manner can be used without verification. Faulty or not, this information may be the only explanation that the employees have, and they grab it, accept it, and talk about it.

Thus, it is vital for the boss to know what the employees are thinking. If he is unusually skillful, he can sometimes use it to serve his own ends. For example, fear is particularly contagious, and in extreme cases the boss might plant the seeds of fear that the factory will close if production goals are not improved. The executive must be warned that fear can also distort facts and that, when it is once on the "grapevine," the information is subject to all sorts of twists and manipulations. It cannot be controlled by the more formal methods of communication. In the flow of communication up the line to the top executive's desk, good news has a tendency to flow very fast. If Department A breaks a production record, it doesn't take long to speed this information up the line to the general manager's desk. Bad news and blunders, on the other hand, are slowed down in the flow. The hush and delay tactics are applied to unpleasant and distasteful facts, and the boss is sometimes without information of a serious crisis in his plant. The foreman would like to have a solution to a mistake accompany the news of his "bust." He does his best to cover up the situation, until it can be corrected and worked out. The "cover up" is, of course, the worst blockage to communications, and it is a symptom of distrust and fear of misunderstanding. When an executive finds examples of blockage and covering of mistakes, it is an indication of distrust. It reveals a fear that the boss will not understand the reasons behind the mistake or that he will be unusually harsh in his judgment. The executive must correct this situation, when he finds it, and teach his subordinates that it is more dangerous for all of them when information and mistakes are stifled.

Some bosses have a reputation for quick placing of blame and the use of some subordinate as a goat. This technique builds up in the worker a defensive "alibi" which he is ready to use at all times. It creates damaging blows to fluid communication. The alibi is born of fear and accompanies this "sackholding," or unwarranted emphasis on the placing of blame. There is nothing more destructive to mutual trust.

BUILDING SELF-RESPECT IN ALL COMMUNICATIONS

Workers as well as bosses demand their own self-respect. It is fundamental that in order to be received adequately an idea must build up self-regard. This works both ways. Workers must be recognized as intelligent, sincere, self-respecting individuals. They must be conceived as willing to work diligently for a cause in which they believe. They will naturally be resentful of decisions and ideas that to them appear to be arbitrary or degrading. The boss, too, likes to be put in a good light. He likes to be thought of as conscientious, honest, and fair. He is susceptible to ideas and attitudes that acknowledge his place and status.

There is no danger in overdoing this business of building high self-adequacy through communications. One psychiatrist says there is no such thing as too much praise. Of course, he is quick to distinguish between flattery and sincere praise. Flattery is false praise and is damaging to the personality of the one who is flattered. If a person is told that he is perfectly wonderful in a field or an accomplishment where he knows he has bungled, he then begins to wonder about the sincerity of the one who praises him. It begins to dawn on him that maybe he has no real ability that is worthy of praise. This tears down the feeling of self-sufficiency and breeds fear. Genuine praise, however, has the opposite effect. When something is done well or when there is a genuine accomplishment, speaking of it in glowing terms merely encourages the worker or the boss and builds up his self-confidence. A good screen to put on all communications is not only "Is it true?" but also "Is it helpful and will it build up the dignity and self-worth of those who hear it?"

When a frontal attack is made on an individual or his values, he does not readily accept it. It is natural for him to build up defense areas which make communication impossible. Some executives who feel that everything they say is discounted or not heard do not realize that in "burning out" an employee they have built up high walls of resistance to anything that the boss might say in the future. Praise and commendation can and should be done publicly, preferably in a loud voice. This confirms the worker's notion that the boss is a smart man and that what he says is true and important. Corrections and reprimand, on the other hand, must be very confidential. The worker's ego must be protected so that he will be responsive to the ideas and suggestions of the boss.

It is important to emphasize again that the foreman is the key to good communication. In the eyes of the workers, he is the management. He represents the top executive in so far as the men are concerned. He is the link between the boss and the worker. He is also the link between the worker and the boss and must act as the representative and interpreter of the employees to the management. He is in the best position to sense the needs of the men in the plant, since he deals with them directly. He is aware of their feelings and their wants. He must translate these things to the top management so that it can know and understand the worker.

To be effective and efficient in communications, the foremen and supervisors must have authority and status. If responsibility is overcentralized and held by the top executive only, the first-line supervisor loses his effectiveness. It is impossible to run everything from the front office, and if the foreman is merely a "figurehead," he will soon be by-passed by the workers in their need to find a better answer for their questions. If the top executive finds that he has a constant stream of workers and subordinates running to him for information and guidance, it is an indication that he has not distributed authority down the line and he is putting himself on the spot of being the only one who can give out the accurate information with authority. All subordinates must be upheld in dignity and responsibility, or else be relieved of their jobs.

MUTUAL TRUST AND INTEGRITY

There is no short cut on manipulative techniques. Good communication rests entirely on mutual trust and integrity. If the worker believes that an attempt is being made to trick him into adopting an attitude or value, it will not succeed. Just as truly, management will not treat fairly an effort by employees to take advantage of the company. Talking down to the men or browbeating the boss can sometimes win a point but will lose the battle in the long run. There is no substitute for sincerity. Without it, you cannot share. "What you *are* speaks so loudly I can't hear what you *say*," defines communication. The ideal is mutual confidence, trust, and integrity, so that problems get to the boss before they happen, and solutions are the product of everyone, and thus are agreeable to all.

CHAPTER 10

THE USE AND MISUSE OF AUTHORITY

*"Well, now you're the boss around here, George, maybe
some of us fellows can get a little authority to do our
jobs. . . ."*

*"If those smart guys up in the office would keep their
noses out of other people's business, maybe we could get
some production out of this place. . . ."*

The situation which George McGowan and his subordinates face
is only too common in industry. Here is a supervisor in a function
that should operate in a staff relationship to the supervisors in
the departments performing the actual production work, and he
is seeking more authority and even line authority. He desires a
greater right to give positive instructions to people in other departments using his "services" of production planning. And here
is a supervisor in a line department who is irked at too many instructions, too much interference with what he feels is his rightful
formal authority by the people performing the service functions.

THE EFFECTS OF "SCIENTIFIC MANAGEMENT"

In Chapter 8 reference was made to Dr. F. W. Taylor's "scientific
management" approach to the business of getting work done more
effectively. An examination of this theory and the practices that
resulted from its application may throw some light on the problem
we are considering.

In the later years of the last century there developed in the
United States a great deal of pressure to make more goods available for wider distribution. This would be of no use if the people
in these wider economic levels could not afford to buy the goods,
so the problem was how to make things more cheaply.

This is where the teachings of Taylor became most important.

105

He taught that it was a function of industrial management to "develop a science of work" and apply it to each and every job, and also to "take this science to the worker."

Under the "old rule-of-thumb methods" referred to by Taylor in his writings, the methods employed in the making of things were largely up to the producing worker and his immediate foreman. The decision as to just when and where and how the work was to be done usually rested with the foreman, and the foreman also had his own ideas as to what constituted a good day's work for each man in the crew.

Under the application of "scientific management" all of this was changed. These functions were now to be performed by specialists. The methods engineer was to analyze each component to be manufactured and determine the steps that should be taken to fabricate the product, as well as the sequence in which each step or operation should be performed. Then, he was to design jigs and fixtures, patterns and dies, measuring tools, and special cutting devices for each of these operations in the process that he had planned. This "science" was then to be taken to the worker. It was already fully worked out and all that was required was for the worker to put pieces into the machine and take them out and to start and stop the machine as instructed. Of course, if the quantities to be processed should get very large, then the loading, unloading, starting, and stopping become almost automatic and very largely independent of the worker. The same procedure would hold for time standards and production planning. Highly trained technicians were to analyze and measure each element of performing a task and from the data obtained come up with a standard time that would represent "par" for the operation. Using the sequence developed by the methods engineer, and the time standards developed by the time-and-motion study engineer, the planning engineer would be able to work out complete plans and schedules for the movement of materials through the various steps of fabrication, deciding which should be worked on first, and which second, and the quantities that should be routed to which point and at what time.

This procedure, applied as it was to most consumer and producer goods industries, accomplished what was originally intended.

We had found the device that made goods more cheaply. We had discovered the technique of *removing the skill from the production of goods* by putting all the skill into the *means of producing the goods.*

In order to apply these specialized functions to industry, it was felt necessary to depart from the common "military line" structure of organization, and Taylor's functional type of organization came strongly to the fore. Under this method, a specialist was given the job of applying his own particular technical knowledge to each part of the plant where it was needed. The "speed boss," as Taylor called him (or the time-and-motion study man, as we call him today), would set job-performance standards for all production departments. That was his job—to see that proper standards were set. The same applied to the methods boss. He worked out the ways and means of doing each production job in each department. Indeed, under the Taylor system of supervision there were not just the speed boss and the methods boss but seven or eight different bosses, each handling a separate function. This feature of Taylor's system had many limitations, but the influence of the functional approach to the job of supervising is still strong in industry and has spread into our mercantile establishments, such as insurance companies and banks. Its greatest influence has been in the field of work specialization and in a distortion of the staff relationship.

This latter was brought into focus during the 1930s when, under the encouragement of the United States Government, labor unions grew very strong. In the Wagner Act (National Labor Relations Act, 1935) there were provisions known as "unfair labor practices" that were very broadly interpreted by the administrative boards set up under the Act. Industrial management found itself in a highly vulnerable position when the Act was invoked against a company because of something that a foreman had said or done that was said to constitute an unfair practice. To protect itself against the position of having scores or hundreds of foremen and other supervisors "violate the Act," management gave much authority to personnel managers in matters of hiring, discharging, and disciplining employees. This authority, of course, was taken away from the supervisor.

We already had in industry a structure of technical and other specialists who were shown on the organization charts as being in a staff relationship. Under the pressure of "maybe some of us fellows can get a little authority to do our jobs" and with the influence of functional supervision quite strong, our "staff" specialists were given more and more authority over areas previously bossed by the line supervisor. Indeed, sometimes we even went to the trouble to draw our charts something like this:

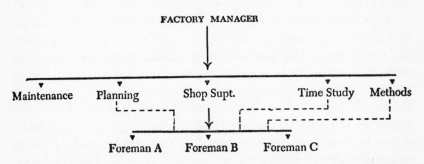

FACTORY MANAGER

Maintenance   Planning   Shop Supt.   Time Study   Methods

Foreman A   Foreman B   Foreman C

The broken lines in the above diagram indicate actual or implied formal authority over the function, and show the expanding control of the staff function.

There are at least two aspects of this situation, clear enough when we look back upon them, that we seem to have overlooked. In the first place, by bringing in the staff people as we did, we created the very thing that Taylor advocated—a thing we had already discovered to be impractical—we gave the worker two or more bosses. Thus, when the personnel director insisted on making decisions about personnel matters, he often became in effect another boss of the worker. And in the second place, we brought about a weakening effect on the "line foreman." He no longer had a proper amount of formal authority, and because he did not have the full right of rejection of the services of the specialist, he was no longer in a position to build for himself an "authority of knowledge."

With the industrial engineers in the position of issuing instructions as to how work should be done, when and how much should be done, and how long it should take to do it, and the personnel department saying who should be hired, transferred, or promoted, there wasn't much left for the foreman. And with the personnel department also having the authority to approve or disapprove who shall be fired or laid off, and the wage-and-salary administrator in the treasurer's department saying yes or no to raises, his authority was restricted still more. Keeping these restrictions of authority in mind, it might be well to ask at this point, just how much formal authority have we left in the hands of the foreman today? The answer is, *very little indeed*. And yet the tragedy is that in so many cases we expect him to meet his old responsibilities in full.

What is the effect of the multiple-boss condition? Most important is that it generates a feeling of uncertainty and consequent insecurity in all of those subject to having more than one boss and more than one source of instruction for accomplishing a piece of work. This situation exists not only for the foreman, but for the nonsupervisory employee as well, and each feels uncertain and insecure. The nonsupervisory employee will sense a situation in which his boss does not have sufficient formal authority. He tends to translate this into his own situation.

"Where do I stand if the guy (the foreman) doesn't rate enough around here to have any authority? He can't do anything for me. If he hasn't any authority, all he can do is pass the buck." And we wonder why Joe, who made the above remarks to his cronies, feels uncertain and insecure.

From the foregoing it will be seen that the multiple-boss situation and loss of sufficient formal authority have a close interrelationship so that it is difficult to say which is cause and which effect, which is the chicken and which the egg.

BY-PASSING AUTHORITY

The by-passing of formal authority is an area of difficulty for all levels of management, and it represents another major misuse of authority. In the vertical chain of formal authority the by-passing can take place in each direction—that is, up or down. Considering the downward direction, suppose the factory manager gives orders to the group foreman and ignores the shop superintendent who is the group foreman's direct boss. What is the effect on all three of the people involved directly and what may be the indirect effect upon others? Perhaps a case would illustrate this point more clearly.

Bob Trevor, the plant manager, was walking through the maintenance shops one day, and seeing Pete Thomas, the foreman of the welding shop, called him over and said, "Pete, I want you to send a couple of gas welders over to Department K. They've busted a press and I want it fixed right away."

Pete hesitated a few moments and then explained that Frank Stevens, the maintenance superintendent, had told him to keep the two gas welders going on a winding drum he had in the welding shop and "not let anything get in the way of getting it out." Bob Trevor brushed the objection aside with this: "I don't care what else there is around here, I want that press fixed and I want it done now."

Well, of course, that put Pete Thomas right squarely on the spot. Here he was the welding foreman, and his boss was Frank Stevens, the maintenance superintendent. But Bob Trevor was the plant manager and the boss of all of them. He wanted to do what Frank Stevens had told him to do. But who was he to argue with the Big Boss? And so he called the two gas welders and told them to go over to Department K and work on the press.

A little later Frank Stevens, the maintenance superintendent, came back to the shop and noticed that the drum was lying on the floor partly welded up but cold. And of course nobody was working on it. Frank found Pete at once and asked him, "How come you're not working on the winding drum? I told you to keep going on it until it was finished."

"I know you did, Frank, but Bob Trevor told me to drop everything and send the gas welders to K to fix a press," Pete said. "I explained what you told me, but he said the press came first, so what else could I do?"

Pete is uncertain. Who *is* his boss?

"What is Frank going to think?" says Pete to himself. "Should I have stood up to Bob Trevor? Gosh, I don't know where I stand around here."

And Frank Stevens, Pete's boss, is also upset.

"How does Bob think I can run this department with him upsetting it all the time? Why couldn't he have asked me about the press? Who's going to get the blame when the yard crane can't unload tomorrow because we don't have that drum fixed?"

And as these thoughts go through Frank's mind he, too, feels uncertain of where he stands. In fact, he feels mighty insecure.

And as the two welders get their gear set up in Department K, one says to the other, "Say, that guy Trevor sure throws his weight around!"

"Yeah," the other replies, "I guess he wants to show he's the boss. Pretty tough on Pete when Stevens catches up with this."

"I dunno about that," says the first, "but I figure it puts Frank Stevens in a heck of a spot. Gimme that wrench, will ya."

Now the fact is that the position of Bob Trevor, the plant manager, is also weakened. He probably does not realize it and perhaps does not give the incident a second thought. But he has also undermined the authority of Frank Stevens, the maintenance superintendent; he has made Pete Thomas uncertain where he stands with his boss; and even the welders know that there are things going on that are not right. Trevor has created an insecure feeling all down the line and has, therefore, weakened his own position.

To suggest that the boss cannot talk to anybody except those reporting directly to him is of course absurd. Any organization that is so rigid that communication of any sort can only take place through the strict line of the chain of command would be horrible to contemplate. There is nothing wrong about Bob Trevor's asking the welding foreman to do something, and certainly he should be perfectly free to talk to him. But Bob Trevor must recognize the probable effects of what he is doing. If the job the welders are working on is of minor importance, at least as far as when it should be completed is concerned, and if Pete and his welders know that Frank Stevens will be kept fully informed by Bob Trevor, the situation will no doubt be harmless. But otherwise, it is dangerous indeed.

Now for Bob Trevor to apologize to Frank Stevens for doing something in the maintenance department that was really Frank's job, is a recognition of Frank's authority and an assurance that it wasn't being undermined. To explain to Pete Thomas, at the time, that he would keep the record straight with Frank Stevens also is assurance that Pete's relationship with his boss is being recognized. But it is very easy indeed to forget some of these seeming trivialities. They turn out to be matters of the greatest importance at times.

And so we have seen something of how communication in an organization can have a very damaging effect at times. But our illustration also points up the difficulties brought on by the multiple-boss situation. When Bob Trevor gave orders to Pete Thomas, Pete had two bosses, two people exercising direct formal authority over his work. Unless there exists a very high degree of confidence in the entire gang, including those in the formal chain of command, even a temporary double-boss situation will cause a feeling of insecurity among those involved. But of course, the dual-boss situation is most unlikely to arise where the condition of confidence based on authority of knowledge and respect exists.

The by-passing of formal authority in the upward direction should now be considered. Using our same characters but at a different point of time, we will suppose one of the welders goes into Frank Stevens' office and talks to him about a job involving a new welding rod. There is little doubt in Pete Thomas' mind what they are discussing, because the rod is very much in evidence. There is nothing necessarily wrong with this, except as to the effect it may have on the people involved. Unless Pete feels quite secure in his relationship with his boss, Frank Stevens, on the one hand, and also with his subordinate on the other, there is danger in this by-passing. Thus, Pete may think to himself, "Why are those two so chummy? I know all about that new rod. Why doesn't he ask me? I guess I don't amount to very much around here."

If Frank Stevens is wise he will suggest to the welder that he talk to his foreman about this. Or having discussed the merits of this particular welding rod with the welder, he might very properly say something to this effect, "Say, be sure to talk this over with Pete. He knows a lot about this sort of thing, but I appreciate your calling it to my attention."

And then, at the first opportunity, Frank Stevens should tell Pete Thomas that he and the welder had a chat about the new welding rod, and then add, "Pete, I'd appreciate your views on this. And by the way, I told the welder he ought to talk to you about anything that comes up, and that I value your opinion about things."

This approval tends to keep things straight in the minds of all concerned and at the same time is a positive contribution to the building of an "authority of knowledge" and an "authority of respect."

THE ASSISTANT

Misuse of authority through improper assignment of responsibility and delegation of authority is very common in the title and job of "assistant." There is probably no more flagrant case of dual bosses than the appointment of an assistant with full formal authority over a function when the boss continues to exercise the same formal authority as he did before the appointment of his assistant. For example, if the foundry superintendent appoints an assistant foundry superintendent, we have the following change:

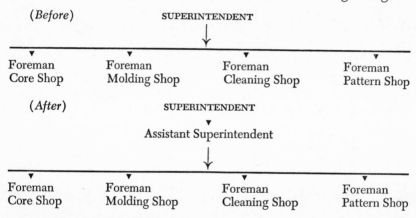

The difficulty that the superintendent or any other boss usually has, in such a case as this, is to realize that he has delegated all the tools of his authority to his assistant. In other words, he is no longer the direct boss of the core-shop foreman, for example.

This difficulty is usually most serious when there is just one assistant. Suppose our foundry superintendent had appointed two assistants. To one he assigned the responsibility for the core-making and molding functions and to the other, the pattern-making and cleaning functions. The failure to delegate the necessary authority does not happen nearly so often in this type of case. But in any event, if he withholds any essential authority from his assistants or continues to exercise formal direct authority over the functions he has assigned to them, he has created a multiple-boss situation.

Actually, in many cases the superintendent does not intend to delegate his authority to an assistant, but merely hopes that such an appointment will help "lighten his load." Nothing is wrong with this desire, of course, but in that case, what the boss probably should do is to appoint an "assistant to" the foundry superintendent, so that our structure would look something like this:

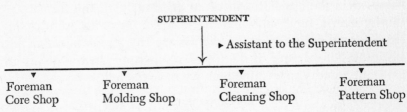

SUPERINTENDENT

▶ Assistant to the Superintendent

| Foreman | Foreman | Foreman | Foreman |
| Core Shop | Molding Shop | Cleaning Shop | Pattern Shop |

Now the relationship of the assistant to the superintendent and the foremen is a pure "staff" relationship and should carry no formal or command authority. In the event that the superintendent is unable to perform his duties on account of sickness, being out of town, or for some other reason, then it is quite proper to have the "assistant to" act as superintendent during that time, providing there has been a proper delegation of authority to him. But naturally, there must be a very clear understanding of the situation by the foremen, as well as a full acceptance of it. Provision must also be made for a definite and full reversion to the "status quo" when the superintendent returns to the job.

AUTHORITY AND THE THREAT

So much of the traditional concept of authority is in the power to impose punishment there is small wonder that we find this view interfering with the development of good human understanding in our organization processes. We are not suggesting that we have arrived at that ideal state of affairs where our industrial and business organizations can be built without regard to formal authority and the implied power in the chain of command. To imply or suggest this would be unrealistic and foolish. What is being suggested is that the boss who depends entirely or primarily on the power of formal authority is in a highly vulnerable position. But even more important, depending only on one's formal authority to secure compliance will result, within a surprisingly short time, in minimizing performance on the part of subordinates. Where those who work, no matter in what type of job, are constantly in fear of the consequence of not performing, the eventual result is in performing just enough work to avoid the punishment.

The slave who is subject to the whip if he does not work hard enough to please his master may apparently do a lot of work, but he learns very quickly not to do any more than enough to avoid the whip. In fact, he will do all he can to reduce the point at which the whip will be applied and be very careful not to increase his expected quota by ever doing anything beyond the critical point.

The worker who is constantly under the threat of being fired or otherwise severely disciplined responds in much the same way as the slave. There is nothing to gain by doing any more than the minimum to avoid being fired. If he does more than the minimum, all he accomplishes is to increase his load without increasing in any way his security or job satisfaction. In fact, he makes his situation less secure if he steps up his own work quota because the greater the amount expected of him the more likely he is to fall down, and thus the greater likelihood of his losing his job.

The thinking of much of present-day industry appears to be improving in this crude misuse of authority. However, as a warning, we should remind ourselves that full employment for more than a decade may have lulled us into a feeling of having "learned better." The test will come if and when the loss of the job represents a real threat to a worker's economic needs. The temptation to threaten workers is not very strong at present because of the fact that most anyone, losing one job, can get another. But can we successfully resist the temptation to threaten when and if it becomes possible really to threaten again?

One other point in this regard: In many a business today it is the members of the management team who can be most effectively threatened. Ordinary workers often have a union contract to protect them, and seniority provisions and grievance procedures often make threats rather unrealistic. But supervisors *can* be threatened.

However, threatening them has all the bad effects of threatening anyone else—and others besides, for they are members of management!

Another aspect of this subject of threat that requires much more attention than it has received in the past is in the other satisfactions that people get from their jobs. To lose status with one's fellow workers can be, and often is, more serious than the loss of a job. The demoting of a foreman to a nonsupervisory job is likewise most damaging. The demoted foreman has very little status with the foreman group, and because of his previous associations as a foreman he is not acceptable to his new group. Threats to these other satisfactions from a job can be, and often are, as serious as threats to the continuation of one's job.

The threat, actual or implied, to the individual ego, resulting from the misuse of authoritative power, can be very damaging. The foreman who steals an idea from one of his crew and passes it off as his own or who fails to give proper credit for special accomplishment is using his position of power as a threat to the ego satisfaction of members of the group. The foreman who plays favorites is doing much the same thing. He is constantly demonstrating his power by the withholding of things that Joe needs or by implying he has the power to do so.

The misuse of formal authority by the threat will eventually create a situation in any group that can prove destructive to the "point of no return," as far as that particular supervisor is concerned. The group will act as a group to protect itself against the threat. They will gang up on the boss by common consent.

"If he picks on one of us, he'll have the whole crew to contend with."

SUMMARY

Authority is a means of getting things done, a tool necessary for accomplishment when humans indulge in group action toward an objective. Like all tools, it is a means and not an end in itself and, to continue the analogy, like all other tools, it is capable of being misused and damaged even beyond repair. The wise leader will recognize the highly temporary nature of the formal authority that stems from his position, and he will move forward to greater acceptance of his leadership position by becoming an authority of knowledge and then continuing to build his relationship by understanding people, by demonstrated integrity of character, to the point where he will have the ultimate in authority which is the power that he earns from the group he is leading.

And it must also be remembered that the effective exercise of authority is no easy task. It is possible to fail by recklessly cutting across formal lines of authority—though it is also fatal to observe them with absolute strictness. It is possible to fail by unwise delegation. And it is easy to get the impression that *authority* and *threat* are closely related, whereas in the well-run organization threats are used sparingly, if used at all.

CHAPTER 11

WAGES AND INCENTIVES

Why wasn't the bonus plan for the production group working out as well as they thought it would? He always thought it worked all right, but . . . he realized that costs have gone up . . . that there is constant bickering about standards and allowances. . . . Sometimes he feels the foremen are siding with the men. . . .

The idea of "payment by results" is not new to industry. The "piecework" method of paying for production work goes back into early industrial history and is still used in modified forms today. But the idea of paying extra money as an incentive to turn out more work received its greatest boost in industrial thinking as a result of Frederick Taylor's teaching. By measuring the net work content of a job or operation and by applying calculated allowances for other needs of the job and the man doing the work, a standard time or "norm" was arrived at that represented "par" for that job. Under the various "wage-incentive plans" that grew up under this idea, a bonus of money was paid to the worker in relationship to the amount by which he exceeded the "par" output.

Most of these "production bonus plans" were built on the assumption that the *only* incentive needed to motivate people to increased output was the opportunity to make more money. That the chance to make more money is a strong motivation to most people is not questioned. That it is a *prime* motivation is open to serious question. That it is the sole motivation is fallacious and absurd.

INDIVIDUAL INCENTIVE PLANS

So many industrialists during the history of the development of modern industry have spoken with implied authority, usually
118

based upon a self-interpretation of their own experience, to this effect: "Give a man a chance to increase his pay and he'll work harder," or "Put a man in business for himself in his job, and you use the good old competitive spirit that built this country." So speak the self-styled rugged individualists and undoubtedly with sincerity and full belief in what they say. The trouble with such an expression is that it stems from an insufficient knowledge of human behavior, not only from a lack of understanding of other people's motivation but also from a failure to evaluate one's own.

The experience of many industrial and other business executives, particularly those who are applying unbiased and objective thinking to this problem, added to the work of Mayo, Roethlisberger, McGregor, and many others, prompts this statement: Any system of wage payment based solely on the premise that material gain is the only consequential motivation to work accomplishment is *doomed to failure*.

People in industry are usually working in some form of group. Sometimes it is a group within a large group. Often individuals are identified in various aspects of their work with different groups. A foreman is usually in this position. He is a member of the group of which he is boss and also a member of the group that is composed of the foremen, which in turn is part of the larger group that is "management"! It was pointed out in Chapter 4 that groups have their own "folkways and mores." This is just as true of the groups in industry as it is for society in general.

The work group will establish its own "code," or set of behavior rules, to which members of the group will conform, perhaps in part because of the ostracism that will take place if anyone violates this code. It is probable that the individual *wants* to conform because he must have the group "accept" him in order to satisfy his basic "social" needs. This does not mean that an individual will subordinate his judgment of right or wrong to the code of the group, but usually if he has a desire to be a member of a group he will at least outwardly accept the standards of behavior of that group. As was pointed out in a previous chapter, he, the individual worker, is much more comfortable under conditions of group acceptance.

An understanding of this group behavior is important when

evaluating the effectiveness of wage incentives. When we apply a standard in the form of a time period in which to do a job, we may think we are dealing with an individual worker and that it is "nobody else's business," but the fact is that Joe is going to respond to that time standard pretty much as the group expects him to respond.

Joe Stewart is just starting work for the XYZ Company. He has been shown his job by the foreman and is working away alone, when the man at the next machine, Bill Lewis, comes over to Joe, and after they exchange names in introduction, Bill says, "Did they explain the bonus setup they got here?" "Yeah," says Joe, "they told me something about it." "Well," continues Bill, "I suppose they gave you the usual line about not caring how much you make so long as you get out the work. I thought I'd tell you, Joe, we don't make more than 20 per cent around here."

Now Joe would like the money—there are a lot of things he could buy with it—but Joe does not make more than 20 per cent extra pay even when he finds he could make 25 per cent or 30 per cent quite easily.

With very few exceptions the Joes of our factories need the acceptance of their group more than they need the extra money. *They will not risk the exclusion that will result from violating the code of the group* for the sake of extra dollars.

Why does the group have this code, which seems silly on the face of it? They are purposely limiting their own earnings. The things that groups do can almost invariably be traced to a feeling of what is in the best interest of the group. To condemn the action or behavior of a group as stupid, illogical, or ignorant only means that it looks that way to the person voicing the condemnation, not that it necessarily is so, and it certainly is not to the group itself. Whenever a group in which we are interested behaves in a fashion that we do not like, it is wise to examine things *from the point of view of the group*. This is not always easy, but is an essential requirement if optimum performance is ever to be experienced from group action.

Why does our group that limits its production so that earnings are never more than 20 per cent above the base rate feel that its interests are best served that way? The chances are that the group is protecting itself against reductions in standard time which would result in an increase in the amount of production expected from each worker. In other words, the group feels it is reasonably safe from "attack" at the present rate of work output but that any increase would encourage the management to re-examine the time standards. This type of behavior is particularly evident when increase in the output might result in a reduction of work force. It is an exasperating yet common experience for management to observe the "spreading of the work" by a subtle slowing-up process when the group sees or even only senses a lessening in the amount of work available.

In an attempt to break down the individual and group "protective" attitude toward time standards, most managements today who have incentive systems based upon such standards offer guarantees to the employees that the time standard will not be reduced no matter how much production is turned out.

"Make as much as you can, boys. We'll guarantee not to re-time the job so long as the method or the material is not changed." "Watch the gimmick," says Joe. "If I up the output they'll find a way to change the method all right."

The management promise not to reduce the time allowed to do a piece of work is probably quite sincere. But the people in the work group suspect that high output when the standard time is generous will draw the management's attention to it and thus make it a natural target for an excuse to remeasure the job. The logical reservation, "so long as the method or material is unchanged," is often looked upon by management as an escape provision to rectify, by some rearrangement of the method of fabrication, an error in establishing the time standard.

GROUP INCENTIVE PLANS

Another interesting attempt to meet the problem of making "wage incentive" plans work is to be found in the so-called "group bonus" plan. This takes various forms depending on the process or product, but basically they are the same. It involves the pooling of the standard times for each operation that the group works on and then comparing the total *elapsed* time that the group has recorded with the total *allowed* time under the standard. If the elapsed time is less than the allowed time, premium wage is paid, based on this ratio. Usually each member of the group gets the same additional percentage payment over his base pay.

It will be seen quite readily that as long as this approach is based solely on a money motive it is not going to work satisfactorily. In some respects it is probably worse than the case of individual performance measurement. Now, any and *all* standards affect *all* members of the group alike, and a common bond of group protection is established against all of them.

Some time allowances will be generous by comparison with others. The operations so favored will be guarded by the group as "gravy," but the standards which are difficult to meet now become the personal business of the entire group. Opposition to these difficult standards usually takes the form of an attack on the fairness of penalizing the entire group by having "tight" standards. This whole thing is not vicious behavior necessarily, but more often is another aspect of the group-protection attitude.

At about this point in a discussion of this subject someone will break in with an observation to this effect, "Why do they install so many of these incentive plans if they are so bad?" or somebody else may say, "Well, I know of dozens of wage plans like you are talking about, and they seem to be working all right—some of them for years and still going strong."

Now, as we discussed the probable causes of failure in so many of these plans, it will be noted that no statement was made that production wage-incentive plans were necessarily bad or wrong as such. However, it was suggested that they would not succeed if extra money was the *only* incentive. When any plan or system is being installed in a factory or office, the fact of having something new around the place represents a subject of interest. This creating of an interest will usually result in some response from the group, commonly in the form of increased output. Further, the process of measuring work content and analyzing jobs will often result in the discovery of better methods which tend to lower the cost. If a careful analysis of our industrial incentive-wage plans were made, it most likely would be found that the increases in production and lowered costs came from methods improvement and not from the cash reward for additional work.

Where any plan has a history of continued success, it is suggested that the *entire* administration of the plan be examined to find the reason. It is a safe prediction that within the framework of the operation of a wage-incentive plan that has been successful over a considerable period of time there will be found other than economic rewards for the participants. Perhaps there is a high degree of participation by the production workers in the establishing of the standards; or possibly this is a case of where the group is *in* on all that is going on. In any of these cases there most likely will be a high degree of noneconomic satisfaction over and above any extra money that may be forthcoming.

INCENTIVE WAGES AND NONPRODUCTION WORKERS

Another problem for incentive wages arises in a factory operation in which incentive wages are offered to the production workers and not to the people employed on other than production work. This latter group includes the maintenance employees, the clerical workers, the inspectors, and others who are engaged in nonproduction functions. The reason for having the production group on incentive wages and the others not on such an incentive is usually because of the comparative ease in measuring output standards for the repetitive jobs and the difficulty of setting time standards on the others.

Under conditions where the production groups receive additional payment for work performed beyond a "par" and where the nonproduction or contributory workers do not have such a plan for them, the consequence is usually a larger "take-home pay" for the lower-skilled production workers than that for the higher-skilled or craft workers. Such an inequity cannot be brushed aside by the statement, "Well, the men on production are being paid for what they do over a normal day's work." This is quite fallacious because the bonus-earning potential is usually built into the time standard. Anyway, ask any maintenance, toolroom, or other hourly paid nonproduction worker, and you will get an enlightening answer usually in more lurid language. That men are very conscious of inequities in wages is evident in the amount of union demand for "elimination of inequities in wage rates" during the past two decades. This stems very largely from a sense of justice that we all have. A man feels just as keenly about somebody who he thinks is being overpaid for his work as he does when he feels that he himself is being underpaid. The justice of the situation is as important as, and probably more so than, the amount of money involved.

That this problem is recognized as a serious one is evidenced by the number of attempts that have been made to evolve wage-incentive plans based upon the quantity of work performed in most nonproduction jobs. There have been varying degrees of success in the fields of maintenance, clerical, and even inspection work on "incentive bonus," but as a practice such types of payment are not widespread. The mechanics of setting fair and just standards and the administration of the plans become too complex. Furthermore, such attempts to meet the problem of inequitable take-home pay still have the inherent weaknesses of the "payment-by-measured-output" approach to the business of wages.

INCENTIVE WAGES AND THE FOREMAN

A still further troublesome consequence of many wage-incentive plans is the difficulty often created in the worker-foreman relationship. A clue to this is George McGowan's worry that "sometimes he thinks the foremen are siding with the men."

If the foreman's salary is keyed to the base rates paid the people under his supervision, any additional wages as the result of a production bonus tends to close this wage gap. Incidentally, this same problem exists where there is a period of overtime worked in which the premium and additional pay received by the hourly paid people often results in a greater take-home pay than the foreman's. Often the overtime situation is temporary, but the bonus for the production worker is built on the assumption of permanence, even on the presumption that it will increase as worker efficiency increases. Thus, the foreman can see the differential between his wages and those of his subordinates becoming negligible. This situation is usually met in one of two ways—either by raising the foreman's salary so that the differential is quite large or by bringing the foreman under the wage-incentive plan. It is with the latter approach that we will deal here.

If the foreman's bonus is keyed to the amount of production or the amount of incentive wages earned by his group, his immediate interests become very closely associated with the group interests. If the group interests (*mores*) are primarily protective, then the foreman finds himself in a very conflicting situation. Any attack made upon time standards by an individual or the group with the idea of getting more allowed time will, if successful, increase the cost of labor in that operation or process. Any action by the foreman resisting the change is not only against his own immediate financial interest but impairs his relationship with the group with whom he has now become identified as a bonus participant. To act on behalf of the management (of which he, the foreman, is presumably a part) against a raise in allowed time to perform a task puts him in the critical situation of being rejected by the group and thereby seriously impairing his leadership position. If, on the other hand, he "sides with the men" he is impairing his identification with the management function and by this process tends to destroy his leadership position.

To meet the above situation (much more common than is realized) many managements argue that the foreman's bonus should be based on his over-all performance in meeting cost standards. This is usually accomplished by setting a budget as a "par" for each foreman and then paying a wage bonus determined by the actual costs matched against the budget. The difficulty with this approach lies in doubtful accuracy in the budget figures and the definition of the areas of cost that the foreman is responsible for and those which are outside of his jurisdiction.

Most budget figures are compiled from past experience, with a considerable amount of judgment as to their application to the future. The foreman or any member of management who is going to be judged against a budget will, like the employee and his time standard, get as generous a budget as he can in order to make his showing as easy for himself as possible. (If you doubt this at all, look at the history of government budgets and the bureaus that are being budgeted.) Where past performance of the departments or other subdivisions of the company is a strong influence on the setting up of a budget against which future performance is to be judged and used as a basis for extra pay, we encounter this travesty of justice: The supervisor whose administration has been lax will have a much greater opportunity for a good showing than will the one who has done a top-notch job and therefore has set himself a standard difficult to beat. Such a situation should be avoided.

In determining the cost areas to be included in the budget covering a supervisor's responsibility we run into another type of problem. The tendency here is to establish a sense of jurisdictional importance that will operate against the over-all corporation effectiveness. For example, if the foreman in charge of process Y finds that he will have to work his group overtime in order to get enough material moved to process Z, he is faced with a conflict of interests. The over-all job calls for keeping Z supplied, but it will "hurt his budget" because the overtime will be charged against him. Costs of an indirect nature are usually charged to an account or work-order number, and from these accumulations the charges are distributed to the area of responsibility covered by the budget. To expect a foreman to be meticulous in his accurate recording of charges when it is against his "interest" to do so is expecting a great deal from a fallible human.

Under these conditions of measuring a supervisor's performance, one is faced with the superhuman task of equitable distribution of costs while at the same time dealing with the administrative problem of demonstrating fairness. In fact, in the matter of "extra pay for extra performance" as applied to the foreman, we find the same set of human behavior problems as we did with the production worker, with money considered the sole motivating force. Actually, by the assumption that cash reward is the preeminent urge to accomplishment, management has just made things hard for itself.

Like all discussions of a subject that is highly critical in nature and destructive of present practice or tradition, it is valid to counter with the question, "Well, if things are that bad, what should we do that's better?"

THE USE OF INCENTIVE WAGES

The most important thing that we can do lies in the area of thinking our problems through. When considering the possibility of incentive plans of any form, it is essential that we remember we are trying to motivate people to more effective effort. People are complex and each is different from the other, so any approach to the motivation of individuals that is reduced to a simple formula should be suspect. Any plan that is based on any *one* of the satisfaction needs of people is most likely doomed. Each of us has an urge to satisfy at least our economic needs, our need for acceptance within our natural groups, and our need for personal recognition, with opportunity to demonstrate capability.

When it comes to the motivation of people in their work, any system, plan, or scheme that does not take all these *needs* and *urges* into full consideration is in serious danger of failing. Further, any approach to this problem must recognize that the degree of drive that each and any of these satisfactions have in an individual will vary considerably from person to person and also in the same individual from time to time.

Therefore, it is suggested that our approach be in terms of what the complete group is trying to accomplish. In other words, if we are talking about an industrial company, what is the company in business for? Suppose that this is defined as "to make and sell products to our customers at such a quality and price that they will continue to buy from us indefinitely." This becomes the objective of the complete group, no matter how small or large. Then the objective of each group that makes up the whole should be aimed toward the accomplishment of the main objective. This gives us the reason for motivating everybody in the organization—to accomplish the objective.

To do this effectively, everybody must *participate* in what has to be done toward the objective. The main objective of the business is the important thing to which each group, subgroup, and individual objective should be contributory. In other words, if we attach more importance to the job (objective) or to any subgroup in an industrial organization than to the over-all job, we are creating a distorted perspective. The ideal, but by no means visionary, approach to motivating people in our industry would, therefore, be to create conditions in which the meeting of individual satisfactions coincides with the serving of the whole company.

This involves a maximum amount of participation in the affairs of the group and the whole organization by everybody—participation to the extent of the ability of each one to contribute. It also means participation in the successes and the failures. It means participation in the determination of the rules and conditions under which work is performed; it means a recognition of the responsibility aspect of participation.

Profit sharing is a phrase that is kicked around with probably as much loose application and misunderstanding as any of our industrial phrases. How often one hears, "Yes, they'll take a share of the profits, all right, but try to get them to take a share of the losses!" This is an example of incomplete reasoning, failing to think a thing through. Why do they (the nonmanagement employees) refuse to "share the losses," but take a "share of the profits"? To assume that "they" are dishonest is an indictment no man should dare to make, so there must be some other reason. Perhaps it is because they feel they are to some degree responsible for making the profits, but had no share in the responsibility for the losses. If the participation is sufficiently far-reaching through the entire organization, the sense of responsibility that stems from a knowledge of having "been in on" things will also include the failures as well as the successes.

To talk of profit sharing as the only real technique of motivation is probably no more sound in its human-relations application than to talk of a production incentive bonus in that way. To talk of participation in the things that affect people's urges is much safer ground. To participate in the material profit is a natural portion, but only a portion, of the total satisfaction that people get from the work they do.

As a note of warning, the above suggestions coupled with all the other and similar ideas on human motivation in this book might be interpreted as "another formula" for motivating people. Such an interpretation might lead to this: "Say, that's a swell idea. Let's set up a complete participation plan."

Nothing could be more dangerous. This is no substitute for time in the process of increasing the degree of participation and the related responsibility. Give it to people as fast as they can take it but no faster, as much as they can take but no more. Remember, when weaning a child from a milk diet you do not at once feed him a full meal of steak and mushrooms.

Above all, there is one requisite to which there is no exception, and that is the element of complete sincerity on the part of the management which is prepared to include the whole group in a plan of participation. This is probably the most critical of all aspects of our human-relations problem. Joe, the nonsupervisory worker, Bill, the foreman, Steve, the superintendent, and Bob, the manager, are more sensitive to sincerity than to any one other thing. They will respond more quickly to it than to any other condition, and probably the most sensitive of these is Joe.

CHAPTER 12

DEALING WITH THE UNION

*"It's about time the foremen around here learned to re-
spect the contract!"*

THE UNION AS A PROTECTIVE ORGANIZATION

To be able to deal successfully with unions certainly requires
patience, but patience alone is not enough. While patience is of
great importance, an understanding of unions is perhaps of even
greater importance to anyone faced with the job of bargaining with
a union and then living with the bargain.

Historically the trade union and the labor union are protective
organizations. They provide protection for their members against
forces stronger than the individuals who make up the membership.
It is a peculiar fact that the historic ancestor of the trade union
is the same as that of the business association, namely, the craft
guild of the Middle Ages. This is quite logical when it is realized
that the reason for the existence of the guild, the trade association, and the union is the same in each case: that is, protection
of mutual interests from encroachment by outside forces.

While it is felt that the need or desire for mutual protection is
the prime force that motivates the trade and labor unions (as also
it does the trade associations), nevertheless we must admit that
there are other forces adding to their development. We shall discuss them later in this chapter, but meanwhile this question is of
great interest: "Why does the union member feel he needs protection and against what?"

A basic human urge is to survive. To do so it is necessary that
we provide for ourselves food, clothing, and shelter. This is accomplished by using our skills and physical effort. In a simple economy
such as an agricultural one this is quite obvious and straight-
130

forward. Food is grown by cultivating the soil. Cattle are raised by grazing. Shelter is provided by cutting timber, and clothing, by weaving wool or cotton or by utilizing the skins of animals.

The "Craft" Union, or Trade Union. In the much more complex economy of today, however, the process of providing for our needs is not so clear-cut. When he is selling his services (or skills and efforts) or exchanging them for his basic economic needs, there are many forces that could interfere with the individual in his efforts to provide these needs. The individual in an agricultural economy who has a much higher skill than his fellows in the forging of plowshares might "go into the plowsharing business." When he does so he must exchange his product for the ways of satisfying his basic needs. He cannot eat plowshares nor can he wear them or use them as shelter. He is now subject to the law of supply and demand. The farmer must want the plowshare badly enough to be willing to exchange farm products for one. The artisan must make plowshares good enough and cheaply enough to pay the farmer to make the exchange. If the maker makes more plowshares than the farmers can use or if too many artisans get into the plowshare business, the exchange value of plowshares goes down. Also, if one of the craftsmen finds means of making more plowshares per day than his fellow craftsmen in the same business, then, assuming that his economic needs are about equal with theirs, he is able to exchange each of his plowshares for less. In other words, he depresses the market for his fellow craftsmen. The farmer is naturally looking for the best rate of exchange between the things he produces and the things he needs that he does not produce. Therefore, our original craftsman finds his plowshares are worth less because his competitor will exchange his plowshares for less. He must get along with less food, clothing, and shelter, or learn how to make plowshares more cheaply.

At this point you are perhaps saying, "Ah, ha! But this is competition, this is the very thing that has raised our standard of living. Make things more cheaply, produce a lot more to meet the demand, and more and more people are able to buy them. And you create more jobs besides." Quite correct, your argument is valid, and this country has demonstrated its truth. However, if you are on the short end of the competition, as is our plowshare maker, the im-

mediate effect of lowering the value of plowshares is an assault on
your economic position. It represents a very real risk, and may leave
you unable to provide for your basic economic needs. And we
must never forget that even though this process does provide more
things for more people and also more jobs in the long run, it poses
some very real threats to the people who cannot adapt themselves.

Here is where the idea of protection begins. It stems from a
feeling of insecurity. To feel insecure is, of course, a condition
common to all of us, and to strive for a condition or feeling of
greater security, or perhaps less insecurity, is one of the strongest
motivating forces in nature. Therefore, it is quite natural for people who are faced with forces capable of increasing their insecurity
to take some appropriate action to defend themselves.

The craftsman who sells his skill in the making of things and
gets in exchange the satisfaction of his basic needs in food and
shelter, as our forger of plowshares does, is faced with a very
practical form of this problem. Obviously, he cannot eat his product, so his problem is one of insuring a satisfactory exchange value
for his product in relationship to his food, clothing, and shelter
needs. He cannot completely insure such an exchange value, but
he can lessen the insecurity if he can reduce the risk. As the above
illustration shows, there are three major forces that can affect our
craftsman's security: first, too many people making plowshares;
second, somebody making them much more cheaply than the
others; and third, technological change that makes the farmer no
longer need plowshares.

Another natural force in human behavior is our tendency to
think in terms of groups. If we feel insecure as individuals, we look
for others in a similar position and form a group for the purpose of
collective security against a common force that is threatening. So
our craftsman who can forge plowshares combines with others of a
similar trade who also feel somewhat insecure for the same reasons
he does, and we have a craft or trade union.

In dealing with a craft type of union it is well to keep in mind
the reasons for the existence of the union and the various forms of
insecurity feelings that motivate it. Many of the so-called "unreasonable" actions of union officials and union members can be

understood if we take the trouble to "think through" to the basic reasons for such attitudes.

When the union limits the number of apprentices it will train, it is often doing so in order that the craft will not have "too many people making plowshares" or too many people laying bricks. The jurisdictional dispute is another aspect of the same protective function of the union. If those of another craft with some overlap of the skills involved perform work that I think my craft should normally perform, I expect my union to defend me by taking action to prevent this invasion of my craft territory. For example, the craftsman who installs steam lines and who calls himself a "steam fitter" encounters the craftsman who installs water lines and who calls himself a "plumber." Suppose that this plumber is working on the repair of a steam valve. Then the steam fitter will feel that his natural jurisdiction is being invaded. He feels that his, the steam fitter's, skill will be less valuable if he lets "anybody with a wrench in his hand" perform tasks that he usually performs. He is afraid of what he calls the dilution of his trade. It is largely because of such situations as these that the craft-union members have resisted the specialization that we so often need in mass production. Incidentally, we shall discuss the impact of high production on craft unions a little later.

When our craftsman encounters any fellow craftsman "making them much cheaper," the group action of the union is likely to come into play by applying social pressure to bring the offender into line. If the offending craftsman is a member of the union, then the pressure may take the form of a threat to expel him from union membership. Or if this attack on the value of a craft is the work of a group in one certain company, the craftsmen, through their union, may get cooperative action from fellow unionists of perhaps another craft, who can withhold material or their labor from the offending group or company needing them. Here we find the "sympathetic strike" and the type of action often called "secondary boycott."

Resistance to technological change is one of the "unreasonable" areas of craft-union action. It can be argued that improvements in the ways of doing things have always resulted in more jobs for more people as well as more things for more people. But how logical does this appear to the skilled house painter when asked to substitute a spray gun for a brush? He may be quite willing to accept the broad argument that reducing the cost of painting houses will eventually increase the ability of more people to buy houses and that in the long run there will be many more jobs and much more painting. However, in the meantime our painter is wondering what happens to him. Is he willing to risk using up the available work and being out of a job, against the big increase in the number of jobs in the more distant future? Or does he say to himself, "I'm going to protect what I've got,"? Perhaps when looked at from his point of view, he does not seem quite so unreasonable.

Let's summarize what we have said. The craftsman protects himself from an increase in his insecurity by limiting the number of people that work at his particular craft. He resists the invasion of his craft by those who in his opinion are not qualified or who have not met his (the craftsman's) requirements. Also, he attempts to prevent displacement of the need for his craft, a result that sometimes follows the introduction of mass-production methods. And he tries to enforce a continued use of his craft by bringing economic pressure to bear. All this he often tries to accomplish through the group action of a union.

The "Non-craft" Union, or Labor Union. As has been pointed out earlier, the United States of America has been going through a form of industrial revolution since the 1890s and 1900s. Under the leadership of such men as Frederick W. Taylor, industry developed the philosophy of "mass production." As a result of this philosophy, a science of the work process was evolved and made available to the production worker. This meant that industry analyzed the kind of work required to produce an article and divided the work up into separate operations. Then, by determining the order in which each of these operations should be performed, a definite flow of work was established. This procedure involved the use of the highly skilled specialist who engineered the operational steps and the sequence. It also involved specialization in the work performed by the production worker. This worker was able to perform his work without spending time and effort in determining how the job should be done—that had already been done for him. This pre-engineering of the "how" opened up a great area of development in the engineering of tools for the performing of detailed steps in the production process so that the production worker often had no greater function than to follow the method "built into the tools of production." By using the engineered "tools of production," to which horsepower, usually in the form of electrical energy, had been harnessed, the production worker was now able to turn out many, many times the quantity of products that he had produced heretofore. And by concentrating his efforts on one or a few simple repetitive operations he was often able to attain a very high degree of productive efficiency.

Let us pause at this point and examine what has happened. Have we not revolutionized the whole approach to the production of the goods that we need and use? By doing the thinking, planning, and deciding before the actual work of producing, and having these planning functions done by people other than the production worker, we have transferred the "point of skill application." We now use craft skills in industry to make the tools that make things, and very rarely use craft skills in the making of the things themselves.

You will notice that the term "craft skills," rather than the word "skills," is used here. The reason is that so often the argument is put forward that there is no such thing as "unskilled work." We have no intention of quarreling with this. Nevertheless, there is a basic difference between the skill required in the performance of a craft and the skill needed for a repetitive production job in the mass-production industry. The difference lies in this, that the production worker whose means of production has been engineered for him does not have to make a choice in how work should be performed. He is not permitted to decide what method to use, what tools to employ, or in what sequence to perform the steps of the work. On the other hand, the skilled artisan, the craftsman, does make decisions as to how to go about performing a piece of work, what tools to use, and when to use them. Consequently, the craftsman assumes a responsibility for the work he does because of the degree of latitude he has in performing it. On the other hand, the production worker who has no choice in how the work is per-

formed has very little responsibility for the result. Just as significant is the fact that in order to be able to earn a living, the person
engaged in such pre-engineered work does not have to have any
more knowledge than to be able to read simple English, understand simple oral instructions, and perhaps add and subtract whole
numbers. So it will be seen that there is some meaning to the term
"craft skill" as it applies to our modern industry.

As this mammoth production machine that we call mass production grew, more and more thousands of people engaged in
the actual production processes—people who, because of not having a craft skill, had no protective organization to go to for a sense
of collective security. And, if we examine their problem, we see
that while the craft-skilled artisan had his security problems he
at least had the knowledge of his craft and a considerable range
of opportunity to use his craft skill to provide for his needs. But
not so for the non-craft-skilled production worker. He was dependent upon industrial management to provide him with the means
of meeting his needs. Management had to sell a lot of refrigerators
so that there would be enough work in making refrigerator parts
to provide him with a job. And, remember, before he could go to
work on the particular refrigerator parts that he made, an engineer
had to devise the tools and machinery that Joe used in the production process.

This dependency is the basic cause of a feeling of insecurity,
a much greater insecurity than that of the skilled craftsman. From
such a growing group of people came a need and a demand for
collective protection, and the whole matter came to a head in the
early 1930s. The craft unions were under pressure to admit these
non-craft workers to membership, but the very nature of their own
security was being threatened by this proposed "dilution" of their
ranks and they (the craft unions) refused. As a consequence, in
1935, an insurgent group from within the American Federation
of Labor, known as the Committee for Industrial Organization,
broke away and formed another federation of unions. This group
was composed of unions whose membership included both non-
craft and craft workers in the different industries. For example,
the rubber workers, the automobile and agricultural-implement
workers, the steel workers, etc. These unions and other similar

ones, whose growth during the 1930s was phenomenal, became what is now the grouping known as the Congress of Industrial Organizations. They perform the function of providing the workers of our industries who are not craft-skilled with a sense of collective security much the same as that provided for the craftsman by his union. However, in dealing with different unions, and particularly with unions from different federations, it is important to remember that the form of insecurity that motivates them is often quite different.

THE NONECONOMIC NEEDS OF WORKERS

The differences between the craftsman and the non-craft worker and their respective unions becomes even more apparent when we examine the noneconomic satisfactions that people must get from their jobs. The man with a craft skill gets much satisfaction from the "job of accomplishment" in the things he produces. The toolmaker will get a deep feeling of personal satisfaction from a tool or a gauge he has made, even though he may never know much about the end point of the production article that the tool is for. Naturally, knowing the use and application of the device he has made will probably add to his satisfaction. But in his day-to-day work in using his skill to make things for which he has a considerable measure of responsibility and which he can identify as "his," he gets a feeling of personal importance and of consequence. The general manager of a large corporation in the aviation field was once showing the author around the city of Cincinnati. He stopped at a downtown building and, pointing to some beautiful iron grill work, said, "I made that while I was a co-op student at the University here." The pride and joy of personal satisfaction was so evident in his voice and bearing that it will always be remembered. When dealing with a craft union, remember you are dealing with a group who are protecting their craft, not only because it provides them with the means of satisfying their economic needs, but also because they are jealous of their means of obtaining personal satisfactions of accomplishment.

In comparing the noneconomic satisfactions of the non-craft worker with those of the craftsman, we are entering the area of greatest misunderstanding in union-management relations. It is very difficult for Joe, the production worker, to get personal satisfaction of accomplishment out of a job where he has no choice of method, when all the brains and skill are built into the tools and machines. His relationship to the product is quite different from that of the skilled craftsman. Joe cannot identify himself with the results of his work except in a very general way, as part of a whole "mass" of production. He cannot get a feeling of importance (unless he has quite a vivid imagination and exceptionally comprehensive knowledge of the whole process) from his little niche in the production factory. Stamping out a queer-shaped part identified by a number gives little or no opportunity for self-expression or creativeness; in other words, it is most unlikely to provide satisfaction for Joe's ego, his desire to be recognized as an individual. The willingness of many union members to contribute time and energy to union affairs as officers, stewards, and committeemen of the "local" is strong evidence of an urge to be recognized as an individual and someone of importance among one's fellow men. Perhaps if those of our management and supervisory forces would realize that the predominant urge behind the man who becomes a steward, for example, is likely the same urge that impelled them to become supervisors, we might have a greater amount of understanding when dealing with the union.

The urge for status, for the position of leader, for recognition by one's fellows, is a powerful one, and any additional economic gain is usually secondary, whether one is a foreman or a steward. As Peter Drucker points out in his book, *The New Society,* there has been a trend toward the appointment to management jobs of the "staff man" and the college graduate, thus reducing the traditional opportunities for the rank-and-file worker. Consequently, we can understand his conclusion that to the worker a position of leadership in the union is especially attractive because it affords him a good deal of prestige.

THE UNION AND MANAGEMENT AUTHORITY

Perhaps the closest thing to absolute or complete managerial authority is the slave economy, where there is the legal right to ownership of human beings and the right to dispose of them in terms of life or death. Obviously, present-day management in our society has much less authority than this. There have been two major forces at work tending to lessen managerial authority: government and the trade or labor union. Government action (which in a democracy means public action) limiting managerial authority has a history almost as long as history itself. It goes from the Factory Acts of the early nineteenth century up through the safety codes, Labor-Management Relations Act, and Fair Labor Standards Act of our present day. Each time the federal, state, or municipal government passes a law imposing some rule or regulation on business or industry, it is a limitation of management authority.

Likewise, when a management signs a contract with a union representing the employees under that management's jurisdiction, it (the management) has agreed to some limitation of its authority. For example, the law provides (in interstate commerce) that no employer shall pay any employee less than 75 cents an hour. That is a limitation of management authority. Should an employer company (represented by management) agree with its employees (represented by their union) to pay a scale of wages none of which is less than one dollar an hour, this is a further limitation of management's authority. If management agrees, in the contract it makes with the union, that only in accordance with strict seniority standing will it lay off employees in the event of reduced business, this too is a limitation of managerial authority. This management has given up the right to say who shall go and who shall be retained in the event of work-force reduction.

As the management cannot delegate authority that it does not have, then it naturally follows that any limitation will apply all the way down through the organization. If the general manager does not have the authority to pay anybody in the bargaining unit less than one dollar an hour, obviously he cannot give authority to do so to any of his subordinates in the entire organization. Usually the supervisory force will recognize this fact and do its best to work with limited authority. However, when managements fail to delegate essential authority that they have, down through the line of supervision, damage can be done. Some of the dangers of this have been discussed in the chapters on authority. But in dealing with the union it becomes quite critical.

A group under the jurisdiction of a foreman will feel a lack of confidence on the part of the management in the foreman if essential authority has been withheld from him. It takes exceptional leadership qualities in a foreman to overcome this handicap. In many cases where the foreman lacks important authority the group will look to the union steward to provide it. While the steward does not have the formal authority by virtue of having it delegated to him, he will often assume it for the purpose of demonstrating union power.

Another point to be considered is that a union by its very nature is a political organization. It exists by the will of its members, and in most unions the democratic process controls its internal operations. The officers, stewards, and committee chairmen are usually elected by the membership, using one of the established democratic methods. This means that, since he is beholden to an electorate for his position, a union official must serve his constituency in the way they expect to be served or make way for somebody who will. A traditional method of a union to justify itself to its members is to demonstrate it has the power to enforce its demands. Quite often, during the last few years, a union has called a strike on an issue of comparatively little consequence. This in many cases is what Drucker calls a "symbolic strike,"—a symbol to management of its power, and also a symbol to its members of its ability to bring into play the most powerful weapon the union has.

A much more subtle method of demonstrating power that is used by a union is the invading of management's authority. In fact, so serious has this become that many union contracts contain a clause defining "management's prerogatives." It should always be borne in mind that the union, being a protective organization, is in opposition to the enterprise whenever it feels the interests of its members are in jeopardy. Therefore, from the point of view of the union, the more power it has in its relation to the management of the company employing its members, the better its position when it comes to performing its function of protection.

As has already been made clear, mass production, with its centralizing of authority and its wide use of the staff man, has led to a definite limitation of the authority of the first line of supervision. Indeed, this limitation has progressed so far in many industrial organizations that the foreman's formal authority is practically zero. This represents a very weak situation in the relationship between the foreman and his group, and the unions have been quick to realize that where there is weakness in the management chain, there is the possibility of strength for them. By presuming to act with "authority," the officials—stewards and committee-men of the union—have strengthened their relationship with their members at the expense of management's area of authority. This condition sometimes takes the extreme form of cutting the "lines of communication" between the supervisor and his men. Where the foremen, voluntarily or under strong pressure, have abdicated their position and perform much of their function "through the steward," this cutting of communication lines is virtually complete.

We have engaged in this discussion of management-union authority not for the purpose of blaming either managements or unions for anything, but simply to point out the reasons for many of the actions of union officials. Also we have tried to illustrate the dangers to the whole management team, at all levels of super-vision, of weak organizational structure and to show how it can seriously affect relations with the employees and their union. It is always a strong temptation to a union to build its strength by the assumption of management's authority. To prevent this sort of weakness in our organizations will not weaken the union, but will tend to compel the union to build its strength in its true func-tion. The unions are not slow to recognize that their existence and strength depend upon strong and healthy enterprise.

BARGAINING AND GRIEVANCES

The right to bargain as a group with management, and the right to present grievances for redress without fear of reprisal, represent the strength of unions in their relationship with management.

Most bargaining and grievance-handling structures involve the "getting together" of employees and supervisory and management people for the purpose of settling differences. The first step in a grievance procedure usually takes place at the level of first-line supervision, with the employee under his jurisdiction who has a grievance. (If this is *not* the first step, it should be.) Subsequent steps in the procedure will normally follow organization lines up the management ladder.

The most important step in this whole procedure is the first one. This is the point where grievances should be settled to the satisfaction of both the employee and the foreman (acting as a representative of management). The first-line supervisor will be able to handle the first step of grievance providing he is working in an atmosphere of policy and practice that is conducive to effective action. In other words, the foreman cannot be expected to create good personnel relationships if the general manager does not believe in good human relations.

Suppose Joe, the press operator, is complaining to Fred, his foreman, about not getting a transfer to a higher-paid job in another department, and Fred (who tries hard to be a good foreman) says, "I'll be glad to look into it, Joe, and you can be sure you'll get a fair break from the big boss." If Joe replies "O Yeah! That's what you say. Who d'ya think you're kidding, me or yourself?" it will be very difficult for Fred to act, for there is probably little or no feeling of confidence that he is being backed by a fair and understanding management.

The important point in grievance handling is that it involves a close relationship between people. It is an excellent opportunity for the first-line supervisors to get to know the people under their direction, how and why they think the way they do about their jobs and the conditions under which they are working. Also, in meeting the problem that is a grievance, the supervisor is in a position to bring the management's point of view to the employee. The wise foreman in a good organization is able to present the broad interest of the whole company in dealing with an aggrieved employee and to do it in such a way that the personal interest of the individual worker will be more closely related to the interest of the company. Again sincerity and honesty are essential in such dealings, but the steps of the grievance procedure (especially the first step) are excellent opportunities to further our understanding of Joe's point of view and to help Joe understand ours.

The bargaining process, involving as it does actual meetings between the operating management and the employees in their union capacity, is another opportunity to deepen and broaden the areas of understanding. For management to assume that the employee "should be interested in the success of the business," is naive, if management has failed to show the employee where his success, his security, and the satisfaction of his other needs are closely tied up with the success of the business. Remember, when a business is "taking a long-term view," the actions involved may conflict with Joe's situation, which is often short-term in nature. Or Joe's knowledge of where he stands in relation to the long-term picture may be very limited. Therefore, the wise management will use the bargaining session as a means of presenting its point of view, but the success of such a course will be largely dependent upon how well the employee's point of view is understood.

In dealing with the union at the bargaining table or in committee meetings, we must never forget the political structure of the union. As we have said, the officials and other chosen representatives of the employees are only in their position by virtue of the support of their union "constituents." The steward may make a grandstand play to the foreman, or the official may make a vitriolic speech before the union members. This is usually a part of the business of demonstrating to the membership that their interests are being watched and that they are not "selling out to the bosses." This is not in any way a suggestion that the union officials and stewards are not honest. Actually, they are in fact "communicating" with their group in a language that can be understood. The significant thing is that these manifestations are not necessarily "unreasonable" or "two-faced" actions but stem from the problems involved in internal union leadership.

LEADERSHIP AND THE UNION

It is a fair general statement to make that union leadership will be patterned very largely upon management leadership. The union members will tend to pick their leaders from men similar to the managements with whom they will have to deal. This is, of course, a generality but history tends to bear out the truth of it. The tough, uncompromising management will usually generate a similar type of union leadership. In other words, the members will be inclined to pick tough, uncompromising men to represent them. If management is "tricky" and "slick" in its dealings it will commonly find itself dealing with sharp practice on the part of union leaders. On the other hand, the management that is honestly trying to deal fairly and to see points of view of the employees, the stockholders, and the public will discover a strong trend toward the choice by the union of leaders who will match the management attitude.

This response of unions to management attitude can be observed at the foreman-steward level. The foreman who is inclined to belittle the steward in the eyes of the group will find himself on the receiving end of the belittling. On the other hand, the foreman who is aware of the needs of the employees in his group and of the steward's relationship to the union members will usually find himself dealing with a similar attitude on the part of the steward. In other words, the group will tend to pick the steward to match the foreman. This does not mean that a weak foreman will bring about a weak steward, or a weak management, a weak union leadership. It does mean that management's attitudes toward the whole matter of human relations and the function of leadership will tend to bring about a union leadership with a corresponding attitude.

A common example of this is the matter of mutual trust. Where union-management relationships are on a strictly formal basis it is usually a sign of mutual distrust. This may take the form of having a phonographic recording of meetings and discussions so that, "they won't put words in my mouth I didn't say," or, "we've got to stop these fellows from agreeing to something today and running out on it tomorrow." There are many other illustrations of this distrust—carefully worded memoranda between the parties, insistence on having "everything in writing," the formal requirement for a "written grievance," and the technical insistence upon time limits for each step, and the like. The list of things could take up much space but we all recognize at least some of them.

But at this point the argument is raised, "But you have to do these things or those fellows would run all over you." Yes, no doubt there is a period in management-union relationships in most companies where distrust is the natural condition. This is particularly true following an election for union recognition; that is, when union representation is new for the company. The important thing to remember is that it does not have to remain so. The relationships can be progressively more pleasant as time goes by, and a sign of success in this direction is the gradual dropping of the formalities. But in this area of human relationship there is little doubt about which is the chicken and which is the egg.

The function of management is essential to all human endeavor of a group, or collective, nature. Business can function successfully without a union but it cannot operate and survive unless the functions of management are performed. As we have seen, the union is often a means of providing security that workers find it difficult to get otherwise. Thus, there is no doubt, from their point of view, that the union serves a purpose of social benefit at the present stage of our economic and social development. We do not know what the future of the labor and trade union will be, and, besides, such a question is beyond the scope of our present discussion. But basic leadership in this area is in the field of management, and management people must take the lead. The initiative is theirs because the ultimate responsibility is theirs.

CHAPTER 13

SELECTION AND EVALUATION OF EMPLOYEES

George was feeling more uncomfortable as he thought of his problems. Right now he had the difficult job of promoting a man to foreman down in Department F. There were one or two likely candidates, but it was a big move, an important step, and a lot depended on it. George wondered just how he'd come up with an answer to that one. And thinking about the business of promotion turned his thoughts to the selection of people for special jobs. How do you pick people for jobs? You watch a man for a time; he seems all right. Then you put him in the job and he just blows up or falls flat. Something seems to go wrong some place. George heaved a big sigh . . . just another one of those things!

Many employers believe that selection of employees is their most vital problem, for, they say, no stream can rise higher than its source. And if a company hires only average or below-average people, the company can never amount to much. There is, of course, a lot of truth in this belief. Certainly, people who are inferior and cannot be otherwise are not often much of an asset to their employers.

It is quite possible, however, that we have been more concerned about selection than we should have been. There are two reasons for saying this. In the first place, we really never know for sure what we are actually hiring until long after the hiring is completed. True, in some cases we feel quite sure, but in others we do not know, or we miss our guess badly. As George McGowan discovered, you can select a person and be confident that he will work out very well indeed, only to find that he is a failure. And it is also true that some people succeed when we don't really think they'll make it at all. The truth is that while we have learned a lot about how to select and evaluate people, our present methods are far from perfect, and we still have a lot to learn about selection.

In the second place, *who* is selected for a certain job is often not as important as how the person is treated after he is hired. Success in a job, in other words, depends on a lot of things besides ability and skill, important as these are. It often involves how the worker *feels* about his job, his foreman, his fellow workers, the company, and the like, and the way he is treated by all these.

It would be easy here to misunderstand the point we are trying to make. Very definitely, we are *not* saying, "Don't worry about selection, for it isn't important anyway!" What we are really saying is this: Selection is important, and a company ought to do the best job it can in selection. But when a good selection has been made our opportunities have just begun. How the new man or girl will work out will most likely depend more on how he or she is treated on the job than on facts discovered in the interview and by tests. And if you, as a leader of workers, are having trouble with your work group, think twice before you say, "How could anybody get anything out of workers like these? What we need around here is a decent employment department!"

THE PROCESS OF SELECTION

Principles to Be Followed. As we have just remarked, it is easy to expect more of the process of selection than it can deliver. We must never forget that selection is fundamentally a matter of "playing the odds." No selection device or program bats a thousand, of course. What we are looking for is the methods that have the highest batting averages. Then we will use and try to improve on them, all the while remembering that strike-outs are not rare, even among the best hitters. It is important that management recognize the limitations of even the best selection programs, and that it expects neither to work wonders nor to remake an organization by means of proper selection alone.

In the second place, responsibility for final hiring should *usually* rest with the line, not with the employment department. The supervisor, in other words, should have an opportunity to choose the person he thinks best for the job from among those considered suitable by the employment department. This right to choose, at least to say "yes" or "no," certainly should not be just a matter of form. The supervisor should have the right to do this and be expected to do it well.

There are at least two reasons for making the supervisor the final authority in hiring. For one thing, if the foreman picks the man, he is *his* man and not someone pushed off on him by some interviewer up in the front office. Needless to say, the new worker has a better chance under these circumstances. And then, two heads are better than one. The foreman knows his jobs and his men. He certainly should be able to add to the accuracy of selection.

A third consideration in selection: Be careful not to oversell the job to the applicant. Indeed, if you are going to make a mistake here, it is better to *undersell* the job. How much better it is to have a worker surprised and pleased to find the job better than it was pictured than to find that he was "sold a bill of goods!"

Very closely related is the matter of induction training. Induction training is fine, and large firms, especially, would probably have difficulty in getting along without it. But on the other hand, many mistakes have been made by picturing the jobs, the bosses, and the company in a very favorable light in the hiring interview or the induction sessions or the employee handbook when in reality things are very different. Under these circumstances the induction program may do more harm than good. Misleading employees probably never pays in the long run, whether done consciously or unconsciously.

In the fourth place, we often make the mistake, in hiring, of assuming that every job should be filled with the very best and most capable person available. The big trouble about hiring only the brightest and most talented people is that practically every firm has many jobs that are done better by just ordinary people. The ambitious, capable person may quickly tire of his assignment, and you have an inefficient, unhappy employee.

Another aspect of this problem is the difficulty of finding enough promotions for these capable people. After all, there are only a limited number of promotions in most firms, and nothing hurts the morale of some people more than to realize that they are "stuck" in a job because there are and probably will be very few or no openings ahead of them. Thus, most employers have a real need for a lot of ordinary folks and few places for the *unusually* bright and capable.

Finally, the fundamental aim of all selection devices should be kept in mind: It is to provide a true picture or appraisal of the applicant. We are trying to find out what sort of a person he is, what his values are, how well he is motivated, what sort of ethical standards he has, what his skills and abilities are, etc. We hope all the evidence will be consistent and will point to the same kind of person. Sometimes that is the case, but often there are facts that seem to go in the opposite direction from the picture formed by the other facts. For example, work history may indicate a very good office worker, but educational background or test results might lead to considerable question. Then it becomes a matter of trying to fit all the facts into the most consistent picture possible, and while there is no way to be sure when this has been done correctly, experience in selection and serious study of the process will be of great help to us.

Selection Devices.   Among the several selection devices available to the employer, the two about which most has been written are the interview and the psychological test. We shall discuss these, and a few other devices besides.

The Interview.   The interview is without doubt the chief device at present for employee selection, and there is no serious reason to believe that any other device is likely to take its place. Others may be used to supplement or help it, but the interview is apparently here to stay.

ERRORS IN INTERVIEWING.   The interview, of course, has definite limitations. For one thing, bias or prejudice is very influential. Different interviewers with different feelings about women or redheads or Southerners will often appraise people differently. Also there is a tendency to overgeneralize from the results of an interview. Neatness in dress may be taken as a strong indication of neatness of work, and nervousness in the interview may be interpreted as lack of emotional balance. In some cases these may be sound conclusions, but often they are not.

Another common error in interviewing is what has been called the illusion of previous experience. All of us are inclined to prefer the applicant who has had experience on the job to one who has none. And yet experience as such is often much less important than the ability and willingness which an inexperienced worker may have. Also it must never be forgotten that five years of experience on a job may literally be nothing more than six months of experience repeated ten times.

TRAINING OF INTERVIEWERS.   But what can be done to improve interviewing techniques, to help interviewers become better interviewers? A number of suggestions are in order.

First, general reading in the field of interviewing should be encouraged. Not nearly enough has been written on the subject of interviewing, but some good materials are to be found nevertheless.* Such reading should not be confined to employment interviewing but should take in all kinds of interviewing. And indeed, much broader reading is very helpful.

Likewise, experience in any sort of interviewing should be sought. Exit interviewing, vocational counseling, employee counseling, nondirective interviewing—these are some of the sorts of interviewing from which valuable experience can be acquired.

Formal training in interviewing is helpful. A good many colleges are now offering courses that help fill this need, and the training department of a large company could be of real help to interviewers by providing or supplementing such training. A significant part of these courses should be practice under supervision. Recording of interviews and careful study of them later is one way of doing this. Certainly, mere practice alone is not enough, for it must never be forgotten that if practice makes perfect, wrong practice makes perfectly wrong.

Getting practice in interviewing while being observed by an experienced interviewer is not as easy as it sounds, simply because the presence of an observer, a third party, in a real interview, is often disturbing and may well do more harm than good. The practical answer to this problem apparently lies in a device known as "role-playing," in which one person pretends to be an interviewer

---

* For example, Bingham and Moore, *How to Interview*, 3d Ed., Harper & Brothers, New York, 1951; Drake, *Manual of Employment Interviewing*, American Management Association, New York, 1946; and Rogers, *Counseling and Psychotherapy*, Houghton Mifflin Company, Boston, 1952.

in a certain set of circumstance and another pretends to be the interviewee. A make-believe interview is then conducted, and afterwards the weaknesses and strong points of each participant are discussed. Needless to say, criticisms by a third party are often helpful. Actually, these can probably be secured best if the interview is *recorded* and later played back.

This device has a great deal more usefulness than is ordinarily recognized. It can be used by employment interviewers to improve their skills. But supervisors and executives can use it, and are using it. And while they may "role-play" employment situations, they also role-play disciplinary interviews, exit interviews, information-giving and information-getting interviews, interviews for explaining to an employee the results of his merit rating. There is hardly a limit, in fact, to the possibilities of this technique.

Finally, a lot of help can come from staff meetings of interviewers. These meetings are held to provide for professional growth, and discussions and role-playing may be carried on without any aid from an "outside expert." All these methods of training interviewers will ordinarily pay real dividends. And it must never be forgotten that interviewing is an important part of the work of nearly every member of line management.

IMPROVING THE INTERVIEW. Some valuable suggestions can be made to the individual interviewer. It has been found, for example, that most interviewers talk too much and hence the interviewee talks too little. There are at least two bad results from this situation: The interviewer does not find out as much as he should about the interviewee, and the interviewee does not find out as much as he should know about the job and the company. Every interviewer should ask himself constantly, "Am I doing too much of the talking?"

And then there is the tendency to cross-examine the interviewee before he has a chance to tell his story. Authorities are agreed that the greatest accuracy usually follows allowing the applicant to first tell his story—what sort of person he is, what he has done, why he wants *this* job with *this* company, etc. In other words, general questions are used to start him talking, and most specific questions should come after he has told his story.

It is commonplace, of course, for the interviewer to know the purpose of the interview and decide how it is to be conducted. The requirements of the jobs that are open should be known in detail. The way of opening the interview, conducting the main part of it, and closing it should be carefully planned. One may not follow his plan to the letter—indeed, he should not, many times—but he will be better for having planned, nevertheless.

Far more mistakes are made here than is usually recognized. We take too much for granted, or else we get busy and simply do not do the desirable amount of planning. But plan we must, especially for the more important interviews. This point is covered in some detail in the chapter on disciplining employees.

An easy error for interviewers to fall into is to prize cleverness and diplomacy above sincerity. Of course, an interviewer should be diplomatic and, in the best sense of the word, clever. But there is no substitute, in interviewing—as there is none in most other human-relations situations—for honesty and sincerity.

And then, it is not uncommon for interviewers to use questions which imply an answer, when direct, factual ones would be more productive. For example, "I guess you left this job to return to college, didn't you?" is usually poor. It suggests an answer and may hide important facts. "Just why did you leave this job?" would be better, even if the answer appears to the interviewer to be obvious.

Another suggestion to the interviewer is the usefulness of a written record of the interview, made either during or just after the completion of each interview. Such a record is very valuable for later follow-up and other study of the interview, and it also is of great help at times in recalling facts about the particular person concerning whom a decision has to be made.

Still another point concerns the necessity for broadening the base of many interviews, for getting at the underlying motivations and reactions of the individual and not simply checking on skill, ability, experience, training, and the like. In Chapter 3 we referred to some of the basic needs of workers and to the fact that important needs are often unconscious. The interviewer needs to understand these things and to try to get at as much of this material as possible.

Finally, we need to notice the gains that come from using a panel of interviewers rather than a single interviewer. This is no doubt a process that is too expensive to be used in many jobs, but it can unquestionably justify itself in selecting people for key positions. For example, if an engineer's job is open, applicants might be interviewed individually by the chief engineer, the shop superintendent, the treasurer, the personnel director, and perhaps one or two other persons. If this method is used, each interviewer should arrive at and record his own conclusions about the applicant before discussion with any other member of the panel, and then the panel may meet for discussion. A good part of the advantage of this scheme comes from having several *independent* judgments about the applicant.

In most endeavors there is a real reward for careful study, attention to details, and sincere efforts at improvement. The field of employment interviewing is certainly no exception.

The Psychological Test. Much has been written about the use of psychological tests in selection, more perhaps than has been written about interviewing. In a way this is undesirable, for, as we have said, the interview is the basis of nearly all selection programs. Psychological tests do have a place in selection, but it is a more limited one than is often recognized.

There are a number of difficulties in the use of tests for selection. One of these is the assumption that scores on the test must be related to success on the job. For example, if a test is to be useful in selection, applicants making high scores on the test should, in most cases, turn out to be good employees. Those making average scores on the tests should usually be average employees. And persons who make low test scores should usually turn out to be poor employees. (Of course, this relationship could be reversed, with good employees making poor scores and poor employees making good scores. While this is not likely to happen, it could. And if it does, the test will still be useful, except that we'd select people with low scores after the test becomes a part of the selection program.)

Now, the real difficulty here is proving that such a relationship exists. *It is not usually safe to assume it,* even in cases that look obvious. And it is more difficult to be sure of such a relationship than one would usually expect. What are some of the problems connected with proving that test scores do correlate with success on the job?

In the first place, there is the question of getting a dependable measure of job success. Production figures are useful here, if available, but some sort of rating or ranking method will usually be useful. In the second place, there should be a fairly large number of people working on the same job or on closely related jobs. Obviously, it is difficult or even impossible to show that there is a real correlation of test scores and job success unless one has a fairly large group of people to work with. A final requirement, if you are using persons already employed as the "pilot group," is that you be reasonably sure that actually working on the job has not changed the scores of the people (as might happen, for example, if the test is one of job knowledge). Obviously, it is not easy to meet all of these conditions, a fact which definitely limits the use of tests.

There are other difficulties in the use of tests. The evaluation of a test in a particular situation requires expert assistance. There are many so-called experts in this field, but before one is hired it should be determined that he not only knows tests and statistics, but that he is well grounded in the fundamentals of testing and the use—and limitations—of tests in industry.

Another difficulty is the ease of "putting a tag on a man," of "marking" him with a test score in such fashion that he is not evaluated for what he actually is. The I.Q. is a fine example here. If it ever becomes known, even to the management group, that a man has a high (or low) I.Q. (or is an "introvert" or "has paranoid tendencies"), the man may be tagged for the rest of his days with the company. And, of course, this is often unfair to this man and to the other employees because many things besides a set of test scores should be taken into account when evaluating a man's worth to the company and his future with it.

Still another difficulty comes from the fact that the test results may influence the standard against which they are evaluated. Test results may become a powerful suggestion to the supervisor or department head or general manager to see in the individual what the tests say is there. Thus, if a test says that a certain individual is subject to wide swings in emotion (from joy to sorrow and back again, that is), if we really believe in the test, it is very easy indeed to see that characteristic in the person. Actually, it may be that the test is wrong. And perhaps we had never thought of the person in this way until the test suggested that interpretation. And so we see that we have to be careful in our evaluation of the correlation of test scores and job success, or else we may be using the test itself as a basis for checking its own success. This is an especially great temptation in dealing with the personality test of the questionnaire variety. If this sort of test is to be used at all in a selection program, it should be done only after careful, unbiased study of the particular employment situation.

Finally, tests at present can do very little with that important aspect of the employees which we call motivation or willingness to work, and willingness and ability to cooperate. Some of the newer tests may prove to have real value here, but their worth in the ordinary selection program still has to be proved.

And so we see that while tests may, and do, have a place in selection, their use should be based on careful research in the company. And it must never be forgotten that tests only supplement—they do not supplant—the ordinary hiring procedures.

Other Devices. It is obvious that the application blank is helpful in selection, partly because it serves as a basis for the interview and partly in its own right. Application blanks probably deserve more study than they receive, especially since there are two notions as to what should be put on them. On the one hand, we want them to be as inclusive as possible, so as to give us as many facts as possible about the applicant. On the other, we want them to be as short as possible, so that they will be easy to fill out, and and besides we don't want to offend the applicant with prying and "personal" questions. It has been suggested that this difficulty can be met by finding out what items on the blank are related to job success and cutting out those that are not. But actually, it is difficult to establish such relationships, and therefore, a number of good items might be eliminated. Besides, since the application blank is a basis for the interview, it should contain information helpful to the interviewer, whether or not that information can be proved to relate directly to job success. There is, therefore, no way to be precise about what ought to go on an application blank. Most blanks probably represent a compromise between being very long and being very short.

Another device for supplementing the interview is letters of reference. These are generally agreed not to have much value. However, if they contain answers to specific questions asked by the prospective employer they may well be worthwhile. Obviously, personal calls on former employers for references will be more useful. It is usually more practical, of course, to call these persons by telephone, a procedure that has much to recommend it.

A final supplementary device is the physical examination. The purpose and function of this examination are well understood, with the exception of perhaps one fact: The physical examination should not ordinarily be simply a "yes" or a "no" to the question of whether the person should be employed, but rather it should represent a serious attempt to match the physical demands of a job, or several jobs, with the physical abilities of the applicant. It is not necessary, in other words, that every person employed should be without limitations physically. All that should be required is that the applicant be able to meet the physical demands of the job or jobs for which he is scheduled.

EVALUATION AND PROMOTION OF EMPLOYEES

Some Fundamental Considerations. The way in which the employees of a firm are evaluated is one of the most significant things about the firm. Evaluation must take place, of that there can be no doubt. Well done, it may be one of the finest assets of the company. Poorly done, it may do damage that all other good personnel procedures cannot overcome.

One problem in evaluation is caused by the fundamental beliefs of a democratic society. In this country we have abolished the king and the noble class, and we assert our belief in the equality of all men. How can we permit one man, or a group of men, to control the destinies of many others?

The practical answer is that we *have* to do it. No one wants chaos or anarchy, and having leaders with authority to act is the only alternative in most cases. But *how* those leaders act is of great consequence. And the fact that this is a democratic society seriously restricts what they can afford to do.

One thing that American workers look for in their bosses is, as we have previously said, respect for the dignity, integrity, and intrinsic worth of the worker. Bosses have to make decisions, and sometimes the decisions are unpleasant to the workers. But if the decisions are wise and are made not in a spirit of conceit but in a spirit of helpfulness, if the boss recognizes that he is only a human being, legally and spiritually on a level with other human beings, he can usually find support for his actions. But misery follows the boss who is "high and mighty," who feels and shows his belief in his own inborn superiority. Workers may tolerate and even follow him where they have no other choice. But they do not respect and really *work* for him.

This is one of the reasons why the opinions of the workers must be considered when one is evaluating an employee. It is not suggested that the boss should call a meeting of the employees, find their opinion about the worker or supervisor in question, and then adopt that opinion as his own. All that is being said is that the opinions of the social group must be *seriously considered*. And if the opinion of the boss about the employee goes against that of the work group, the boss must certainly reexamine his position very carefully. He may still decide to go against group opinion, but he wants to be sure that he does so on the basis of fact and not out of prejudice or discrimination. And in most instances, in a well-run store or shop or office, he will not have to go against group opinion very often.

Mistakes at this point are one of the reasons why workers have insisted so strongly on seniority as a basis for promotion. If seniority is the basis for promotion, *arbitrary* decision by the boss is thus avoided. Even if the best man is not promoted, the sense of integrity of the workers has not been violated.

In summary, then, evaluation must be carried out with due regard to the rights and feelings of others. It must always be done in accordance with the long-run aims of the enterprise, and not for the short-run gain of a special group. And it must not be done in a spirit of haughtiness or great superiority to those evaluated.

Principles of Promotion.   There are a number of considerations that ought to govern the promotion policies of a company. First, wherever practicable, promotions should be made from within the organization rather than from outside. There are few ways in which a company can demonstrate its real interest in its workers more clearly than in this.

Incidentally, here as elsewhere "the grass is usually greener on the other side of the fence." We do not see the ordinary, every-day limitations of the applicant who comes from afar. But we see those of our associates all too well. The upshot is that we often pass by good employees for people from the outside that are no better. And that is a tragedy, for one promotion from within may mean many promotions in the lower levels, while filling a good job with someone outside the company means no promotion for the present employees. It has to be admitted that a case can be made for filling some key positions from the outside, for otherwise the organization may very well become stagnant and fail to change with the times. But generally speaking, promotions should be made from within.

Second, under some circumstances a good employee should be helped, or at least should not be blocked, in securing a better job elsewhere if the company cannot make full use of his abilities. In a way, this policy seems foolish, for good men may be lost this way, but actually it is far from foolish. The talented individual for whom there is no suitable opening in the company will probably become unhappy and even mediocre before long anyway. Besides, one of the best ways to keep a good man is to show him that you really care for him, that you would be willing to help him improve his position even at your own expense. When such an attitude on the part of management becomes known, it definitely influences the morale of the organization. And if the man leaves, you have a lifelong friend for the company wherever he is, and some promotions for the people who have worked under him.

Third, the principle of putting the best-qualified man in every job is another one that works far better in theory than in practice. This is a theory in which almost every youngster believes as he starts to work for an organization. But as he gets older and receives some promotions he probably begins to doubt whether he wants the *best* man to have *his* job. He probably feels that he would rather keep it *himself!*

Long and faithful service to a company must be considered

very seriously when promotions are to be made or salary increases handed out. Surely, no one actually believes that a promotion should go to the senior worker, regardless of merit or qualification. But seniority should certainly be an important factor, and the faithful should be rewarded as often as practicable. Putting the *best* person in every job is fine in theory, but if, in bringing this about, the confidence and trust of the workers in the boss are seriously weakened, we no longer have the best man in every job. Perhaps, indeed, we no longer have the best man in *any* job. The authors of this book yield to nobody in their devotion to efficiency or their desire to bring it about. But efficiency in human relations is often quite complicated, and what appears to be the most efficient practice may in the long run prove to be the least efficient.

Perhaps all this can be put this way: In promotion, the policy and the practice must be to see every person as having intrinsic value, and every effort must be made to see to it that promotions and salary increase go to those who through faithful and efficient service have earned them.

Efficiency Rating, or Merit Rating. A development, relating directly to employee evaluation, is sometimes called "efficiency rating," at other times "service rating" or "merit rating." It began about the time of World War I and has spread rapidly. Many firms, some large and some small, now have such plans. It has worked quite well for some of them, but not well at all for others.

Like some other devices we have considered, merit rating is probably sound in theory, but it presents a number of problems in actual practice. The theory is that every so often (perhaps every six months) each employee will be told where he stands and just what he can do to improve. Furthermore, a record will be made of those evaluations and they will become the basis for, or an important part of, the wage, salary, and promotion plans of the company.

Some of the limitations of such a scheme are evident at once. For one thing, foremen are only human, and they make errors in judgment. Besides, there is no guarantee that the rating form means the same to all foremen. Sometimes an employee may be rated low because he is a poor employee; sometimes he may be rated low because his supervisor just does not give any high ratings.

And then there is the fact that the rating should be and usually is discussed with the employee who is rated. The foreman would be less than human if he were not influenced by that fact—and by the additional responsibility of having to suggest to the employee ways in which he might improve. The rating often becomes what the foreman thinks he can justify, not precisely what he really believes about the employee.

The truth is, then, that merit rating is far from the complete answer to the problem of worker evaluation. In some cases, as we have already said, it has helped in the solution of the problem. In others, it has no doubt made the problem even more difficult.

But suppose a company has considered all aspects of the problem and wants to install a system of merit rating. What are some of the "do's" and "don't's" of such a project?

In the first place, if a rating plan is used, the employees ought to be informed of the results. It has already been admitted that doing this will make the rating less accurate, but there really is no alternative. If employees know that they are being rated but no information is furnished them about what the ratings are, they will quite naturally resent the whole system. Under these circumstances ratings would very likely do more harm than good.

In the second place, the raters, that is, the supervisors, must be trained. It is far better if they have been "in on" the scheme from the beginning and have a hand in setting up the plan. But there must be as much agreement as possible on the meaning and use of the words or phrases on the blank, and that comes only from a number of conferences—perhaps only from continuing conferences—and some personal counseling. Training will not overcome all differences in interpretation, but it will help. In fact, without either formal or informal training the plan is very likely to fail.

In the third place, the ratings should not be tied closely to wage and salary increases or to promotions. The temptation to reward the employee with the highest rating is great. But ratings are simply not that definitive. They may be put in the employee's personnel folder and examined when he is considered for salary increase or promotion. But they certainly should not be the *sole* determining factor.

In the fourth place, it is probably well to avoid the "tricks" that are used to "improve" the ratings made by foremen. One of these is to adjust the foreman's ratings after he has made them. Thus, if a foreman rates everyone at average or above, the people that are rated lowest by him as in the "average" group, for example, are forced into the "fair" or even "poor" group. Or if he rates everybody as average or below, his highest ratings (again in the "average" group) are forced into the "excellent" or "very good" categories.

This is a very questionable practice. In the first place, it overlooks the fact that the work group in question may, as a matter of actual fact, be decidedly good or decidedly poor. In the second place, it says to the foreman, "We don't trust you, or at least not your ratings!" Wouldn't it be better, under those circumstances, to help him improve his ratings through training and counseling, or just to abolish the system?

A somewhat less objectionable "trick"—but still not a very sound practice—is to arrange the descriptive phrases so that the complimentary ones are at the right of the line on one quality to be rated, at the left of the line for the next, etc. Thus, if the foreman wants to rate a particular worker high in "quality" or "output," for example, he may have to check toward the *right* end of the line. But if he wants to rate him high in "job knowledge," he may have to check to the left. The gain from this scheme is negligible. On the other hand, it, too, implies a lack of confidence in the foreman, and probably does more harm than good.

For the same reason, there is question about the use of the "forced-choice" type of merit rating. In this form the rater is never sure just how he really has rated the employee, for the statements are chosen so that only half of them really "count," and no rater is ever allowed to see the "key" to find out which ones really do affect the employee's score. Again, this seems to say to the foreman, "We don't trust you!" Isn't the gain in accuracy that this method yields bought at a price that is too high to pay?

This is a final remark on merit rating: Whether it works or not depends largely on the feelings that exist between the workers and management. If these feelings and attitudes are fine and sincere, almost any sort of a scheme (including no formal scheme at all) will work, simply because the workers trust management and management trusts the workers. And if these feelings are hostile, the best plan that can be devised will not really accomplish its objective. The fundamental thing here is worker-management attitudes. We certainly need to avoid getting so concerned about the mechanics of merit rating that we forget to try constantly to make the company a better place in which to work.

SUMMARY AND CONCLUSIONS

In this chapter we have emphasized the importance of the attitudes of management as these attitudes affect the processes of selection and evaluation. There is no substitute in these processes for sincerity and genuine concern for the individual and his welfare and for the group.

With regard to selection we concluded that the interview, which is the basis of most good selection programs, can be improved considerably. It may also be supplemented by other devices, and a better job of selection often will result.

In connection with employee evaluation, we insisted that such evaluation must be carried out with concern for the feelings of those evaluated. Furthermore, what the workers think about those considered for promotion or increase in pay must be taken into account. And there is sound reason for giving seniority a good deal of weight in promotion. Finally, merit rating, while it may be helpful at times, introduces many problems that are difficult to solve.

CHAPTER 14

EMPLOYEE COUNSELING

> *For example, there is the stenographer who has been doing quite a lot of work for George recently. He noticed that she seemed to be very keen and enthusiastic at the beginning but something's gone wrong. Being a man, George feels that "Oh, maybe she wouldn't want to talk to me." He knows that somebody ought to talk to her or perhaps she should be able to go to somebody that she could talk to. Yet they don't have any setup that he knows of to take care of it.*

A relatively recent development of modern industry is the grievance procedure. Provision for the formal handling of grievances is found in most union-management contracts, and many firms without unions have also made provision for taking care of them.

This development in business and industry is no doubt a phase of a larger social movement, which holds that the complaints of people are important. The counseling movement is part of this same way of thinking. We have counselors now in our schools, in government agencies, in stores, shops, and offices. Undoubtedly, this means that we are concerned about people and their troubles, and wish to provide means of helping them.

THE NATURE OF COMPLAINTS

Some of the most interesting work that has been done on the complaints of employees comes from the so-called Hawthorne experiment of 1927–1932. An interviewing program carried on as part of this experiment is of special interest to us.

Each of the more than 21,000 employees in this plant of the Western Electric Company was interviewed by one of a group of persons selected for the task. The interviewer always introduced

163

himself clearly to the employee and told him that the purpose of the interview was to find out how he felt about his job and anything connected with it. The interviewer did not ask questions, nor did he suggest the subjects to be discussed. He did not argue with the employee nor try to clear up any mistakes in the employee's thinking. The interviewer, in other words, did whatever he could to keep the employee talking about things *of interest to the employee* and tried very hard not to direct the conversation. It is interesting to note that the employees were glad of an opportunity to talk about their jobs, and that the average time per interview was an hour and a half.

Incidentally, while this was a somewhat surprising conclusion at the time, it is entirely in keeping with what we would expect now. A great many companies of today are using the so-called morale survey, a group of printed questions to be answered by each employee without signing his name or revealing his identity. These questions concern the employee's opinion of his job, his supervisor, his wages, his working conditions, the company, and related topics. And the surprising thing is how willing—and even in many cases, how eager—the employees are to answer the questions. It's a funny thing, but when people are given an opportunity to talk about things that they really care about, they seem to take great delight in doing so, provided, of course, they know that they will not be penalized for talking. That seems to be the way it was at the Hawthorne plant.

As each of these interviews was completed, the notes that the interviewer took on it were analyzed. Two things were determined about each comment that the person being interviewed made. In the first place, the comment was classified according to the *subject* that it dealt with. Thus, a particular comment might have to do with wages or the pension plan or the supervisor or the employee club or the machines in the shop or the washrooms or something else. Naturally, some things (for example, supervisors) were mentioned by most of the workers, while other things were mentioned very seldom (for example, free legal service furnished under some circumstances by the company).

The second way in which each remark was classified was as to whether it was favorable or not. It was possible in this way to find what percentage of the comments about a thing represented *favorable comments*. Thus, everybody could have said something about wages (though a fairly large number of people did not comment about them), but *any* percentage of the comments about wages could have been favorable. That is, every comment made by every employee about wages could have been favorable, every one could have been unfavorable, or some could have been favorable and some unfavorable. (Actually, nearly three-fourths of the people did mention wages, and somewhat more than half of the comments were favorable.)

You are interested, of course, in what things, in general, were commented upon favorably and what, unfavorably. It is hardly possible to cover all of the things in a single statement like this, but this was true in the main: The benefits and services program of the company received the largest percentage of favorable comments, and working conditions, including tools, the largest percentage of unfavorable ones. Thus, fans and tools and washrooms and lockers did not fare so well at the hands of the employees. Why did things turn out this way?

The most obvious answer to the question is that that's just the way they should have turned out: The benefits and services were fine, but the working conditions were bad. But actually that is not a good explanation. The benefits and services program was pretty good, *but so were the working conditions*. There is no serious reason to believe, for example, that lockers and washrooms were poorer than they were in other plants in the Chicago area—indeed, there is good evidence that they were *better* than average—and yet they were talked about frequently and unfavorably.

Now why is it that employees will gripe about lockers and washrooms in a plant where lockers and washrooms are at least as good as they are used to—both on the job and at home—and actually perhaps, definitely better? One possibility is, of course, that the lockers and washrooms really were in bad shape, that there were things wrong with them that management didn't know about and that those who conducted the Hawthorne experiment couldn't see. But that is quite unlikely.

And then the employees might have picked on lockers and washrooms because the lockers and washrooms can't talk back or even get their feelings hurt. After all, if you talk about your boss, he might find it out and make you wish you'd not said anything. And if you talk about the company or the retirement plan or wages, management may take offense and make you wish you hadn't. But talking about lockers and washrooms isn't likely to hurt anybody's feelings, or if anybody does get his feelings hurt he's not likely to be anyone who has any influence anyway.

The chief argument against this explanation is that the employees seemed to talk freely about whatever they wanted to talk about and furthermore they talked as freely at the end of the experiment —when the last people were being interviewed—as they did at the beginning. In other words, the promise to the employees that their confidence would not be violated was kept.

Before we try to say what actually does explain this situation, let's mention one or two other things. How employees feel about food in the company cafeteria is often much like this. In most company cafeterias the food is cheaper and better prepared than it is in other nearby eating places, and it, too, is sometimes better than what the employee has at home. But in many, many places food in the cafeteria is a constant source of griping on the part of employees. And there is no doubt about it: In many, many cases it is not the fault of the food, of how or when or where it is served, or of what is charged for it.

And here's a situation that arose in a certain shop: The company gave its employees a rest period in the morning and another in the afternoon. But the plant was too far from a drugstore or cafe for the employees to be able to get a cup of coffee, so for some time the company had been fixing coffee and selling it to the workers at a nickel per cup. Then management got the idea of *giving* the coffee to the employees instead of selling it to them. In spite of the fact that the coffee continued to be served as it had been and was as good as ever, the workers began to complain about how poor it was, and they actually drank a lot less coffee after it was given to them than they had drunk before. A thing like that just doesn't make sense, does it?

By now it is evident that we are not dealing here with simple problems. The "common sense" thing to do would be to make lockers and washrooms bigger and maybe keep them cleaner; or to reduce the cost of the food or prepare it differently. (I don't know what the "common sense" thing to do about the coffee would be!) But it is almost certain that these things wouldn't correct the situation, and probably wouldn't really help!

The only reasonable way to account for these strange happenings is this: People have a need to gripe, and gripe they will unless they are held down by fear or lack of someone who will listen. And what they gripe about may have *no logical relationship* to what they are unhappy about! Actually, people usually gripe about whatever it is popular to gripe about, whatever they hear others griping about.

Now it's pretty easy to misunderstand what is being said here. It's easy to think that we are saying that people *know* what they are unhappy about and that it is something other than what they *talk* about. But since they hear other people griping about the lockers or the coffee or the food in the cafeteria, they figure they'd better gripe about that, too. Sometimes it probably happens just that way. But that is not what *usually* happens in cases like this. Ordinarily, the people are unhappy without knowing what they are unhappy about. It may be the way they are treated at home or in the community. It may be worry about a sick child or a son in the army. Most likely, when a *group* of workers is unhappy it's because of things that are happening in the work situation—lack of security or sufficient wages, a feeling that they are just cogs in a machine, doubts about whether their bosses are in every sense honest and truly ethical, or any one of many other possibilities. And they express these feelings of unhappiness in the best ways they know.

Let's illustrate with some things that happen at home. Every parent has had this experience: One of the kids gets up some morning all out of sorts. He gripes about the bed he has to sleep in, the clothes he has to wear, the little amount of money he has to spend, the school he has to go to, and so on. Now what do we parents usually do? We argue with the child, and tell him how wrong he is. We show him—or try to—how his clothes are as good as those of his friends or at least as good as we can afford, and how school isn't so bad, and all that sort of a thing. But did you ever notice this: that when the child *needs* to gripe, *he will* (unless you force him to keep quiet)? You no sooner refute all his arguments about clothes than he shifts to school. And if you take care of the school arguments, he shifts to how he's treated at home. He *needs* to gripe.

All this puts complaints and grievances in a very different position from the one they are often thought to have. No doubt about it: Complaints and even formal grievances are often the *manifest aspects* of a *latent* feeling of unhappiness. And the management that treats the manifest and neglects the latent is no smarter than a doctor who merely tries to bring down a patient's fever without trying to find and cure the *cause* of the fever.

OUR WORDS AND OUR FEELINGS

Maybe all this can be made more meaningful if we make a different approach to the subject. The common conception of the nature of language is that it is designed and used to express ideas or logical meanings. Thus, when I *tell* you something I am getting some ideas (or "facts") across to you.

Now obviously that is *one* function of language and conversation, but it is far from the *only* one. A function of language often overlooked is that it either *releases* or *conveys* feelings, attitudes, and emotions (and it may both release *and* convey these things). Undoubtedly, much of what we say is concerned only a little or perhaps not at all with logical meanings.

The use of profanity is a case in point. When you hear one person curse another, it is almost certain that the intellectual content of the words used has little or nothing to do with the situation. What is really happening is that the person doing the cursing is saying to the other, "I am unhappy! In fact, I am very, very unhappy!" And we miss the real point here unless we see that the person doing the cursing usually gets some *emotional release* from the cursing. In other words, he feels a strong urge to say these things, and he says them. And afterwards he feels better, temporarily at least!

Most of the *sweeping generalizations* we make are like that. "Ability doesn't count in this company." "You never use any kind of good judgment in spending money." "The world is going to the dogs." "You're the noisiest kid I ever saw." All these and countless other expressions are designed to release or convey feeling, primarily, and not ideas or meanings. At present most of us believe that there are only two kinds of statements, the *true* and the *false*. It would be well if we also made a place in our thinking for the statement that is *nonfactual* (neither true nor false but designed to release and convey feeling).*

By now you are probably wondering what this chapter is all about. We've been going on and on and so far have said nothing about how to handle complaints and grievances. Well, frankly, there are mighty few rules about how to do this job. What we're trying to do in this chapter is to help in an understanding of what complaints and grievances *really* are, with the hope that these facts will aid the supervisor or executive as he uses his very best judgment in dealing with them. And the only field in which good judgment is needed any more than it is here—if there is one any-where—is the area of discipline. Perhaps from time to time we may say something about *how* to handle a grievance. But even then the comments will be general. And the supervisor's hard work, broad experience, serious purpose, and good judgment will have to supply the solution for the individual cases.

METHODS OF COUNSELING

The employees in even a small business organization will, of course, have many problems. Some of these will be handled suc-cessfully if the employee is given certain information which he does not have (for example, why did he receive $56 instead of the $58.25 he was expecting this week?) or else is supplied with some tangible thing he needs (for example, a loan from the credit union). But many of his problems are essentially *emotional* prob-lems. They are concerned basically with the *latent* or the *nonfac-tual*. How can we solve problems for employees? How can we know what they should do, and how do we tell them effectively?

The truth of the matter is that only rarely can anyone solve an-other person's problem for him. We might provide him with the facts or the money he needs, or we might make some good sugges-tions as to the best courses of action. But, in the last analysis, the employee himself will usually have to decide whether and how

---

* The ideas in the first part of this chapter are drawn primarily from Roethlis-berger and Dickson, *Management and the Worker*, Harvard University Press, Cam-bridge, 1939.

to use the facts or the money or the advice. And in most cases when the facts or the advice and maybe even the money are supplied, they will be changed to suit the needs of the individual.

Actually, as we have said before, we don't have much luck *telling* American workers what to do. We can make suggestions, and they are often grateful for them; and in some cases we can give financial or other aid. But most people would like to solve their own problems if they could, even to the extent of "thinking up" the suggestions.

All this is to say that there are two kinds of counseling, the *directive* and the *nondirective*. These terms, taken literally, oversimplify the situation. Actually, there is little or no counseling that is *fully* directive and just as little that is *fully* nondirective. And obviously there are situations that contain elements of each kind. But the distinction is a useful one just the same.

Directive Counseling. As we have already indicated, there are some situations in which the counselor can and should supply the answer himself. And certainly every organization should have some person or groups of persons (supervisors, personnel technicians, counselors, or someone else) to help as needed on this sort of problem.

But a word of caution here: It must never be forgotten that what the employee is talking about may be very far from what is troubling him. Sometimes this is true because he is reluctant to talk about what really troubles him. But sometimes it is a case of the *manifest* and the *latent*. And a wise counselor will always keep this possibility in mind.

In truth, then, the directive method of counseling, while it is most appropriate in certain cases, leaves much to be desired. Even the experts in counseling often fail to get to the root of the trouble, and when they do get to it, the person being counseled is often unwilling and even unable to accept or use the advice given.

Nondirective Counseling. Just what is nondirective counseling? That is not an easy question to answer, any more than the method is an easy one to learn. When a person is being nondirective in his counseling methods, he is doing but little of the talking, the counselee doing by far the greater part of it. When he is being nondirective, the counselor does not agree or disagree with the counselee. He does not argue, he does not praise or blame, or reassure or discourage. He *listens*, intelligently, alertly, understandingly. He follows not only the thoughts of the counselee but also (what is usually more significant) the feelings and emotions and needs and wishes of the counselee. In other words, he tries to understand as fully as possible what is going on in the other person. This understanding includes the emotions of the counselee. The counselor *understands* these emotions though he does not become emotional (in the sense of being angry or sad or afraid) himself.

Another belief of the nondirective counselor is that in these problems involving the deep needs of the individual the best insights as to their solution will usually come from the counselee himself, provided the counselee is freed from emotion, so that he can bring his best reason to bear on the problem. This point has been overdone by some of the nondirective counselors, but we have to admit that it has a lot of truth in it, if it is wisely applied.

And so a nondirective counselor tries to get the person with whom he is counseling to talk—about anything and everything that he wants to. The belief is that if he talks long enough in the nondirective sort of atmosphere he will eventually get a good deal of emotional release and also a good deal of insight into his problems.*

There are at least two remaining questions about nondirective counseling. First, does it have any usefulness to the supervisor or executive in dealing with his human-relations problems? And second, how do you get people with problems to talk? The answer to the first question is a definite "yes." Most of us, of course, will not have the opportunity or the inclination to become skillful nondirective interviewers. But if the leader of workers understands the nondirective method and really becomes fairly good at it, there are two mighty good results that are likely to follow. In the first place, he will find the interviewing method itself of considerable usefulness at times. Surely, on some occasions a supervisor must be *directive*, just as directive as he can be. But there are other

* The fundamental ideas in this section come from two books by Carl Rogers. Published by Houghton Mifflin Company, Boston, they are *Counseling and Psychotherapy* (1942) and *Client-Centered Therapy* (1951). We do not, however, go all the way with the views of Rogers.

times when he'd be better off and so would the person being interviewed if the supervisor were nondirective. Leaders could learn a lot about a lot of things, and people could get a great deal off their chests besides, if the members of line management had skill in nondirective interviewing methods and occasionally used them.

The second way in which the nondirective method would be useful to line management is in the effect it would be likely to have on the general attitudes and outlook of people who use it. The use of the method encourages *permissiveness* in dealing with people. It tends to lead us to let them be self-determining and to encourage free expression in them. And this is true in a lot of situations other than just the interviewing one. Now, without a doubt you can be *too* permissive in dealing with people. But we have made more mistakes in dealing with workers by being too rigid and authoritarian than we have ever made by being too permissive. It is true here, as it is in so many other places in the leadership of people, that there is no substitute for good judgment on the part of the leader.

But how do you get people to talk, especially people who are under emotional stress? How do you get them to say what they want to say but can't? How do you get them to say what they *need* to say but don't want to say?

The first point that should be stressed is the *attitude* of the counselor. The counselor must be, deep down inside and not as a trick or technique, *nondirective,* or *permissive.* He must be able to hear whatever is said without being aroused by it. He must not praise or condemn, be shocked or made very happy. He must feel a genuine concern for the counselee as a person of worth, entitled to treatment with dignity and respect (and his behavior must reflect the feeling).

In the second place, it probably helps at times to say, "Tell me more," or words to that effect. Actually, however, this response is not particularly good. It probably encourages superficial material without getting to the more basic needs of the individual.

The third point: Silence may be used effectively to get other people to talk. Everybody knows how it is when the conversation between two people begins to slow down and finally stops—with neither person able to think of a thing to say. They're both embarrassed by that, and each tries hard to think of something to say—and says it as soon as he can think of it. But the nondirective counselor has learned that he can use these periods of silence effectively. If he restrains his impulse to talk or ask questions when the interviewee has stopped talking, he often finds very significant material coming forth following these periods.

Now, of course, this is not to say that silence alone is required for nondirective counseling. Certainly that is not correct. And silence can be misused also. Again it's the old story of good judgment on the part of experienced people.

The final method of the nondirective interviewer _is to reflect to the counselee what has just been said._ Thus, this sort of interviewer very, very often says right back to the interviewee what the interviewee has just said to him, except that he usually shortens it. Thus, he may say in a sentence or two what the interviewee took several minutes to say. And the reflected material is usually put in the form of a question. For example, if the interviewee has spent some time telling about how Joe has been keeping some information from him, discriminating against him somewhat, and even telling things about him that should be kept secret, the interviewer might say, "So you feel that Joe hasn't been very fair with you, do you?"

One other point: There are at least two sorts of things that can be reflected by the interviewer, just as there are two sorts of things that can be expressed by the counselee. These are (1) intellectual or logical meanings and (2) feelings, emotions, and the like. It is easy to see which of these can be most effectively reflected, if the problem is primarily an emotional one. The _reflection of the emotional content_ of what the interviewee has said is probably the most important single method of encouraging more expression on his part.

It is to be regretted if anything said here should lead you to believe that nondirective counseling is easy to learn and easy to use. Quite the contrary is true. Nondirective counseling is difficult, and there are pitfalls in its use. For example, there is real danger in reflecting to an interviewee feelings which he has but which he has not yet expressed. But while one needs much training and experience to become a professional counselor, the ordinary person can profit from the spirit and even the techniques of this method of counseling.

COUNSELOR IN THE PLANT OR STORE

Within the last 25 or 30 years, a number of companies have set up formal counseling plans for their employees. These plans differ considerably from company to company. Some use the nondirective method altogether (or nearly so), while others tend to be more directive in method. Some plants put in counselors chiefly for their women workers, and others have provided counselors for all employees. The training required and the background sought in the counselor have varied, but the plans have all had in common the idea of providing skilled help in the solution of their problems to employees who are in trouble.

There can be little quarrel with the intention of such programs. Employees do have troubles, and they often need help. And supervisors and other members of management are often too busy to help or are not especially skilled at doing so. Besides, since they are in positions of authority over the employee, they may find it difficult to keep their feelings and their positions sufficiently in the background. There is no doubt about it; counseling plans have been quite successful in some of these places.

But there are some difficulties with these plans also. There is always the problem of finding the persons who are really suitable for the job of counselor, especially since it is not yet agreed as to just what sort of training, background, experience, and the like they should have. No less important is the question of how you get the people who really ought to go to the counselor to go to see him. And there's always the question of just what the counselor will try to do and how he will try to do it.

The biggest limitation of a formal counseling plan, however, is probably the ease with which it interferes with the functions of the first-line supervisor and with supervisory training and development. Let's discuss both of these points.

On the first one, it's easy to see how a counselor might come between a foreman and his worker. If the counselor has or takes authority, and tries to correct the actions of a supervisor, he is definitely setting the stage for interference and resentment. Incidentally, this is usually more true if the counselor goes to the foreman's boss than if he merely talks to the foreman. But if the counselor takes any positive steps at all, relative to certain problems of employees, he runs this risk. And, of course, if he takes no positive steps—but only listens, however sympathetically—he has increased the difficulties of employee acceptance.

The matter of supervisory development is almost the same point over again. Surely there is nothing that American business and industry needs more than strong line management. (*Strong* here does not mean authoritarian and highly directive; it means able to command respect and admiration because of its all-around character and effectiveness.) This certainly means that supervisors and executives must learn to counsel effectively. They can no more afford to turn counseling over to a specialized staff group than they can afford to do that for training or employee evaluation or discipline. These are, in the last analysis, line functions, and so is counseling. The staff can be of help in all these areas at times, but counseling as a staff function probably brings with it more problems than most of these others. Let's put counselors in, if we need them, but let's don't forget to train supervisors and other management personnel in effective counseling, too.

All this means that there is real doubt about whether the formal counseling movement will spread or diminish in years to come. The problems are there, and they must be met. Shall we meet them with resourceful line people only, or shall we have counselors? Even if we have counselors we must never forget that supervisors must be good counselors too.

THE NEW WAY OF LOOKING AT EMPLOYEE COMPLAINTS

In this chapter we have been trying to say that our age has adopted a new way of looking at complaints and grievances. Our fathers tended to see them either as logical statements of fact or else as results of man's inherent weakness and perversity. But we now realize that many of them at least—and perhaps the great majority of them—are expressions of deep, underlying needs of people. They usually arise, indeed, from the thwarting of these needs, and the words and logical meanings that the griper uses *may* bear little relationship to the real problem. These words and meanings are often merely his way of seeking emotional release or of conveying feelings and attitudes.

All this means that if we are going to deal effectively with these complaints we must understand their origin and development and handle them in terms of the feelings they release or convey. The professional counselor may be of real help here. But, in the last analysis, there is no substitute for an informed, resourceful line management.

CHAPTER 15

PROBLEMS OF DISCIPLINE

Sam didn't answer the phone, so George went down to the department, right out on to the floor, and told Sam he'd better move the man back to his own job and watch his step in the future, before he got them all in trouble.

Now George wasn't sure he'd handled that just as he should have. He had a feeling that he was wrong, but he couldn't say why.

THERE MUST BE DISCIPLINE

One of the unpleasant but inevitable facts of human existence is the necessity for discipline. It would be fine indeed if people always did just what they ought to do, so that no discipline would be necessary. But that, of course, is not always the case—at home, at school, at play, or at work. In any organization, from time to time, and in some organizations almost constantly, people do things that interfere with the aims of the enterprise. They break rules that have been set down for the good of all, and in extreme cases they commit serious crimes. Life would be a great deal more simple if people didn't act that way. But they do—and there has to be discipline.

Of course, discipline isn't always bad, even to those who are disciplined. We can learn from being disciplined and can come to mend our ways. We can be saved from dangers and made more productive, through discipline. And obviously, effective discipline is sometimes all that keeps certain groups from failing completely in their objectives.

But discipline is very close to the feelings of people and may easily arouse them to fear or anger or jealousy. Anyone who is in charge of discipline—in a penitentiary or a school or an office or

177

a family—knows that he is dealing with explosive material. Rightly used, discipline may do wonders for an organization. Wrongly used, it may damage beyond all hope of repair.

The truth is that a supervisor or an executive has to be very careful in the disciplinary actions that he takes. This is more true today than ever, because workers have more power to influence what goes on—and what goes out the door—than ever before. If they respect and agree with the disciplinary measures used in the factory or store or office, these measures undoubtedly contribute definitely to increased production. But if they don't like them, especially if they think them decidedly arbitrary and unfair, there is almost no limit to the harm that can result. Minute for minute and hour for hour, the time that a supervisor spends on matters of discipline is probably the most important of all the time he spends on the job.

THEORIES OF DISCIPLINE

Here is a question that it is apparently useless to ask because the answer is so obvious: Why do we discipline people who break company rules or the law of the land? There are really only two reasons: to *reform the offender* and to *deter others* from making the same mistake. But there is another and an older reason for punishment, one which cannot be seriously defended but, nevertheless, one which has had wide following, if we judge by the evidence that we find all around us. This is the theory of *retribution.*

The theory of retribution holds that when a person has committed a crime, he must be punished simply because he has broken the law. He must pay for his crime, in other words. Thus, we sometimes say of an individual, when he has served his sentence or has been executed, that he has paid his debt to society. The theory also implies that there is a suitable punishment for each crime, and thus it has something in common with the idea of an eye for an eye and a tooth for a tooth.

At first this may not seem to be very different from the more modern conception of punishment as a means of reform of the offender or deterrence of others, but actually it is far from that theory, especially in the kind of discipline that it calls for. Thus, if our purpose is to reform the criminal we do not make him pay a debt to society but rather we take steps to help him become a law-abiding, respectable citizen. One pays his debt to society by serving out his sentence. But according to the *reform* theory, a prisoner might be released in a relatively short time if he has truly reformed, or he might be imprisoned for the rest of his life even for a minor crime if he does not reform.

The *reform and deterrence* theory also implies that at times we may treat the offender in such a way as to make an example of him for the benefit of others. Thus, even if he has genuinely reformed, we may continue to imprison him because his early release might encourage others to commit the crime. And hard as it is to accept that conclusion, it still has to be accepted: If the good of the group demands it, we may have to punish a person severely for the effect that it will have on other people.

Another real difference between the theories of retribution and reform is to be found in the way we treat prisoners while they are serving their sentences. If retribution is our goal we are under no obligation to make life easy or even bearable for the man while he is in prison. Indeed the more uncomfortable he is, the greater the punishment. But if we sincerely desire to reform him, we shall probably treat him with dignity and respect even while he is in prison and shall look for opportunities to help him become self-disciplining and responsible.

Perhaps all this can be illustrated best by referring to some of the practices of at least a few modern prisons. An example is the Federal Correctional Institution at Seagoville, Texas. Here is a prison that is literally without walls. The men are not kept in cells, the guards have no firearms or other weapons, and the inmates are encouraged to take part in recreational activities, discussion groups, the educational program, and many other activities. They are allowed to go to meals with anyone they choose, to sit where they want to in the dining room, to congregate in the "day-rooms" on each floor of the dormitory, to have their own radios, to make suggestions concerning the operation of the prison, and the like.

The remarkable thing about these prisoners is that they are very much like other federal prisoners in the United States. A number of them are "two- or three-time losers" (have served two or three previous sentences), and many are serving long sentences, including life. Besides, a number of them have other charges hanging over them to be faced when they have completed their sentences at Seagoville. In most prisons such men would be watched most closely, locked in cells at night, kept from congregating into even small groups at any time, and otherwise very closely supervised. But this does not happen at Seagoville; yet the remarkable thing is that the escape rate of that prison is about the same as the escape rates of the regular federal penitentiaries with walls, armed guards, cells, etc. Each man at Seagoville has a regular job in the prison, and he is expected to work diligently at it. And most of the prisoners do just that.

It would be hard to find a better illustration of what we have said from time to time in the earlier chapters: You usually get from people about what you expect from them and about the kind of treatment you give them. Apparently this philosophy, wisely and intelligently applied, will work in a prison as well as in a store, office, or shop.

By now many of you are probably asking, "But what has this to do with leadership and the discipline of workers? We don't work prisoners, and we're not concerned with the theory of punishment. What we want to know is how to discipline effectively." Let's see what we can do in the way of applying all this to the leadership of workers.

HOW DOES THIS APPLY TO DISCIPLINING EMPLOYEES?

A few years ago a study was made of company rules governing the conduct of factory workers in the United States.* This study was made with the idea of seeing what changes were taking place in these rules. A number of interesting developments were brought to light: (1) rules were getting to be fewer in number; (2) automatic penalties for the breaking of the rules were provided less and less often; (3) rules were more and more often stated in positive rather than in negative terms; (4) the reason for the rule often appeared with the rule whenever and wherever posted; and (5) cartoons were used to illustrate the rules and make breakers of the

* By the National Industrial Conference Board ("Company Rules—Aids to Teamwork," *Studies in Personnel Policy*, No. 95, 1948).

rule appear ridiculous. Why did each of these developments take place?

It's a funny thing about the decrease in the number of rules. Not long ago there were many of them; now there are considerably fewer. And in some companies, at present, there is only one rule: "This company expects of its employees conduct becoming to ladies and gentlemen." It may not be certain why this change took place, but here's a good guess: Management has learned that you can't make people good by *making* rules. Some are necessary at times, of course. But the ideal work situation would be one in which the employees are self-disciplining and no rules are necessary. Maybe we're moving in that direction. Maybe we're trusting people more, and in matters of everyday decency and common sense maybe we're letting them think for themselves more, and are trying to *think for them* less and less. Ideally, maybe we need only one rule, the one cited above, and maybe even it won't need to be written down. It's remarkable how hard it is sometimes to control people when you try to *make* them do things, and how easy it is sometimes when you just expect them to control themselves. And there is probably no other place in the world where this is as generally true as it is in the United States of America.

The second development was to drop most automatic punishments for the breaking of a rule. You know, of course, what I'm referring to: drunkenness on the job, discharge; three unexcused absences, one day's layoff; tardiness of even a minute, loss of one-quarter of the hour's pay; and similar punishments. Now some of these may well be continued, but the tendency is to drop the *automatic* feature of most of them. Thus, an employee *may* be discharged for being under the influence of liquor, but he does not *have to be*. This development is a good one, for the simple reason that each breach of discipline ought to be considered on its individual merits rather than being dealt with the same way each time.

An illustration: A foreman saw one of his workers walking from the time clock toward his work area, obviously under the influence of liquor. He called his boss and told him that he was taking the worker home, and then did take him home. The next day, when the man came to work, he expected to be punished, perhaps to be discharged, but the foreman said nothing about the offense.

Nor did he mention it the next day or the day after that, and indeed nothing was ever said to the employee about his offense. For days, however, every time the foreman came near he could almost hear the man saying to himself, "Here it comes. Now I'm going to catch it!" Was this wise action on the part of the foreman?

The answer to that question depends in turn on the answer to two other questions: First, what was its effect on the man, as far as his future conduct was concerned? And second, what was the effect of this action on the other workers? Were they more inclined to come to work drunk than they had been before?

The foreman felt that his action was wise, as far as the worker was concerned, because the man had never come to work drunk before and, though the offense occurred months ago, had not come to work under the influence of liquor since the incident. As far as the group was concerned, this sort of thing had never been a problem, and it has not become one. The foreman thinks he handled the matter wisely in these circumstances, and it would not be easy to disagree.

Let's see if we can state the principle that is involved here: If, after a worker has committed a serious offense, he genuinely reforms, and if the spirit of his fellow workers is such that they are not encouraged by his offense to "let the bars" down, the foreman can afford to be lenient. But suppose the worker has not genuinely reformed but only *thinks* that he has, or *pretends* to have reformed; or suppose that the use of liquor on the job or before coming to work is a real problem in the work group. In either case punishment may have to be swift and severe. Certainly nothing is said here to suggest that workers should *not* be fired for drunkenness on the job. The only point is that any punishment should be used only when it will serve a real purpose in attaining the objectives of the organization—and not used if it doesn't.

One other remark in this connection: There is no substitute for good judgment when it comes to matters of punishment. No book and no authority of any sort can tell you specifically which punishment to use and which to avoid—always or in any specific case. The foreman or executive has to "use his head," has to consider all the facts he can get, and make his best guess as to the effects of various actions. Success here requires good judgment, and *there is no substitute for it.*

The third development of rules concerned their statement in positive rather than in negative terms. Thus, in the past it has been fairly common to phrase rules in terms of, "Thou shalt not. . . ." At present the tendency is to say what is *expected,* rather than what is *commanded,* and to state what *should* be done instead of what *should not* be done. Those of you who are familiar with modern safety programs will agree that almost exactly the same thing has happened here: We are now emphasizing the positive effects of safe working habits rather than confining ourselves to the negative effects of unsafe ones. Thus, we talk about how safe practices help, rather than simply about how unsafe ones are costly. We stress the fact that "your neighbor's safety depends on you." And in general we talk more about the advantages of safety than we do about the disadvantages of its lack. Very much the same development has occurred for company rules, and for the same general reasons.

The fourth change was to put the reason for the rule right alongside the rule—on the bulletin board, in the handbook, or elsewhere. This, too, is very sound practice. Somehow, there is apparently nothing that Americans resent more than they resent *arbitrary* decisions, and a rule for which workers do not understand the reason often *looks arbitrary.*

Suppose that you are standing at a street intersection where you can see a mile or two down one of the streets. In the distance you see a car coming, observing all the traffic regulations, including driving at a reasonable speed. Now, suppose that just as that car gets to your intersection a policeman's car catches up with it and forces it to the curb, and right in front of you, two policemen get out and begin to "bawl out" the driver for the way he was driving and then get ready to arrest the man and take him to jail. You'd resent that, as all of us would, and you might even try to help the driver by interceding with the policeman. That surely is a high-handed and arbitrary way to treat a law-abiding citizen, and you don't like it even if you have never seen the driver before.

But now suppose the officers tell you what happened just before this car came into your view. Maybe the man had been driving recklessly; perhaps he had hit someone and then driven away from the scene of the accident. How quickly all this changes your feelings about the matter! Now you'd help the cop arrest the driver, if necessary.

There's an extremely important lesson here for modern management, one that applies to disciplinary action and many other things as well. Workers usually resent arbitrary decisions, even when they are not affected by them. But many *decisions which look arbitrary when we see only the decision are not arbitrary at all when we see the reason for the decision.* As in the case of the offending driver just mentioned, the actions of the officers looked arbitrary until we understood the reasons for them. The application is obvious: Workers want to know the reasons for rules and disciplinary decisions, and furthermore, in most cases they are entitled to know them. Woe be unto the management which thinks that all it has to do is to decide and act on the basis of the facts, and say nothing!

The last change in rules was to illustrate them with cartoons, pictures, and the like. As we said, these cartoons often put the breaker of the rule in a ridiculous position. Somehow this helps make rules more acceptable. One of the reasons why this is successful is that we probably all tend to resent rules somewhat, and this sort of treatment probably softens the feeling a bit. Besides, the cartoons help to put social pressure on the side of the rule. And group discipline is usually powerful discipline.

By now it is clear, no doubt, that we have used these changes in rules to illustrate the use and importance of the theory that punishment is to reform and to deter. Not only does the theory have important implications for how we should discipline offenders, but apparently many of these implications have been recognized and are being used by modern industry.

METHODS OF PUNISHMENT

The punishment that workers have received when they did not do their jobs well has often been very severe in times past. The slave and even the serf could be beaten or starved or otherwise forced into line, and of course, in the recent past, workers were disciplined by discharge, demotion, layoff, and the like, with all such actions taken by the boss. In these cases the worker usually had no appeal, and there was very little that his fellow workers could do to help him.

Great changes have occurred in this field, and they have taken place in a very short period of time. Needless to say, American employers do not beat their workers or starve or imprison them. Even the right to discharge or demote or transfer or lay off for disciplinary reasons has been seriously restricted. It is not that these forms of discipline *cannot* be used any more. It is simply that they have to be used with caution. In many cases, it is not sufficient for management to know that it is justified in taking disciplinary action. It is necessary for management to be able to prove to an outsider, an arbitrator perhaps, that it is justified. Naturally, this has made a lot of difference in how and under what circumstances employees are disciplined.

But what are the methods of punishment available to management, and how satisfactory are they? In general, there are four of them: (1) reprimand, either oral or written; (2) layoff; (3) demotion or other undesirable transfer; and (4) discharge. Let us look at each of them in turn.

The reprimand has long been and continues to be one of the most widely used and effective means of discipline. Obviously, it can be and often is misused, but that does not alter its soundness as a disciplinary measure. Some supervisors use the reprimand too frequently, so frequently, indeed, that it loses most of its effectiveness. Some use it in the heat of anger, an action that is probably always unwise. Some use it as a threat, and then do not carry out the threat when challenged. Some have not learned that to be effective, reprimands nearly always have to be given privately, and not in public where all may see and hear. Supervisors make many mistakes in the use of the reprimand, but it is still a fundamentally sound disciplinary device.

A word about the difference between the oral and the written reprimand: The written reprimand is reserved, of course, for the more serious offenses. Many companies put a copy of it in the employee's personnel folder, and if this practice is followed, such a reprimand becomes a real punishment. In any reprimand, however, the employee is entitled to know why he is being reprimanded and exactly what is expected of him. And obviously, the wise supervisor uses the reprimand only when, in his judgment, it will contribute to the reform of the individual or the improvement of the group.

Not as many favorable remarks can be made about the disciplinary layoff. If workers actually worked only for money, it would be almost the ideal form of discipline. But workers work for money and many other things, including status and prestige. Unfortunately, the layoff may bring the offending employee a great deal of prestige. When he returns to work, instead of appearing to the other workers as a rule breaker who did wrong and was justly punished, he may well be a sort of hero, one who broke the rule and then had a vacation. Or—what is more serious—the other workers may come to identify with the worker in his struggle against the boss, and thus the worker gains respect and admiration. The layoff may work successfully at times, but in general it has not done as well as it would seem it might. Incidentally, of course, the company also punishes itself when it uses the layoff, for it deprives itself of the services of a needed employee.

Much the same thing can be said about the disciplinary demotion, although for a different reason. The demotion is very likely to cause the employee to become disgruntled and unhappy. At the time when the punishment is imposed, he may feel that the demotion will not be so bad, and he may accept it willingly, with a feeling that it was entirely deserved. But as time goes by, the situation is likely to change, and resentment is likely to develop and grow. After all, the loss of status and higher pay is not easy to take. Again, we are not saying that demotion must never be used as a disciplinary measure, but only that as a general rule it is not very satisfactory.

The discharge is, of course, a disciplinary measure of last resort. That is, discharge is to be used only when no other means of punishment is available and effective. And unless management faces an unusual situation, discharges will be few and far between. But discharges are sometimes called for by the facts; if the man cannot or will not reform and his offense is a serious one, it may be necessary to discharge him. Or if the offense is such that (while it could be overlooked this one time in the worker) it cannot be tolerated in the work group—and if, furthermore, there is evidence that if it is not dealt with directly and forcefully it will seriously damage the work group, then discharge is in order. But in all cases, the good of the offender and the larger good of the work group must be the basis for making the decision and taking action.

PUNISHMENT BECAUSE OF THE SUPERVISOR'S FEELINGS

It is very likely that our biggest fault in discipline—the thing that causes us most regret and leads to most of our failures—is a lack of emotional control. Actually, don't we often discipline our children and even our employees *not for what they have done but for how they have made us feel?* How easy it is to let things go, sometimes big things, too, with each one provoking us a little more, until finally some little thing becomes the straw that breaks the camel's back, and we really "let go." We are then reprimanding—or punishing in some other way—not because of what the offender has done but because of *how he has made us feel.*

One of our best illustrations of this point comes from a home in which there was a little girl about 2½ years old, a little "brat" if ever there was one. She was a constant source of trouble. One night, when company was present, she insisted on going into her room and bringing out all her toys and stacking them in the middle of the room. She had a horn and drum, and made the appropriate sounds on them. She got the idea that it would be a mighty good thing to take the books out of the bookcases and pile them on the floor among her toys. Once in a while she would make a side excursion. She walked *across* the coffee table, upset the cream and spilled it on the rug. Her mother and father, during all this time, were saying, "Don't—don't—I'll spank you." After about an hour, she accidentally stepped on her daddy's foot, and he did spank her. That is a good illustration of what we mean: That little girl was disciplined according to how she made her father feel and not for what she had done.

Now, our feelings are notoriously inconsistent. Sometimes little things make us feel just terrible, and sometimes big things don't bother us much. If we discipline in accordance with how we feel, we are almost certain to be inconsistent in our discipline. There is no more fundamental fact in disciplining people than that discipline must be fair and adapted to the circumstances. Employees must not get the idea that they can get by with anything today because the boss is feeling good, and may walk a tightrope tomorrow because the boss is feeling bad. There is probably not anything that hurts general morale and confidence any more than inconsistency in matters of this sort.

But perhaps you are saying, "That is all very good. Nobody could argue with that, but what can we do about it? After all, we are only human, and human beings are just naturally subject to these emotions." Well, nobody reaches perfection in these matters, but one can improve his emotional control and balance if, first, he sees the necessity for it, and second, he stays everlastingly at the task of doing so. If every one of us makes a sincere effort every day to bring ourselves under better and better emotional control, we will make some progress, and, after all, that is about all one can ask. We must discipline for what has been done, and not for how we feel.

THE DISCIPLINARY INTERVIEW

So far we have been talking about when discipline is necessary and the kinds of discipline that are suitable. Little or nothing, however, has been said about an important aspect of the problem, namely, the disciplinary interview itself. In this area of human relations, as in many others, it is far from enough to decide what the facts are and what punishment should be exacted. It is necessary also to decide *what* to say in talking to the offending employee and—this is no less significant—*how* to say it.

There are a number of things that determine the success of any interview. Some of them, of course, are not fully understood at present, and some depend, no doubt, on the personality of the person conducting the interview. But the one factor that we should like to stress in this sort of interview is the necessity for *planning* the interview. What features of the disciplinary interview require special planning?

Well, for one thing, the time and the place for the interview should be carefully considered. Needless to say, disciplinary interviews should be held in private and in comfortable surroundings. And how tired or how irritated or how angry the employee is at the time of the interview can have a lot to do with its success.

Another point that should be stressed is to decide upon the purpose of the interview. This has already been discussed in connection with the reasons for discipline. Is this interview designed primarily to help the individual to reform, or is it a situation in which the effects on the group get chief emphasis? Most likely both these reasons will be present, and it is often not necessary to try to separate them. In the final analysis, however, the purpose of the interview is never simply one of making the offender pay for his crime.

Another place for planning is in the opening remarks and introduction to the interview. There are at least two ways in which a disciplinary interview may be begun, and the supervisor should certainly decide in advance which of these will be best for this particular situation. The interview may be opened diplomatically, with the seriousness of the situation played down for the moment, or it may be opened "straight from the shoulder" or "with all the cards on the table." Now there is no way in the world for an outsider to tell a supervisor which approach to use in dealing with a given case. Naturally, as a general rule, we favor the diplomatic approach as more consistent with the idea of helping the person to reform. But all of us have seen cases where the "straight from the shoulder" approach is clearly superior. The question which the supervisor must ask himself is, "Which of these two approaches will come closer to accomplishing the purpose of the interview?" And naturally, he will choose the one which is more likely to succeed.

Another critical point in a disciplinary interview is how the defenses of the offender are to be met. In the great majority of cases there will be defenses, that is, excuses or alibis. And the wise supervisor will try to figure out in advance what these will be and how they are to be met.

Many mistakes are made in handling the employee's excuses. It is not at all unusual to find that the employee has put the supervisor on the defensive and even thoroughly discredited his account of the incidents—if the employee's story is allowed to stand. Most of us, as supervisors, of course, having taken the position that the employee is guilty, go on and meekly—or with much blustering—impose the penalty. But, needless to say, that is an unfortunate way for things to develop.

Incidentally, the only way to meet the offenders' defenses, if they are to be met, is with facts. In disciplinary matters the supervisor must, to whatever extent he can, be sure of his facts. But it is not always necessary to meet these defenses if it is known that any defenses for the action are bound to be weak and distorted. Particularly in the "straight from the shoulder" approach, they may simply be brushed aside and disregarded. Obviously, however, the supervisor must be very careful in doing this. The employee may go away feeling that he was convicted without any chance to defend himself—that this was an *arbitrary* decision.

In the next place, much attention must be given to what the punishment is to be. The various possibilities must be carefully weighed, and the one most likely to accomplish all the objectives of the punishment should be selected. This often demands the best that there is in a supervisor or executive. Success here is no guarantee of success in leadership, but it is a very great help indeed.

Finally, the closing of the interview should be planned. As everyone knows, closing even an ordinary interview can sometimes be difficult, and disciplinary interviews are no exception. What is the frame of mind that you want the offender to take with him? What remarks, incidents, or illustrations will help create this frame of mind? What *concrete and specific courses of action* are you insisting upon? How are you going to tell him? These are questions of real concern.

In conclusion, the influence of emotional control should be mentioned again. We simply can't do a good job of disciplinary interviewing if we are under the influence of strong emotion, and if at all practicable, the interview should be postponed until the interviewer is no longer angry or otherwise emotional. And emotional control must be maintained, if possible, throughout the interview. All decisions must be made on the basis of the facts and of our very best guesses as to the outcome of various courses of action. And this sort of thinking is not helped by emotion.

EFFECTIVE DISCIPLINE, A NECESSITY FOR EFFICIENCY

In this chapter we have emphasized the great importance of wise and effective disciplinary action. Discipline must be imposed for constructive reasons, for the good of the individual and the group, and not for revenge or to afford a release of feeling on the part of the boss. The goal of effective discipline is self-discipline on the part of the child or the worker or the supervisor or the executive. In all these matters we are striving for the time when all people will do what ought to be done because they *want* to do that, and for the day when it will not be necessary to *make* people do things. Of course, we can never reach that stage completely, but we can *try*. And there will be great profit to all of us if we are wise in our trying.

CHAPTER 16

MAKING WORK ATTRACTIVE
AND SIGNIFICANT

> *Only today, Jack, one of the men from the shop, came
> into George's office and said he was going to quit. When
> George asked him what was wrong, Jack told him he
> wasn't "getting anywhere around here." He had been
> around for twelve years and he couldn't "see any future in
> the place." Jack did promise to think things over, but. . . .*

WORK, THE LOST VALUE

Something has been added to our American culture. There has
been a change in our attitude toward work. In the early days of
our country, hard work was held in great esteem. A man who could
produce a lot of labor had high status in the community. Idleness
was considered frivolous, and a man was a man for what he could
do. Gradually, through the years, we have changed our point of
view. We have now decided that work is drudgery and that hard
labor is almost vulgar. Great premium is put on the ability to get
someone else to do the hard work, and labor is considered something to avoid at all possible costs.

Children are taught early to dislike labor, and we have removed
the daily chore that was used to train our children in the way that
they should go. Every modern father dedicates his life to prepar-
ing his offspring for a white-collar job. We all feel that if we can
get Junior through college, then he will be in a position where
he will not have to work with his hands. Our American daydream
is that the old, dried-up farm homestead will produce oil, and
then none of us will ever have to work again. Blindly, we have
accepted as the secret of success and happiness the ownership of
some capital structure that we can put to work for us.

The unions claim great victory when working hours are short-ened. If you asked the man on the street what the greatest con-tribution of labor unions is, he would say that under the influence of the union the men get more money and do not have to work as much as they did. Even the new college graduate who is con-templating his first job wants to know how much vacation there is connected with the position and at what age the retirement begins. A hard task is something to be endured in order to earn money to buy happiness. To derive genuine happiness out of the work situation is such a shocking idea that it seldom occurs to anyone. It is obvious, however, that our need for higher wages would be lessened if we could obtain our happiness, our satisfac-tion, our thrills in life firsthand from the task that we do day by day.

Thus, great emphasis is put on ease and comfort in modern American life. We have but to pick up a magazine and thumb through the advertisements to see how the American public is interested and induced to buy. We cannot stand it when our car does not have "knee action," "floating power," "foam rubber," "hy-dromatic shift," "power steering," and the gadget to pull down our windows without a crank. We buy our homes with buttons to push and gadgets to make us cool, warm, and comfortable. The most modest shack supports a television antenna in order that the occupants may be entertained in their idleness. Commercial-ized entertainment screams at us for participation so that we can endure the agony of our boredom. The zenith of status and con-tentment, according to the advertisements we see and hear, is sitting in an overstuffed chair with casual (not work) clothes on and with a beautiful girl (in a bathing suit) handing us a bottle of something or other. "That's living," say the appetite makers.

An interesting commentary on American life is that although a man will go to great lengths to keep out of work, when he is actually relieved of work by retirement or vacation, he takes a little rest and then jumps into some activity for recreation that someone else does in drudgery for pay. He fixes up the lawn and putters around the house. He makes something in his shop. He paints the chairs. He drives around the country at a speed that would make the truck drivers strike. Our vacationer enjoys these activities because they are "a change" or because they are "fun,"

He reveals a happy work attitude toward these things for which he doesn't get a cent.

Of course, those who think about it know that the most unhappy people in all the world are the idle people. Disintegration seems to set in when a person is not active or productive. The most tragic personal slavery comes when we have nothing to do but seek satisfaction of our physical appetites. Happiness never comes from being completely relieved of responsibility or work. It comes only from being busy. A peculiar joy accompanies a long, hard task that is well done. It is derived from a hard battle well fought. It is the result of sacrificial effort for the group, or the creation of something significant. A great teacher pointed out, many years ago, that peace and rest come to those who labor and carry heavy responsibility. Each person must find the thrill of a happy work experience and the peace of mind that comes from it.

Work is God's great gift to man. Our most priceless satisfaction comes from appreciating work and enjoying the thing that has to be done. If we can find a task and a type of work that we would rather do than anything else, then our happiness in the plant, in the factory, or in the office is assured. As we assume the role of a boss, our most challenging role is to help those who work for us find satisfaction in *their* work.

WORK—THE AMERICAN TRADITION

We can see the negative attitude toward work beginning to have its effect on our conception of American government and democracy. The whole idea of a security guaranteed by the state is a new concept for us. Originally our democratic ideal was built on the idea that hard work is the only security needed. The core of what we call freedom was the conviction that every individual was important and had within himself the means to determine his own destiny. The early settlement of our country and, later, the American Revolution, were a protest against outside autocracy from the state. The pioneers who pushed their way West were traveling to find a place where they could obtain their independence and freedom. This revolt against domination by government and church became the great passion of this new country. All that the patriot asked was a chance to use his hands and to work out his own salvation unmolested. The laws, the religion, and the social life of this new country were built on the foundation of the essential worth and dignity of each personality and his ability to determine and seek his own destiny. Later laws continued this emphasis. Public education became the method by which an individual could be given the tools to make him competent. Suffrage was extended, and women were given the right to be individuals and to vote. Modern attempts to abolish discrimination are in the same tradition.

The person who has been reared in this American social climate is sensitive about an arbitrary decision. None of us likes to be ordered about or given unreasonable commands. We feel that this is an affront to our dignity and our worth as individuals. We are early conditioned to the idea that all men are equal, that no one really has the right to "lord it" over another. We insist on knowing the "why" of decisions that affect us.

In the earliest training of the home the child is made to feel that he is entitled to have an explanation of what is demanded of him. In industry, the workers resent arbitrary or unreasonable decisions of the boss, and even when such a decision does not affect us personally, we do not tolerate such infringement on individual rights. This deep-seated tradition may explain our universal sympathy for the underdog and our great love and admiration for the lone individual who strikes out in spite of overwhelming odds. We know that compliance is more enthusiastic when the reason for an order is given by the boss. Of course, a lot of decisions look arbitrary and a lot of orders seem unreasonable only until we know why they are issued.

The United States of America is still "the land of opportunity," and its social-status tradition of "log cabin (or haberdashery) to President" is very powerful. Men in high places still like to recall their meager beginnings. Individual initiative is considered to be all that a man needs to produce success. However, government and industry have become so complex and highly specialized that the individual is sometimes a little frightened, and he is inclined to feel his dependence. This fear comes when the worker discovers that he is at the mercy of our economy or of government edict, and causes some of our industrial unrest. The politicians have exploited this fear and have offered security for the restless. In their eagerness to capitalize on insecurity, the government, as well as the factory or office, are presented as agencies where we "get" subsidies, pensions, wages, vacations, and the forty-hour week. These are the values the worker feels he must fight to get from his job and his country if he is to know security and happiness. Now, no one will deny the importance of economic needs in a specialized economy, but the philosophy of individual initiative and the strength of free enterprise will fail if we lose the thrill of "giving" to our job and government. *Hard work and sacrifice for the good of the group are still the most reliable devices for happiness, security, and successful living.*

PATERNALISM

A person is strong only as long as he feels that he is able to cope with the rest of the world under his own initiative and with his own resources. A healthy self-opinion is most important for happy work adjustment. When he loses faith in himself through insecurity, through dependence on outside factors, the emotional stability and creative ability of the worker are threatened. When George was promoted, he knew he could do the job because he had done well in other tasks. It is this confidence in himself that makes him effective as a boss.

During the last two decades industry has shown a willingness to be concerned with the needs of the worker. This is very commendable if all of the individual needs of the worker are to be considered. Many companies now offer paid vacations, group-insurance plans, recreational facilities, liberal retirement features, and many other indications that management is interested in the welfare of the worker. Sometimes this tendency to provide the worker with the things that make a happy life has been termed *paternalism.* It not only involves the care of the working man by the company as suggestive of the care of the child by the father, but it also suggests the *control* that the father gives his child. At first, the workers appreciate this loving care and concern for their needs and welfare. The plan is attractive to the boss as well. He benefits by the high morale of his workers and exercises a subtle control over their welfare. But when the workers realize that the control of the benefits and even the suggestion as to their need comes entirely from the executive branch of the company, they have a tendency to resent it and look for the trick or "the catch." Often this feeling of resentment develops into more worker demands. They are determined to "get" even more, and the bewildered boss cannot understand what the worker really wants.

Of course, in this spirit of paternalism, the boss has considered only some of the needs of the worker. As much as he needs a liberal vacation, a worker needs healthy self-confidence and the feeling of worth and dignity as an individual. He wants to know that he has a choice and an opinion that is valuable. Paternalism then becomes very destructive and even fatal when it arbitrarily offers a release from work and when it limits the worker in the choices he makes. If it becomes merely a device by management to harness up more securely the worker and his routine, it can do more harm than good. The boss must be very protective and cautious about the workers' self-esteem. The use of sarcasm or ridicule to tear down a worker's self-confidence is probably the most permanently damaging thing a supervisor can ever do. For the boss to build up his own *ego-protection* by constantly tearing down those who work for him is cruel. When the supervisor controls a group situation at the expense of another, he may receive compliance, but he has planted the deep seed of resentment. He has robbed the man of his greatest asset—his feeling of competence. No worker can grow in productive ability under such a blight.

So, the task of a supervisor is to build up the worker's self-opinion in order to increase his ability, skill, success, and happiness. To pretend to be interested in the worker's welfare merely to extract more work results in a vicious boomerang to the boss. Only a genuine, sincere respect for the individual personality will produce the atmosphere conducive to the growth of the worker. Honest and public recognition of his accomplishments and a consideration of his desires and opinions are the best methods of developing this feeling of self-adequacy on the part of the worker.

Of course, you are worried about the conceited worker, who apparently has too high an opinion of himself. The psychiatrists tell us that braggarts, bullies, and cocky egotists are not the result of too much self-sufficiency. In fact, the opposite is true. They

merely have the symptoms of a deep feeling of inferiority and in-
adequacy. This overbearing conduct is the device of a frightened
individual to have every situation on his own terms. With a healthy
faith in their own ability in any circumstances, these misfits in the
group would be able to give up these agonizing ways of behavior.

Genuine and sincere concern over all the needs of the individual
worker is the best morale builder in the world. It is only when the
boss begins to restrict himself to what the worker needs in order
to make him a better producer for the company that paternalism
sets in, and resentment is built up by the worker. He loses his
initiative and opportunities to make choices and to decide his own
destiny for himself. When these God-given rights are taken from
the worker, he can do nothing but be more demanding in his
frightened search for what he calls security. Enlightened management is recognizing that industry is not only producing a product
for market, but that it is producing individual personalities which
are the foundation of strength for future organizational stability.

WAYS TO MAKE WORK SIGNIFICANT

One outstanding factory manager was asked the secret of his
plant's great achievement. He explained that it was his emphasis
on making the workers feel that their work was important and
significant. He said that this is the key to the good production and
the secret of the profits of his factory. He worked out a daily report
showing the units produced in the shops and their value on the
market. He put this on the workers' bulletin board every day, so
that they could feel that they shared in the inner knowledge of
the company, and that their opinion about it was important. Once,
when his own report was misplaced, he had to go out to the workers' bulletin board to see how his factory was doing in the way of
production.

This manager said that he knew he had won the battle one
Saturday night. He had taken a friend through the plant, and,
although the hour was late, he went across the street for a bottle
of beer. On entering the tavern, he noticed two of his unskilled
women workers at the bar, a little the worse for drink. One of them
recognized him and called him over. "We are having an argument,
Jack," she said (calling him by first name). "Please tell this fat-

head how we can't count our profits until we take into account our expenses to operate our factory. She doesn't even know what it takes to keep us running." The factory manager spent the next two of the wee hours explaining net profit to an unskilled worker who was drunk. He was thrilled, however, because *they* had spoken of the factory as "we," and that they knew their work was tied up in "our" profit.

Every person, in realizing his highest potential, has the right to think of himself as significant and the work that he does as important. Each of us has a divine right to express himself through his work. Every boss has a challenge to help the men who work for him to find this satisfaction in work. The effort in this behalf will pay off many times in morale and production. In fact, it is the key to good personnel practices.

Of course, the boss has to feel genuinely that the worker's job is significant. He cannot expect the worker to know the importance of his function if the boss cannot see it. Is *good* elevator service helpful to your efficiency and morale? If it is, the elevator operator has an important post. Are clean rest rooms important in factory production and morale? If so, there is an urgent significance to the task of the janitor. Only management's sincere appreciation for the dignity of work in every form will bring about creative spirit and endeavor.

Some of the great companies of this country have done a wonderful thing in the promotion of what someone has called the "romance of the product." This is the development of a pride on the part of every worker for the brand name or the finished product that is turned out at the plant. There is a certain tool company where all the employees know that the best oil-well bit in the world is produced. In a recent conversation, an employee of a certain oil company was saying that his refinery's product is by far the superior gasoline. His company's know-how, fine equipment, and superior material just naturally make for the best product, he explained. Through the enthusiasm of these workers we can see management at its best.

In the chapter on communications, methods were suggested for conveying management's interest in the worker's situation. Meetings of employers and employees, when done genuinely, are effective in keeping the worker up to date on what is happening in his factory. We have seen the significance of service pins and bonuses. We have devised handbooks and films to explain the purposes and ideals of the company to the new worker and to the public. One progressive company is transferring its men for a limited time to other jobs. Here, the worker as well as the boss has a chance to try out on the other side of the fence. Each sees the problems of the men who do different tasks. This plan not only uncovers new and potential skills and abilities, but it has a tendency to make the worker more satisfied with his own job when he sees the problems involved in the others' tasks.

Occasionally, even a young person stops to consider what he would do if money and subsistence were not factors. Suppose you didn't *have* to work, and that your economic security was assured for all times. How would you like to spend the rest of your life? Of course, your first thought is of some fishing or traveling you would like to do. You think it would be fun to be relieved of all "musts" and responsibilities. Then you finally realize that you couldn't enjoy idleness or purposeless recreation for long. If, then, you come to the conclusion that you would do the thing that you do now, with the fellow workers you now have, with the same boss, and for the best darn company in the world—yours—then you have the real work adjustment, the ultimate in satisfaction. It is the realization that we are doing what we want to do, regardless of whether we get paid, that is the test to tell us whether we are truly happy and working to our capacity.

Usually, such a good working situation comes through the helpful guidance of some friend or counselor. It comes from some boss who took the time to fit the round peg into a glamorous hole and showed the romance of such an opportunity. Each boss, no matter on what level, must have a missionary zeal in his endeavor to help his man achieve the thrill of work!

CHAPTER 17

GAINING THE INTEREST AND COOPERATION OF PEOPLE

George wonders, "Why can't people cooperate? That's all it needs—just some cooperation!"
"After all," thought George, "how do you catch the interest of people? How do you get them to do things?"

PEOPLE CAN COOPERATE

This question of George McGowan's is the age-old question of the leaders of people. It is true that history affords us some fine examples of cooperation. Small groups of men have met armies of several times their number and defeated them in battle, when, according to all the experts, it couldn't possibly be done. Streams and mountains have been crossed by men and women who really shouldn't have been able to cross them. Forests have been felled, crops have been raised, and homes carved out of the wilderness under circumstances that any reasonable person would have said were impossible. Instances of personal heroism are many—and often critical to the endeavors of the group. But behind these endeavors there is a large amount of cooperation between people. People can and do cooperate to achieve the impossible, or at least what seems to be impossible.

Competitive athletics furnishes us other fine examples of cooperation. Here's a bunch of boys with not too much football ability who are welded into a fine team—a team that accomplishes the seemingly impossible. It's interesting to follow some of the members of such a team. They identify with the goals of the team, and they serve and sacrifice for these goals. And often the boys win simply because they won't be denied, because they don't know when they're whipped, when they should give up.

201

Here, for example, is Bill, a fourth-string guard on such a team. For all of the previous years of his competition Bill has just been "cannon fodder." He's the guy that the varsity runs the plays over. Day after day he's supposed to take it, to fight back the best he can, and to ask no other reward than an occasional kind word from the coach. Now in his senior year, he's finally made the traveling squad. He's played only a few minutes, except in scrimmage, and the season is just about over. In fact, it's the day of the last—and the really big—game.

The game has been a tough one from the very start. The first-string guards go out early, one of them with serious injuries. The second-stringers go out too, and finally the third-stringers. And now the coach calls Bill, this fourth-string guard, and says "O.K., Bill, it's you!"

Now if Bill were right smart, he'd say, "Oh, no, coach. I've seen six men carried out of that slot today. I'm too smart to go in there now!"

It's funny, but in all the football games we ever watched we probably never saw that happen. Bill may be scared to death, so scared that you can see his knees knocking together as he goes out on the field. But here's his chance, the thing he has worked for for four long years. And he goes out there and does his best! It's wonderful how you *can* gain the interest and cooperation of people.

And it can be done on the job too. Raymond Landers was a "powder-monkey" on a rock-crushing job. His duties were to load dynamite into holes made by the jackhammer operators, and then, when he had loaded a number of holes, to set off a "bank shot." You can easily see that this was pretty dangerous work, and Raymond realized the dangers fully. Actually, he could have made almost as much money if he'd taken a job as a jackhammer operator, but not Raymond! The very dangers of the job were a part of his pay, and he took great pride in doing his job fearlessly and well. He was later killed in a premature explosion of a bank shot, as he realized all along that he might be. But "the mail must go through!" Raymond Landers was an unsung hero who had his heart in his job, who had learned how to cooperate in the objectives of the enterprise. There is no doubt that you *can* gain the interest and cooperation of people. And acts of heroism beyond the call of duty are not restricted to the battlefield.

PEOPLE SOMETIMES FAIL TO COOPERATE

But, as we said, people don't always work together well, and there are many everyday happenings to prove it. Here's a great football team, at least a team made of great football players. But they fall out among themselves, some of the men try to get all the glory, and the team comes apart, as we say, at the seams. And a team that could have been the conference champion becomes the conference doormat!

Of course, it has also happened in business and industry. A firm starts out with fine prospects, a good product, a good sales force, a fine advertising and public-relations program—but it, too, falls apart at the seams. The salesmen start quarreling among themselves, and the sales manager isn't too enthusiastic either. Gradually a wonderful opportunity for all of them slips out of their hands because they lack real sustained interest and find it impossible to cooperate. George McGowan's question is a very real one: How *do* you get the interest of people? How do you get them to do things?

One thing *is* clear in all this: You can't *make* people have an interest in things, and you can't *make* them cooperate. You may make them *comply,* and even go through the motions of cooperating, but genuine cooperation is a matter of the heart, and not simply of compliance.

Of course, as has been pointed out earlier in this book, there's another reason why we can't make people cooperate, and that is that we have found ourselves, in the last ten to twenty years in particular, in a position where we don't have many ways of *making* people work. As a result, we have to inspire them to work, or get them to *want* to work.

Let's develop that point just a little bit. As you realize, the foreman of fifty years ago was pretty well the monarch of all he surveyed. He hired and fired the people he wanted to hire and fire, he promoted the people he wanted to promote, and he demoted the people he wanted to demote. He had many ways of making peo-

ple work even if they didn't want to. He could discharge, reprimand, or lay off, and he often had a very choice vocabulary which
he didn't mind directing toward employees; and sometimes even
the use of his fists was necessary. But obviously, such a foreman,
no matter how effective he was fifty years ago, would be completely out of place today. Even though we can and must discipline
our employees, under some circumstances we have to be mighty
careful about how we do it. The foreman even has to be careful
about the language he uses in addressing a worker lest he face a
grievance pushed very strongly by the union. We are up against
this simple fact at the present time: The *tools of compulsion* by
which workers could be made to work have either been taken from
us or else their use has been very seriously restricted. The result is
that, for all practical purposes, modern leaders of workers often
have only one possibility, to persuade or inspire people to work.

This is a more important point than most of us realize, for it is
quite likely that the values of the American way of life are hanging
in the balance. We have always believed, in this country, that hard
work and individual responsibility are the necessary conditions for
freedom, prosperity, and happiness. But if it should turn out that
people in managerial positions do not succeed in inspiring people
to work, there seems to be no end except a demand for more and
more for less and less, and in the long run, such a program invites
disaster. On the other hand, if people in positions of responsibility
for the work of others do have the necessary resourcefulness and
ability to inspire people to work, we probably have a brighter
future than we ever dreamed of. An inspired work force can set
production work records the like of which we seldom attain. We
are playing a game, you and I, a game in which the stakes are
tremendously high. If we can bring workers who don't *have* to
work (or at least don't have to "put out" much) to *want* to work,
the game can be won. And it's a game that we cannot afford to
lose.

HOW CAN WE BRING PEOPLE TO COOPERATE?

In the first place, the manager who expects to gain the interest
and cooperation of his fellow workers needs *emotional control and
balance* very much. Let's look at what this means. Everybody has

a tendency to do this sort of thing: If things have gone well for him that morning, the supervisor comes to the job feeling fine, and employees can get away with a lot of things. An employee can do things he probably shouldn't be allowed to do, and the supervisor passes it off with merely a slap on the wrist or maybe no comment at all. But the next day, if the supervisor doesn't happen to feel so well, if he had an argument with his wife or heard some depressing news, those same employees are likely to have a lot of trouble, and little things may bring serious disciplinary action where major things didn't the day before. Now it must never be forgotten that we *all* have that tendency. Of course, some people have it to a far greater degree than others, but we all have some of it. And, naturally, anyone would rather work for a manager who has emotional control and balance. Even if you don't like *where* he stands, certainly it helps to know that he always stands there.

Actually, of course, this is the same point made earlier when we were talking about disciplining workers. There is nothing that helps more in giving workers a feeling of security than to work for bosses who are emotionally well-balanced. In the long run, it does far less good to tell people to be calm and steady than it does to set such an example before them. And the supervisor is often the key man to this situation.

The second point to be made, under this general heading of gaining the interest and cooperation of people, is that the supervisor must *act decisively and wisely.* One limitation of the kind of material presented in this book is that people may get the idea that it means to be nice to people always. To some it seems to say, be persuasive, try to inspire people, be diplomatic, kind, tactful, and never take action that will hurt people's feelings—in other words, hesitate and be indecisive. Actually, there isn't a thing that we've been trying to say that suggests that a supervisor ought to be afraid to take action. As a matter of fact, one of the most obvious things in connection with the work group is that it will lose confidence in a leader as quickly when it finds him unwilling to take action which he ought to take as it will when he takes action wrongly. There is no question about it. There are times when a leader of human beings has to make decisions. Of course, it is not suggested that you make snap decisions, or "rush in where angels fear to tread." But it is a necessity, if you are going to be an effective leader, to take decisive action where it is required. Be willing to take that action if the job demands it, and, by all means, be willing to stand on your own two feet and acknowledge that you made a decision even if it is wrong.

The importance of decisive action is hard to overstress. It must be fair, and take into consideration the feelings of workers, the facts, and certainly the other people who will be affected. All that is true, but workers seldom, if ever, admire an individual who is "wishy-washy," the person of whom it is often said, "You never know where he stands." Workers like decisive action. Workers like wise action. No group will follow a leader very long who is wrong most of the time. They want wise action, and there is no substitute for making correct decisions most of the time. But no one can be right all of the time. As a leader, you have the right to be wrong. You have the right to make decisions that are not correct, at least once in a while. The only person who never makes a wrong decision is the person who makes no decisions at all. And to be a good leader you must take decisive action from time to time.

The third point is that the supervisor ought to be *willing to do anything that he asks an employee to do.* Now that isn't easy, you know. On the other hand, it is very easy for us, when we are elevated to a position of leadership over a work group, to think that we were promoted because we are pretty good. Probably all of us can remember when we were first made a boss. That confirmed a suspicion we had had for a long time that we were pretty good, that we were the best person in that work group, and that other people were beginning to recognize it. We had a tendency to feel that we had arrived, that the other people down there were now our servants. They were pretty fine folks, but they didn't know too much, and here we were away up here. Anyone who has such a feeling as that should remember one line of the Declaration of Independence: "All men are created equal." Now, the Declaration of Independence means to say one more thing: "They are not only created equal, but they are always equal." This is one of the fundamental facts of the American way of life—our belief in the integrity of the individual, that every man is equal to every other man in the eyes of the law and in the sight of God and man. We have be-

lieved that and still believe it. We are not very consistent sometimes, perhaps, but we still believe it. If you ask what the heart of
the American way of life is, many of us would say that it means
that you and I, as individuals, are not one bit better than the people who report to us. It means that I don't have any right to turn
up my nose at anybody that I supervise. It means that I am not too
good to do any job or work that is necessary in this country for
the welfare of the citizens. I am not too good to do any kind of
job that needs to be done.

Of course it is necessary to add a qualification. We have not said
that a supervisor *must* do everything that he asks his employees to
do. We are talking about a spirit or an attitude or a willingness.
It would certainly be a very poor expenditure of the funds of the
company if a person who draws a high salary is put to doing unskilled jobs. But there is this *willingness* to do, even if the actual
doing is unwise under the circumstances. Really, the position of
the leader is more influential than that of any other individual in
the group, and your example as a leader will carry more weight than
that of anyone else that is in your work group. That is not always
true, of course, but it is usually true. This attitude of being willing
to do whatever needs to be done is an extremely important attitude. It is basic in gaining the interest and cooperation of individuals.

A fine illustration is the experience of the president of one of the
smaller railroads in this country. Somehow, during the war, this
railroad didn't get its share of business, and it went down and
down, until the rolling stock was run-down, the track was in bad
shape, the stations were dirty and unpainted, and morale was very
low. The president, who had just come with the railroad, started
riding the line. He'd be on a freight train, and it would come to a
small station where the station agent was the only employee of the
road. The depot would be dirty, not having been swept out for
weeks, and the last several times it was swept out the dirt and
trash were simply piled into one of the corners. This president
would say to the station agent, "I know you're busy and don't have
time to sweep out this place. I'm sorry the railroad doesn't have
the money to hire an assistant for you. But I'll tell you what I'll do.
The train is going to be here for 30 or 45 minutes, and if you'll get

me a broom, a mop, and a bucket of water I'll see what I can do."

And the president of the line took off his coat, rolled up his sleeves, and cleaned up the station! Of course, this railroad president did not spend his time cleaning all the depots, but he did on several occasions, and very soon the improvement in the stations of the line was amazing. The lesson had been taught and learned.

This president also started riding the passenger trains. He noticed that members of the train crews were indifferent, if not openly hostile, to passengers and never went out of their way to be of any help to them. But the president did. He did everything he could do to assist them, with information, baggage, etc. And passenger service on the road also improved a lot. There isn't any way around it: Nobody in the United States is too good to do anything that needs to be done.

The fourth point is that you have to *inform people about the things that affect them.* They want to be "in the know," as we say. Perhaps that has always been true. Employees have always wanted to know about their employer and things that affected the business. However, in the days when industry was small, that wasn't much of a problem. The old-time craftsman may have had a journeyman or two working for him, and perhaps that many apprentices. There weren't many secrets in that kind of an establishment. The apprentices knew and the journeymen knew, at least in a general way, most of what the craftsman knew—what was going on and what was likely to go on. But times have changed, and changed tremendously. There are many people in every large establishment who don't have much idea of what is going on. However, most people would still like to know a great deal more than they get a chance to find out. One reason why they don't know any more is, of course, the bigness of industry. But another is a feeling on the part of management that there are some things that employees don't need to know or should not know. Now, in some instances that is completely correct, but the real difficulty is the failure of line management as a group to get across to employees all the information that ought to be put across—things which employees would like to know and have a right to know.

Here is the situation we are up against. The supervisor is busy with a hundred and one things. He doesn't have much time to worry about the new employee, and furthermore, he takes things for granted. He has been around a long time and is amazed that it takes days, weeks, months, and maybe even years for new employees to learn what they need to know. Somehow it seems to him that he has always known these things, and that any new employee automatically learns all of them.

More important than all of these is our failure to transmit the fundamental aims and objectives of the enterprise, or perhaps it would be better to say, the spirit of the organization. Practically every organization—every plant or store or office—has a unique background and history and accomplishments of which its people can be proud. Furthermore, it has, or should have, some aims, not only in terms of serving itself and growing larger and stronger, but in terms of serving its customers and society in general. And it is the supervisor's job, whether he is immediately over a work crew or several levels above the first-line supervisor, to reflect that spirit, that attitude, and those goals, and to help that attitude to permeate the organization. In all seriousness, unless the supervisor can do that, it can't be done. You can have a fine company newspaper, a suggestion system, a public-address system, and the like, and they may help you get this spirit across. But they won't really do what needs to be done. If the supervisor doesn't do his job well, it doesn't matter how good the plant magazine is or how effective the suggestion system or public-relations program—the employees won't be well informed. Whatever his position is in the line operation, he is one of the key persons in the problem of communication in the organization, and if he fails to transmit facts and spirit both up and down, he has failed in one of his vital duties. There is nothing that gains interest and cooperation more than to know what is going on and to be a part of it.

In the next place, if you are going to gain the interest and co-operation of people, you have to *consult with them about their jobs* and the problems of the work group. Here's an illustration: If you get the feeling, as an ordinary worker, that you are just a cog in a machine, you don't have much interest in the thing you are doing. If they give you so many parts to stamp out, or cartons to store, or papers to file, and you don't have any idea of the significance of the article or significance of the over-all operation, if you are not "in the know," and if nobody ever asks you for suggestions as to how to do the work better, you are not going to have much interest in the work, or if you do have, you will soon lose it. This is one of the most fundamental facts about us. Do you want to know how to get a person interested in a venture? Give him an opportunity to be of service to that venture, an opportunity to make a contribution, and he will often come nearer to taking an interest in that venture than if you give him an increase in pay, better working conditions, or shorter hours.

Perhaps we have all observed, on more occasions than one, that parents who have two or more children, one of whom is deformed or sickly or feeble-minded, often become more devoted to that subnormal child than to the normal child. Now, why is that? That is not a hard question to answer. The youngster who isn't normal requires more of the services of the parents, and the more you serve a person the more you are likely to come to love and be devoted to him.

Here in the United States, in the general area of employee–employer relations, we have made a very serious error in supposing that the only way to keep people happy is to give them more and more—increased pay, better working conditions, and shorter hours. These things are important, it is true. But one of the motives of workers which we have hardly tapped is their desire to be of service to the organization in which they work. Maybe not all people are willing to be of service, but certainly most are. Indeed they are *eager* to be of service, are hungry for an opportunity to make a contribution. Every supervisor ought to ask himself constantly, "Have I given the people who report to me an opportunity to satisfy this need to be needed, this need to feel that they are more than a cog in a machine, that their ideas are at least worth considering, and that somebody wants to consider them? Have I, to the degree to which I might, practiced the techniques of consultation with people so that they have an opportunity to make a contribution to the things they want to serve?"

Now, of course, we have to be careful not to use the technique of consultation with workers as a trick. If you don't really want the ideas of a certain employee, don't ask for them and don't pretend an interest which you do not feel. But if you are *not* interested in his ideas, now is a good time to ask yourself why. You ought to want good ideas, wherever they come from, and especially those that come from your fellow workers.

The last point that we shall make is that if you want to gain the interest and cooperation of people, you have to be *a living example before them* of the very thing you want. This point cannot be stressed too strongly. If you want honesty and sincerity and interest from your workers, if you want them to have confidence in you, you have to be a living example of those very things, not only in your work situation, although that is very important, but in your everyday life.

A while ago we were talking about the use of tricks. One of the most vicious and harmful tricks a supervisor can use is to express an interest in people which he does not feel. Most likely you have read articles suggesting that you must treat workers as individuals and that you should express an interest in them whether you feel it or not. Now that is a very dangerous doctrine. A supervisor should not ordinarily express an interest which he does not feel. Any supervisor or executive who does do that is using a trick, a dangerous one, and he is "cutting the corners." He is doing the very thing that he condemns in workers who try to "cut corners" on him. You understand the kind of thing we are trying to say: If you have a good work group, it will probably be because you are a good supervisor. If you have a good work group, it will be because in no small measure you have lived a good kind of life before these employees who depend on you.

Let us say a little more about being a living example. We conceive a leader in a democratic society as the servant of all. When you come right down to it, who *really* gets out the work? Is it the president or the comptroller or the department head or the supervisor? That's easy, of course. It's none of these. It's the hourly rated, or at least the nonsupervisory, people who actually get the goods out the door. All the rest of the people in a plant are there to be of aid and assistance, and that includes the boss. The boss is truly the servant of the workers.

MOTIVATING PEOPLE, OUR MOST CHALLENGING JOB

As we said in the beginning of this chapter, there is no doubt but that people can be motivated—often to attempt the heroic or even the impossible. But there is also no doubt that they are not always so motivated, and this seems to be especially true in America today. We have told workers that work is unpleasant and that nobody would do it if he didn't get paid for it. Furthermore, we have encouraged the idea of getting more and more for fewer and fewer hours and less effort. Finally, we have kept workers from having much appreciation of what is really going on. Sometimes we've kept them in the dark because our plant or office has grown so large that they are lost in the shuffle. Sometimes we haven't bothered to tell them because we don't think that they care. And sometimes we haven't really made them a part of the organization because deep down inside we didn't trust them—we didn't feel it was any of their business where we were going or what we were trying to do.

These things are nearly always fatal to genuine interest and cooperation. We're going to have to live good examples before our workers and to be genuinely interested in them. Furthermore, our interest in them will have to be an interest in them as human beings of genuine worth, our equals, our fellow workers. There is seldom any other way to get their long-run real interest and genuine cooperation.

CHAPTER 18

THE MANAGER AND THE PUBLIC

"Maybe he's sore because I turned down that invitation to serve on the Chamber of Commerce industrial committee. I don't know why I'm expected to do those things. I've plenty to keep me busy here, and then some. Why doesn't the Public Relations Department handle it? It's their job. And yet, maybe . . . ?"

WHAT ARE PUBLIC RELATIONS?

What has the manager, the supervisor, the foreman got to do with public relations? Before that question is examined for a possible answer, perhaps we should ask ourselves, "What do we mean by the term 'public relations'?"

Wright and Christian, in their excellent book on the subject,* give a definition that is well worth thinking about: "Modern public relations is a planned program of policies and conduct that will build public confidence and increase public understanding."

No business concern today can ignore the public or be indifferent to how the public feels and talks about it. There was a time in our history when business ownership and management did not consider the public's opinion of them to be of much consequence. There are cases on record of actual expressed contempt, such as "the public be damned." The hard road of bitter experience has taught us that this is a foolish attitude and a business with such a "policy" is doomed to failure unless it changes its ways. Modern industry has come to the realization that it is a part of, and not apart from, the community in which it operates. As businesses get bigger in size and scope, the size of the community affected

* Wright and Christian, *Public Relations in Management,* McGraw-Hill Book Company, Inc., New York, 1949.

213

by them gets bigger also, until it may be the whole country that is the "community" with which they are concerned.

Let us examine our definition at this point. You will notice that what we are trying to accomplish is the building of public confidence and increasing public understanding. Also, it should be noted that this is to be done through our policies and conduct. The way we behave as a business is going to determine what the public thinks about us.

Policies.   Too often the excuse is made that top management sets the policy and "there isn't anything I can do about it." True, top management has the responsibility for the decisions establishing broad basic and operating policies and in no way can it avoid the weight of such responsibility. But to a surprising extent these policies result from opinions expressed by those who are considerably lower in the management scale. Nobody in the entire managerial team can escape responsibility. This is particularly true of the industrial-relations policies of a company. The experience gained and the opinions expressed by the foremen, superintendents, and managers of our industrial enterprises play an ever-increasing part in the establishment of the policies our managements set up to guide our personnel practices.

It is part of our supervisory obligation to carry out the policies of the company, so one of the first things to do is to find out what they are. It could be that the public-relations policy of your company is expressed in very broad terms. Perhaps it is something like this: "The XYZ Corporation recognizes the need for good public relations as a desirable objective in its business," or "The Whoosing Company will so conduct its business and other relationships as to earn the highest public regard."

These would be normal statements of policy as handed down by top-level management. The second statement is the stronger. It contains the important truth that public regard—or good public relations—must be *earned*. It cannot be bought with just money, nor can it be obtained by reams of publicity. The public in this free democratic country has an uncanny sense for the "phony." Remember what Lincoln said about fooling all the people.

Furthermore, public regard cannot be earned by just having a public-relations man. W. A. Patterson said, "The public-relations man cannot go out and manufacture a philosophy that does not exist in management." He was right. True, the man who heads up the public-relations function is a most valuable member of the organization. He can and does advise management on good practices to put into effect and bad ones to stop. He should help all the members of the organization in the development of a sound attitude toward the public, and advise in the building of plans and programs. But he cannot create a condition of good public relations himself. If the public-relations director and his staff cannot create public regard for the company, the big questions are: Who does? And where do you fit into the picture?

Conduct. The inescapable truth of the matter is that public relations is everybody's job. Every person in the entire organization is in some way constantly influencing public opinion toward either a higher or lower regard for the company. This influence on the opinions of others is to a great extent based on how we behave. The things we say and the way we conduct ourselves will cause outsiders (members of the public) to form opinions that will reflect on the business we work for. If the laborer from the factory gets mixed up in a downtown brawl, or the clerk from the office doesn't pay his grocery bill, there is a reflection on the company they work for. The status of the individual in the company will have some bearing on the amount of influence he will have on outside opinion. The higher your rank, the more completely your behavior and opinions will be regarded as reflecting the attitude of the company as a whole. Responsibility for the opinion of the public toward our company was not included in the job definition when we received the promotion to managerial rank, but it was there nevertheless. In fact, promotion into and within management can be likened to changing the windows in our house. Before becoming a part of management, our house was much the same as most of our neighbors'. The first step into management made a change that inserted a large window through which the people on the outside could see us more easily. As each step up in promotion is made, another large window is put in, making our lives and actions more and more visible to the outside world, until upon arrival at the chief executive position one finds himself living in an all-glass house.

There is little, if any, privacy. All the things one does and all the things one says are identified with the company. Further, the "increase in visibility" extends to one's family. It may be considered unfair and unjust for the company to expect us to shoulder such a responsibility. But, remember, this situation was not created by the company; it came about because of the way people think and behave. If each of us examines himself, he will find that, logical or not, fair or unfair, it is his normal behavior that has been described.

WHAT SHOULD YOU DO ABOUT IT?

The natural question to ask is, "Where do I fit in this public-relations picture? What can I do? How can I find out what is expected of me?" The answer is found in the capabilities of the individual. In the first place, each member of the managerial force, whether general manager or foreman, is expected to conduct himself as a good citizen of the community in which he lives. He is also expected to act as head of his family group and influence its members to a sense of responsibility in personal conduct. Beyond this, there is an obligation to participate in activities outside the immediate job demand. This is where the particular abilities and likes and dislikes of you as an individual come into play.

Perhaps the first step is for each of us to make an honest appraisal of his abilities beyond the skills needed by his job. Obviously, there is not space here to make an analysis of all the things people can do well, but a few examples should illustrate the point.

Suppose woodworking is your hobby. You do it because you like it, and consequently do it quite well. When some other woodworking hobbyist comes along, you find a mutual interest that gets you into conversation about techniques and equipment, what you have made, and the plans for future work. Your new-found hobbyist gladly visits your shop and is eager that you return the call.

This in itself is good neighborliness. But being part of a community means giving of one's self to others. Have you, the woodworking hobbyist, considered how you can make a contribution to others and *like doing it?* Have you thought that there are boys with some natural aptitude in your neighborhood who would respond to a teacher in using tools and shaping things out of wood?

Consider the effect of forming a small class or club for such a purpose. You are doing a constructive work in encouraging the impressionable youth of your neighborhood in the use of the hands and teaching them the joy of skilled craftsmanship. You earn not only their high regard, but the esteem of their parents. The respect and affection that you earn will reflect on the company for which you work and with which you are identified.

There are many ways of working with young people as a means of making a contribution to others. Participation in Boy Scout work and acting as advisor in Junior Achievement activities are two ways similar to the woodworking illustration. The important point to remember is that such participation in neighborhood affairs can be effective as a satisfaction to yourself only if you enjoy doing it. If you are forcing yourself "because it is the thing to do," it will not be well done, and consequently your identity with a poor job will reflect on you as well as your company. This point should not be used as an excuse for not doing anything at all; let it serve to point up the importance of doing well the things you can do.

Exercise care and thought before becoming too closely associated with an extracurricular activity. While you as an individual might feel very strongly on a subject, the cost in personal prestige should be weighed before actively participating in unpopular, obscure, or "queer" movements.

For those whose abilities do not run in the direction of the illustrations given, there are many other activities, public in nature, that can be indulged in with considerable benefit to one's self and one's company.

For example, there are the technical and professional societies. Active participation in the local group of a society or association closely related to your own interest or knowledge will reflect credit upon your employing company. It also has the advantages that you gain by keeping up in your field and grow by reason of close association with other informed people.

It must be clearly understood that *active* participation is necessary. Merely belonging to an organization without taking part tends to have a negative value in your relationship with your fellow members. You are not doing anything to earn acceptance by the group and as time goes on any regard they may have had for you gets less and less. Finally, they hardly notice when you drop your membership.

Participating in civic affairs, such as the Chamber of Commerce, the Community Chest drive, or the Parent-Teachers Association, represents a form of valuable public service in which personal contributions can be made. Great gain results eventually—gain that is rarely of an economic type, however. More importantly, it is satisfaction of our need for self-expression. It caters to our personal egos and that part of our nature which needs acceptance by our fellows—our "social needs," as Douglas McGregor calls them.

Writing. To many, the term "public relations" means making speeches and writing publicity articles for newspapers and magazines. These methods of "building public confidence or increasing public understanding" are useful and have an important place in our public-relations activities, but they cannot do the whole job nor can they substitute for the individual participation by members of the management team that has been discussed in this chapter.

The preparation of material for newspaper publication is a special art in itself and very rarely falls within the normal requirements of the managerial supervisor's job; but the facts and ideas that form the subject matter of such material frequently are supplied by him. Your public-relations department cannot hope to do an effective job in publicity if the people responsible for the operating function of the business do not give cooperative help.

In their zeal to write readable stories for newspaper publication, it is only too easy for public-relations people to assume facts or get wrong slants on things that happen. Keeping them informed is the only way to prevent such faults. To do so, it is necessary to take time to talk to them and to get an understanding of their problems. You who are actually dealing with the people who make up the organization and are dealing with the day-by-day happenings are in a far better position to know the true significance of your area of activity. You certainly are interested enough to try to prevent any distortion of, inclusion in, or omission from a news story that might make your human-relations job more difficult.

The preparation of articles for professional or technical publication is in a somewhat different category. This means you are in an "authority of knowledge" position and, of course, accuracy is of prime importance. Not that inaccuracy is condoned in the previous case, but now we have a type of permanent record from which quotation will be made and from which the stature of the individual and the company he represents will be judged.

To be willing to inform others whereby they can get help in their own problems is good neighbor behavior. This is just what you are doing when you write a paper for publication or present it at a meeting of a group of interested people.

Making Speeches. The last thought suggests the making of speeches. To the majority of men in industrial management, the idea of making a speech brings on a feeling of terror. "I can talk to my own group all right," says one, "but I just can't get up and make a speech. I'm scared I'll make a fool of myself." How often do we hear that and agree with the fellow who says it because we have just the same feelings!

If there is a serious danger of "making a fool of one's self," or being completely engulfed by fear, then perhaps the speech should never be attempted. But actually that rarely happens. The most important thing to remember is that you would not be asked to make the speech if the people asking you did not believe you were well informed in your subject. Secondly, we do not want flowery oratory every time we hear somebody talk on a subject in which we are interested. What we, the listeners, really like is a straightforward expression of ideas and experiences from which we can learn, delivered in simple language and coming from a sincere person. Remember, if we get the impression that he doesn't know what he is talking about, and is making up for his lack of knowledge by a flood of language, a speaker goes down a long way in our estimation, as does any organization with which he is identified.

On the other hand, giving a talk before a group, although a little terrifying to contemplate, perhaps, can be a most satisfying experience. It can and does offer an opportunity for personal growth as well as earning the esteem of our fellow men. Speechmaking is not as difficult as it appears, providing one is sincere and honest with the listeners.

THE PUBLIC AND HUMAN RELATIONS

As hinted earlier in this chapter, there is a definite relationship between a company's human relations and its public relations. Perhaps it is not too extreme to say that without a good industrial personnel-relations program, no company can expect good public relations. The foundation for good public relations is good human relations inside our plants and offices. If the employees in your company *think* and *say,* "This is a good place to work and a good outfit to work for," it's safe to conclude that you have good personnel relations. Such a good opinion of the company by its work force is the keystone in the structure of public esteem.

It is well to remember that the employees of our industries have a wide and extensive contact. Their relatives, friends, and organizations are, of course, members of the public. Each of these gathers impressions and forms opinions of the company and its management policies and personalities from talking with Joe "who works there." Joe's attitude in the majority of cases will be a reflection of the treatment he has received from his foreman in particular and the management generally. If they practice fair dealing, honesty, and consideration for others, then the chances are overwhelming that Joe will develop a feeling of being part of a "good outfit." On the other hand, he will not be able to hide his feelings, even if he wants to, if he experiences discrimination, double dealing, or insincerity in any of his relationships with the representatives of management.

The local community of which the plant or office is a part is quite sensitive to the personnel relations in the organization. It is an easy subject of conversation, particularly if the situation is not good. If it were possible to survey these conversations, it would be found that they usually take the form of comments on individual behavior of members of management including, of course, the foreman. Reference to the "company," or "they," meaning the management, often is part of such a conversation and will reflect the general or collective impression of policy or action. But discussing people as individuals carries more weight and is more interesting conversation material.

Perhaps our community relations could be summed up in this

fashion: Do the people in the area in which our business is located say, "Too bad that outfit ever located here"? Or are they indifferent to us? Or do they say, "We're lucky to have the XYZ company in this town"? How the public feels about us will be largely the result of our attitudes and behavior in the field of personnel relations.

SELECTION AND PROMOTION

If consideration of public opinion of us is so important, and individual behavior plays such a big part in it, surely it is logical that management consider this aspect when hiring new people or promoting present employees to greater responsibility. When bringing in a new employee, remember that he soon will become identified with the company.

There is no formula for selecting people that will give positive measurement of how any one of them is going to behave either inside or outside the job situation. But through good interviewing and perhaps some testing and the application of large amounts of good judgment, we can form an opinion as to whether or not we should like an individual to represent our company to the public. The important thing is to give consideration to this point. A person who is going to bring discredit on the company by his behavior and attitude on the outside often can do much more damage than his skills or professional knowledge can do good.

In the matter of promotion, the selection of people with consideration for the "public-relations aspect" becomes even more important. As any individual climbs the management ladder, he becomes more and more identified with his company. Therefore his ability to meet the "public-regard" demands of his job must be evaluated along with all the other qualifications at the time the selection is made. The problem of considering his impact on our public relations is not confined to the man who is a candidate for promotion to a supervisory or higher management job. His wife, particularly, and perhaps other members of his family, must be taken into consideration. Again, careful judgment is necessary. In the case of the man to be promoted, association with him on the job and outside can give a good basis for judging how he is likely to behave in the job of higher rank. But in evaluating his wife it is not so easy. However, all the amenities of good taste can be met by observation at the Christmas party, or department picnic, or in other social gatherings. If she is active in community affairs, the job is much easier. But judgment should be formed— of her as well as her husband. As society has matured, the team relationship of husband and wife has become an accepted and realistic matter. No "team" should be judged by judging any one member, but by the performance of the complete unit. The husband and wife team definitely are a unit in the area of public relations; and their attitudes, as well as their individual behavior, will cause public disapproval or earn public regard.

This whole matter of the manager's problem and the public was given in capsule form by someone many years ago: "Public relations is being good and getting credit for it."

CHAPTER 19

ATTITUDES AND MORALE

George is afraid Jack is going to quit. Yet he is a good man, a skilled craftsman, and has a lot of ability.
"I wonder why he has such an attitude toward the company and toward his job. Why does he want to quit?"

WHAT IS AN ATTITUDE?

We blame many of our difficulties in human relationships on that carelessly defined thing called "attitudes." We are inclined to accuse those with whom we disagree of having a poor attitude. The labor leader tears away at management, saying that there would be industrial peace if management didn't have such a poor attitude, and vice-versa. Liberals insist that the conservative attitude retards progress. The reactionary fears that the attitude of the radical will cause revolutions. Even in personal matters we insist that home would be a happier place if the wife had a better attitude toward the budget, or if the son had a better attitude toward school, or if the daughter had a proper attitude toward boy friends.

We have seen examples of demagogues who lead the people by an appeal to their attitudes. Liberal leaders in the North have been able to earn a following by appealing to the neglected rights of the Negro population. On the other hand, there are certain Southern leaders who have risen to power by appealing to the attitude of white supremacy. In the chapter on discipline we find that not only must the offender be made to comply, but his attitude must be such that it, too, will improve. We are harsh on a mild lawbreaker if he shows a poor attitude. We find ourselves defending the worst criminal if we discover that his attitude has changed.

It seems incredible that such attitudes are so important to our lives and to our relationships and at the same time that we know

223

so little about them. We have amassed a great deal of knowledge in the material universe. It is no problem to remove a mountain or put great powers to work. There seems to be nothing that we cannot produce on a production line. We now have the tools and weapons to make or destroy almost anything, but we have very little information about the attitudes which control these powers.

We know that *an attitude is a tendency to act with respect to a certain value*. It is a sort of hair-triggered spring, or inclination, that we have for a thing, person, or idea. Take the boss, for an example. We can test our attitude by discovering what our inclination toward this person is. How do we feel about him and how would we really like to treat him? Of course, we cannot judge an attitude by how a person actually acts. We become skilled in suppressing our attitudes, and many times we act in an opposite direction from the way we feel. Maybe we do not like the boss. Maybe he is obnoxious to us, and our inclination is to do him violent physical harm. Then he represents a negative value to us, but our reason tells us that we must get along with him. Our best interest insists that we please him. So, instead of doing him physical harm, we smile at him and act in a way that would give outside observers the opinion that we love him. The important things to remember about attitudes are that they are under the surface and are latent. They cannot be confused with how we act. They are ever present and are waiting for stimulation. They produce the inner pressure and tensions that accumulate around our feelings toward a certain value.

The key word in the definition of attitude is the word "value." What do we know about a value? There are two kinds of values— material and nonmaterial. They can be things like money, diamonds, and real estate. Or they can be ideas and concepts like democracy, love, and loyalty. The positive values are the things and ideas we like and have a tendency to acquire, as for example, beauty and knowledge and money. The negative values are those we fear or dislike or repel, like snakes and diphtheria. The key fact is that all our attitudes depend on some value.

Now, these values do not stay still. They constantly change and sometimes change rapidly. *As the values change, our attitudes change.* Values that once were negative, like bobbed hair, are now positive. Some of the people whom we consider peculiar and non-conformist today are that way simply because they cannot change their attitudes as fast as society changes its values.

We know that we are not born with attitudes. They are not hereditary. We derive all our value system from the various contacts that we have had. When George McGowan is afraid that Jack is going to quit and wonders why he has such a poor attitude toward the company, he must realize that Jack's attitude can be explained in terms of his experiences. Some of his values he learned in a formal way at home and school. He was taught that certain things and ideas are good and some are wicked. Many of his values he did not learn but seemed to catch. They are contagious, and we seem to pick them up without ever realizing that we have caught them. This is particularly true in our childhood, when most of our values are established. We may never have been told in school that a black cat is a negative value, but, just the same, we deplore them when they cross our paths.

How can you change an attitude? Since a poor attitude is the cause of much of our failure in human relations, how can we develop a better attitude? The secret of attitude change is in the change of a value system. What are the things that we think the most important, most sacred, most true? Some of our positive values have been determined by pure *intellectual* reasoning. We have thought the matter over carefully, and we have come to a logical conclusion. We know that there is a calculated risk in driving on the wrong side of a highway going up a hill. We can reason that good brakes are essential in traffic.

It is interesting to realize that intellectual values are the easiest values to change. It is simply a matter of finding a flaw in one's logic or of changing one's mind. When the attitudes have an *emotional* content (and most of them do), they are much more difficult to change. In this case it is not what we *think* about a matter, but how we *feel* about a value. We cannot change our feelings as we can change our minds. Even when our best intellectual processes tell us we are wrong, we still cling to our way of feeling about a thing or idea. *Spiritual* attitudes that are based on blind faith are the hardest of all values to change. Here are values with a rigid wall around them, and they are accepted without any sort of doubt or explanation. While all attitudes can be changed, the attitudes based on the emotional and spiritual faith are the most stubborn.

HOW TO DEVELOP AN ATTITUDE

Since attitudes and values are the result of our experiences, we must look into the person's background to understand him. We have mentioned that the family influence is very powerful. In many ways we adopt our parents' values just as they are. We are Catholics because we come from a Catholic family. We are Democrats because our people have always been Democrats. We never go hunting because our family didn't like guns.

Most of the things that we learn in life we pick up before the age of six or seven. By that time many of our likes and dislikes are pretty well established. The matter of our attitudes toward the members of another race is a good example of the background influence on our values. No white man can completely know what it means to be a Negro, since we have never had that experience. A little Negro boy on a train made a hit with his forthright personality on a group of men who watched him. He had been shielded, apparently, by his mother from racial antagonism and segregation. He was frank, open, and friendly in his spontaneous contact. His big dimples and smile melted the hearts of those who saw him. As the train sped on, one man was heard to say to another, "Isn't it going to be too bad when that little boy learns he is black?" What the men were really saying is that some day the little boy would have to change his values. He would have to take a different attitude toward the white people with whom he came in contact. He would have to force himself into a minority pattern of behavior.

People who travel in foreign lands easily recognize the difference in values between different nationality backgrounds. We do not "look at a thing" as a foreigner does. Our values are different. In fact, a minority is a minority because of a different and unique set of values. (Sometimes this difference in values is enforced only by the majority.)

More and more we have come to realize that the class structure in our country determines many of our values. Some of the latest research indicates that we can nearly forecast the value system of people by knowing their class status in the community. We all have a tendency to take on the values which our class has developed. Many people do not understand this class difference. They do not know that there are different folkways and mores in each of the classes. Misunderstanding often comes when the people of the upper class, for instance, judge those in the lower class. Their mistake is in judging the other group on the basis of upper-class attitudes. We hear the term "middle-class morality." It is simply another way of saying middle-class mores and folkways. Kinsey's famous report indicated that lower-class people have very different sex attitudes than the middle class. The middle-class attitudes were in contrast with those of the upper class, and yet each group judged all men on their own set of values. As we have said earlier, a great deal of the industrial strife in our country comes from the fact that the owners and the management come from a different class from that of the bulk of the laboring people. In a sense, they do not speak the same language, and their values are so different that it is difficult for them to understand each other. This is particularly so when they judge the other person through the eyes of their own attitude structure.

Similar illustrations can be built on many other phases of background and experience. Whether a person has a rural childhood or has been reared in the city would be a case in point. Whether we are Southern or Northern, man or woman, college man or high-school graduate, minister or trader—all are examples of how varied values can be.

When men are promoted and rise on the status ladder, they usually accept and adopt the new attitudes of their new social position. As George McGowan is promoted into the position of factory manager, he will find that people will expect him to live a little differently. He will be expected to dress a little smarter and perhaps even drive a better car. He will soon readjust his value system and will adapt his attitudes to this new station in life. Some men who are promoted are inclined to forget the attitudes of the worker in the factory. Others promoted do not necessarily forget, but they feel that their new-found values are so superior that they try to impose this new attitude on their former friends. The wise man is the one who, through all his promotions, can remember the former atti-

tudes and use this knowledge to understand and interpret the point
of view of the worker.

ATTITUDES IN INDUSTRY

A constant hazard in industrial relations is the clash in attitudes.
The management pictures the factory or plant in terms of very
different values from those of the worker. On the other hand, the
worker looks at the plant through the eyes of an entirely different
set of values. In order to understand the conflict that sometimes
arises between the attitudes of the boss and the worker, we must
examine the values the company holds for each, and how each
evaluates the work of the other.

Here is management. It is employed by the stockholders to ad-
minister the corporation. Authority is given by the board of directors to the executive. What are the paramount values in this company for this executive and his subordinate bosses? If we can contrast these values which the boss looks for in the company with the
values that the worker seeks, we can compare the variation in attitudes. To the boss, the primary value is *profit*. This means not only
money to be shared among stockholders but money to be re-
invested to strengthen the business. We know that profit also is a
symbol of success in management. If you were on the board of
directors and you were called upon to judge the management, the
first thing you would like to examine would be the books of the
corporation. If they are in black ink instead of red, and if the company has maintained a good profit, the chances are that you would
defend the executives. The profit then becomes not only money
but an indication of success and a criterion of status in management.

There are some who insist that profit is the only value that
management has. They say that everything else is insignificant or
merely a means to a profit. "Look at the customer," they say. "He
rates very high with the company and is treated like a king.
Extravagant expense accounts are allowed to keep him happy."
And it is pointed out that he is not important in himself but only
as a means to show a profit for the company. Industry has been
accused of treating their employees well for just the same reason
and no other. "Keep 'em happy at all costs, since we must keep up
production. It will pay in the long run," they say. Good service and

efficiency are not ends in themselves, but are held to be merely the way by which a profit may be insured.

There are indications lately, however, that the human values of a company are becoming increasingly important in themselves. There was a time, not many years ago, when safety was merely a matter of keeping production going and reducing the cost of compensation insurance. Now, even the most cynical will admit indications which show that management is interested in the individual personality of the workers. In many companies it is a fact that the factory not only produces a profit on the product it makes, but there is also an awareness that it is helping men and women become ever more loyal employees. This latter is not merely a by-product, but a positive value to the company. Most personnel policies, safety programs, and employment practices are now originated from a philosophy of genuine concern by the management for the men and women who invest their lives in the company. Thus, good working conditions, high morale, and pleasant public relationships are all important values to the executive. Fortunately, it has been proved that this concern for the value of the employee and the good will of the community is not expensive in the long run. Neither is it at all inconsistent with profit.

Pride in the quality of a product is also a value to management. All executives like to be associated with the best product in their field. We find this attitude toward quality is contagious, and it is the surest way to sell goods. Thus, the high importance placed on the worth of the product is not damaging to profit. But even if it were costly to the profit, there are many executives who would not compromise their quality because they have an *attitude* toward the value of their product.

Now let's look at the *worker* in the company. What value does he see for himself in this organization? What are the factors that determine his attitude toward the plant and the boss? The primary value that the company offers is *security*. The worker looks to the management to provide him with the wherewithal to keep the proverbial wolf from the door. The list of economic necessities for the common man has grown long, and the worker feels that he has a right to expect these things from the company in return for honest work.

However, a good wage (like profit) is more than money to spend

on the necessities of life. It, too, is a status symbol and is an indication of the company's estimate of the worker's worth. The wage
scale in any company becomes a system of ranks, and a raise means
a great deal more than what the additional money will buy. To
the worker, the value of security is more than mere wages, contracts, retirement plans, bonus incentives, and the like. Security
to him also means an emotional security that is derived by his being
necessary and (in his own mind at least) almost indispensable.
He wants to think that he makes a unique contribution to the company. He wants to feel that his work is so significant that the company needs him and will provide for his needs because he "belongs."

Of course, there are other values to the worker besides security.
He wants a safe place to work, with all the features of good working conditions. He, like the management, likes to take pride in the
product his firm produces, and he wants his company to be popular
in the community. When the company has a good reputation, it
gives him the value of status in the eyes of his friends and thus helps
him meet his need for recognition and accomplishment. A man who
cannot find this value of recognition and accomplishment in his
work will seek it in some other place. His attitudes will be affected
by this transfer of loyalty, and when he does not find these values in
his work, he is in position then to turn into a troublemaker or a
problem employee.

In order to analyze the differences in the attitudes of the worker
and the boss, let us review the values that each finds in the company for which they work. Listed below are a few of the values
for each:

Values of Management	*Values of the Worker*
1. PROFIT	1. SECURITY
2. HUMAN VALUES good working conditions, safety, opportunity for advancement for workers, good personnel practices	2. OPPORTUNITY TO GROW ON JOB the feeling of belonging, the feeling of being significant and important, good working conditions, safety
3. PRIDE IN THE QUALITY OF PRODUCT	3. PRIDE IN THE QUALITY OF PRODUCT
4. GOOD COMMUNITY RELATIONSHIPS FOR THE COMPANY	4. GOOD COMMUNITY RELATIONSHIPS FOR THE COMPANY

When the matter is analyzed, there is really little variance in the list of values for a good management and the list of values for successful employees. The difference is in the meaning of the words. Particularly, there is a difference between the words "security" and "profit." There is something about the word "security" which bothers management. If we can believe management associations and manufacturing groups, security is a bad word and refers to something that has been used to exploit the American citizen. To them a worker who seeks security is selling his birthright of liberty for a mess of pottage.

On the other hand, there is a negative value to the matter of profit for a large group of employees. Sometimes the labor unions have pictured profit as the thing that robs the worker of his just deserts and keeps him poor. As we have seen, in reality these two concepts are not far apart. In fact, security is to the worker just what profit is to management. The worker finds in his security the status symbol for his success, the money to pay the bills of his financial obligations, and an opportunity to put money away for future needs. This is exactly the same thing that profit is to management. Thus, the company offers the same values to the worker and the boss but calls it by a different name. If more people could understand this similarity, attitudes would not have to be in conflict.

The other employer-employee values are parallel and similar. Both groups want safety and good working conditions. Both take pride in their product and the reputation of the company. Management talks about the value of morale, and the worker wants "to belong." The boss is interested in the worker as a person, while the employee wants to feel significant in his job. If everyone, including stockholders, management, and worker, can see the same values in the company, then the attitudes all become positive. When the values of the boss and the worker are inconsistent or in conflict, it is always worth the effort to change the values to the elimination of the conflict. In all attempts to adjust attitudes, whether it be the management trying to change the worker's or the worker (often through his union) trying to change the management's, strictest respect for human personality and integrity must be observed. If not, the conflict of values will become much more intense and more difficult to adjust.

MORALE

Morale was defined in an earlier chapter as the "feeling of belonging" carried to such an extreme that the individual feels the welfare of the group is more important and vital than his own. A person is capable of great sacrifice and self-discipline if the morale of the group is strong enough. Those who work with people know that this thing called morale is very elusive and difficult to create and maintain within the group. Nevertheless, it is the secret of a productive situation. When it is completely gone, there is nothing left but chaos and confusion.

How do you get it? How does the leader create morale in his group? After you find it, how do you maintain it and keep it for an extended period of time? These are the key questions to the supervisor in his responsibility for other people.

At the beginning of a certain baseball season there was a great major-league team. It had more than its quota of outstanding stars, and the sports fans were amazed that so many outstanding players could be brought together in the uniform of one team. In the same league, there was a group of young players who had never made achievements or had success. At the end of the season, the aggregation of stars finished in the second division, while the eager, hustling youngsters played over their heads and won the pennant. The sports writers attributed the success to hustle and hard work. They explained the champions in terms of the will to win. This is an illustration of morale. It is a set of attitudes. It is a tendency to act toward certain values. In the case of morale, the value is the high importance of the job to be done, the game to win, the production goal to achieve, or the quality to maintain. When these values are entrenched in the value system of the worker, his attitudes are conducive to great achievement. Because of such attitudes, the morale of his working situation will be high.

We spend a great deal of time and money to keep our machinery in good running order and in fine repair. We do constant research on lubrication, so that there will not be friction and unnecessary wear on the machines. Now we are beginning to realize that the worker needs something of the same sort of treatment to keep his values sharpened and his attitudes enthusiastic for his work assignment. Every device that will honestly present the importance of the work to be done and the eagerness of the management to encourage and help the worker to achieve must be used. Part of this book has been an attempt to give specific techniques to achieve this high morale. The topics include an understanding of authority and its use, the perfection of communication, the significance of making work attractive, counseling and discipline, incentives, and good selection. And evaluations of workers are used to suggest means by which positive attitudes can be encouraged and a high morale maintained. There is no more important work that the boss can do.

CHAPTER 20

TEN YEARS AFTER

"You know I can't make a speech," complained George McGowan to his friend Jim Frazer, the executive vice-president.

This was the same setting where, nearly ten years ago, Jim had asked George to take over the job of plant manager. George remembered that scene very clearly, and how nervous and even afraid he had been as he tackled the job he had held these ten years. But it was the faith and confidence expressed by Jim Frazer that had reassured him a decade ago, and now he was getting the same encouragement to accept another task.

"You can do it as well as any man I know. To be invited to speak at an executive development conference of our Los Angeles plant is a real compliment for you and for this Chicago plant of ours. They don't want any 'high-faluting,' stuffy paper on theory, but just your own words on what you have learned through the years as plant manager. They want to know how you have broken every production record we have ever had. They are asking you to tell about the things you know best. Just tell them simply, in the same way you talk to people in your office, and you'll go over in a big way."

"I'll think about it and talk it over with my wife," George promised.

That was three weeks ago, and Ruth had said of course he would make the speech, and he had agreed to try. But now that the night had arrived he wished he had not been pushed into this spot. Here, seated before him, awaiting his talk were some of the big names in the company, men he'd heard a lot about, some of them people he'd met at various company meetings. But a lot of them had been with the company longer than he had, and practically all of them had done a fine job for the company. What could he tell them? They probably knew more than he would ever know. Several of them had graduate degrees, and yet he had the gall to stand up and tell them how to manage a plant. But it was too late now to back out. He remembered Jim's advice to be simple and tell them what he had found out in his own plant. Well, he would try.

After a somewhat flowery introduction, George got to his feet, cleared his throat, looked at the microphone, and was surprised to hear his own voice.

"I have been trying to figure out how I got into this spot. I don't know what I can tell you that you don't already know, but I have been asked to speak on the subject of human relations in our Chicago plant, and here I go.

"First, let me say that I am proud of the product that we make at Chicago. We think that it is the best in the industry, as good in its way as the product you make here. But we are also mighty proud of the men who produce it. Some of these men have been with the company longer than I have, and we would not trade them for a brand-new factory—debt free. These fellows, by their day-by-day loyalty, have created a good plant, where production records are broken. They have made a good environment, so that now it's a good place to work, and they like it.

"It's hard to say what makes it such a good place to work. Of course, we have all of the usual benefits. It is true in the Chicago plant, as it is here, that the men work a reasonable number of hours each week, at good wages. We have a liberal retirement policy. We see to it that everyone enjoys a good vacation, and we are not at all selfish about such things as sick allowance and time off. We have a good hospitalization plan, and as you know, our men are allowed to buy stock in the company at a very attractive price. One of the best investments we ever made was a recreation camp on the South Shore where our folks are encouraged to take their families for a little fishing and camping. We have made a genuine effort to improve working conditions. We employ an effective safety program. We attempt to promote from within whenever we can, as I know you do here in this plant, and we have all the gadgets for testing and evaluation.

"But now I must confess that our personnel policy is more than these things. We have outgrown the technical gadgets, and we think that the thing that really does the work is a real, genuine interest in the fellows who do the job in the factory. Take, for instance, Jack, who was hurt when he fell off a hoist. The doctor told us that he had a fractured vertebra, so we sent him downtown for the very best medical care. Of course, his case was covered by workmen's compensation, and he received the usual benefits from the insurance company. We kept Jack on the payroll, however, and for the eighteen months that he was in the hospital in a cast we never let him miss a payday. Whenever any of us were downtown, we would drop in to see Jack, and we encouraged his fellow workers to remember him with letters and chatty visits. Jack is back on the job now, and he thinks we're a pretty good outfit. In fact, you couldn't drive him away with a machine gun.

"And then there's that jolly little Mexican boy, Jose, who lost his leg in an automobile accident. We all liked him, and we knew we had to find a job for him. We had a special conveyance made, which he could operate without his left foot. And now he whizzes around the factory, doing a good job and proud of his special jalopy. These things were expensive and did take a little money, but we think they paid off in a loyalty that cannot be purchased.

"I guess every company looks after their men when they are hurt. But it is not only the hard-luck boys who get attention in our place. Last year, at the end of our fiscal year, every member of management, including the first-line supervisors, had a nice, personal letter from Jim Frazer, our executive vice-president, telling each one how well he had done in the plant and thanking him for his efforts. Enclosed was a simple and understandable financial statement of our company. Here in black and white were the figures to show how, through a pretty tough year, we'd been able to show black-ink profit. The report indicated how, because of tough competition, we were forced to reduce our price, but it explained that, through careful and efficient production, these price cuts were more than offset by savings in plant operation. Jim has a way of making this sound as if every single man had been responsible for this victory, and even the unskilled laborers who sweep up the plant talk about *our* production, *our* efficiency, and *our* profits.

It's no wonder we like these fellows, because they make up our team.

"I have wracked my brain to see if there is some magic formula, some secret to explain good production in a plant or some way to account for human relations working at their best. If there is an explanation, I think it lies in two basic principles. One of these is team work—*the process of people working together and feeling they are a part of a group.* We make every effort, at all times, to see that there are no barriers, no cliques, no cleavages between the people who work for us. Of course there are different grades of pay, and there is the management and worker relationship. But we have conscientiously attempted to make everyone feel that he is on the inside and that he 'belongs.' We refer to the plant as *we* and use the word *our* whenever possible.

"The other basic principle is that *every single job is important and significant.* We know that all of our people have to be paid well in order to satisfy their needs at home, but we also realize that money isn't everything, and that if a person is to work in efficiency and dignity, he must feel that what he is doing is significant. A careless telephone operator or a sassy clerk can sometimes drive away more business than the vice-president in charge of sales can secure. A cheerful elevator operator can tone the day for a lot of workers. A janitor who has a sense of cleanliness and a painter who is neat can make all the difference in a room. We believe this, and we do everything we can to show our people how important they are to us and to show how much their efficient and effective service is needed in our plant.

"Of course we have our problem workers and our personnel problems. They offer us our most disheartening challenge. We attack each problem with the thought that perhaps the trouble lies in us, and 'Well, what have we done to cause such a maladjustment?' Old Jake was a trouble-maker in the finishing department. He created all sorts of tensions and ill-will. We were about to let him go, when we discovered that he had a mentally sick wife at home for whom he could not afford proper care, and he had also lost a boy on the Normandy Beach. Of course he was grouchy and irritable. We tipped some of the boys off, and they did some nice things for Jake and his family. Jake has warmed up a little, and I think he may make it.

"Just last week we had to fire Jimmy who was a promising young fellow with a lot of skill because he was fundamentally an exhibitionist. He always had to be the center of attraction. He could not stand the boredom of working on a piece of machinery. He was always breaking the safety rules and doing something spectacular and dangerous. We decided that a factory was no place to give Jimmy the satisfaction he needed. I guess he will have to join the air corps or the foreign legion and get a chance to do the things that require daring and adventure.

"One of our most difficult problems at the present time is the tension that exists between our Negro and white workers. We are attempting to be fair in all our labor practices, but there are members of both groups who are absolutely unreasonable and have a blind spot on this matter. We can't seem to talk this thing out or reason it out with the men. The subject is so laden with emotion that I am afraid a spark will set it off and cause a lot of trouble. The matter was helped last week when Jack, a great, big, strong Negro, rushed in and put out a fire that could have been very dangerous. Some of those endangered by the fire were those who have caused us the most trouble in this connection. But we are still baffled and at a loss for a solution for this problem.

"Naturally, we've had some difficulties in our relationships with the union, and I doubt that we'll ever see eye to eye with them. They center on the needs and desires of the men, and while we think of those things too, we have to consider the whole company and often have to resist the union's demands somewhat. But this sort of difference of opinion is probably good anyway. At least it keeps us on our toes and helps assure us that we don't overlook our obligations to our workers.

"Some of our difficulties with the union come from a genuine conflict in what we want, but I think many, and maybe most, of them come from a simple failure on the part of each of us to understand the other. Sometimes we haven't taken time to see why they do what they do and why they make what seems to us such unreasonable demands. I'm sure the same is true of the union when they look at us. We've been fortunate at Chicago, however. We still have basic respect for and trust in the union, and I think they return those feelings. And as long as there is trust and respect between us, we'll be able to solve our problems even if some of them are pretty rough.

"Maybe an illustration will help. Several years ago, the union came in with a demand for a guaranteed Christmas bonus. Now obviously, if it was to be guaranteed it was not a bonus but a raise in wages, and some of our management people grumbled that this was just another case of how unreasonable unions can be. On the face of it, I admit, it looked that way, but an investigation revealed the real explanation.

"It had long been the practice in our plant that every year, just after Christmas, we would take inventory. This means that we would close down the factory for two or three days and, of course, the factory people didn't get paid for that period. But this is the very time of year when most workers need all the money they can get, and hence their demand for a guaranteed bonus. When we saw the thing through their eyes, it didn't seem so unreasonable. Fortunately, we've been able to shift the inventory to the annual vacation shutdown in the summer, with benefit, I'm convinced, to all concerned.

"Another factor that has helped our management in worker relationships has been the cleaning up of our organization chart. We found some men who had had administrative rank and pay with little or no administrative responsibility. Still others had too many men reporting directly to them. Some of our department heads were ineffective, and we had to make room for some real leaders who could delegate authority and back up their men with confidence. Choosing these men for advancement was one of the toughest management jobs that I have had. We finally selected some men who, we were sure, enjoyed the respect of their fellow workers. We had no formal committees, but it was really the workmen themselves who chose their leaders since, you see, we picked the men they naturally followed. We also found out, the hard way, that you can't give responsibility without giving authority too. When a man gets some authority delegated to him from the top and at the same time is highly respected by his men, he then has the dignity and power of leadership. This has been our policy for promotion.

"The greatest overhauling came in our system of getting our ideas over to the men. We found that we had been careless in keeping all the people in the plant effectively posted. We had some clogged lines of communication from the top office to the foremen, and, by the same token, in the plant manager's office we never were quite sure what was happening throughout the plant. We found out—in the hard way again—that fancy bulletins and high-sounding promises meant absolutely nothing to the workers unless they were followed through and interpreted, and unless we delivered what we said we would. Gradually we have built up confidence in our periodic letter to the workmen. These letters are enclosed in their pay envelopes from time to time. They deal with all sorts and kinds of subjects—safety records, cost features, new equipment, taxes, and all the other things that we think the men would like to know about. We have never told anything but the truth, and we believe that now they accept these pronouncements as the true version rather than taking the distorted interpretation of the grapevine.

"In the selection of new employees we run into some difficulties. The personnel department has set up the characteristics that they think we must have to fill our vacancies. My personal gripe with them is that they look for a potential President of the United States to fill every single position, and they are disappointed if their new man does not have all of the qualities of St. Paul. I won my point with them a few years ago when they refused to hire a dried up, little, old, sour introvert, who hated people. Our competitors took him on and, lo and behold, he perfected a fine new system for making our product! We had to pay plenty to get that process for our own factory. I maintain that you don't have to try to make every single man a potential general manager. Some people should be hired because they will make very good freight-elevator operators and probably never anything else. Our evaluation system is based on the principle of helping the worker fully as much as helping the factory. It is a method by which we try to encourage an individual to be self-critical in a constructive way and at the same

time to build up his own self-confidence and feeling of self-adequacy. We know that this self-esteem is the most valuable possession of any man, and if, through criticism or rough evaluation, his
self-confidence is shaken, we have weakened a good man. We try
to put all suggestions in a positive manner, and do our best to find
in each man strong points that we can point to with pride.

"Since we are trying to establish a team relationship at the plant,
we let the employees 'have a say' in the policies and decisions that
affect them. We ask their opinions about the working conditions
and the benefits that they enjoy. We find that they are more grateful for what the plant does for them if they suggest the things than
when they are handed down arbitrarily from above with a pater-
nalistic sort of attitude. All of our management is encouraged to
listen to the men as well as to advise and instruct them. We have
found that some of our best ideas have come up from the floor
of the factory. In fact we gave old Joe a banquet last month and
presented him with a beautiful watch from the company for producing an idea on loading that will save us plenty of money every
year. We have found it profitable to employ some plant counselors,
who are available to help the men in their personal affairs. This
seems at first to be a dead expense, but it has paid for itself many
times in increased production and in a reduction of absenteeism.

"Of course in building up good will we find it difficult to discipline and to fire anyone. We are so anxious to be fair that we
lean over backwards. I think we covet the reputation of being fair
above any other that I know. When we have to dock a worker's
pay or lay him off for a period, our foremen know that we must
have the man feel that the management did everything in its power,
even to going 60 or 80 per cent of the way, to prevent the thing
that actually made it necessary to discipline the worker. At first
we thought it would be inconsistent to be firm and at the same
time friendly with our employees, but we found that they expect
us to be consistent, and they resent it when we allow any worker
to run over us. We know that the workers will like us best if they
respect us, and therefore we maintain fair limits and will not
tolerate serious violations of them. But disciplinary problems can
be tough ones, and we certainly don't know all the answers.

"Again let me brag about my department heads and foremen.

They know that we are all working for the same goal—their security and the security of their men. They understand that it is all tied up with our production and profits. They fight for the men in their departments and see to it that the company knows the needs and problems of these men.

"Excuse my rambling, gentlemen. I haven't said anything except that I like to work for my outfit. They have been good to me and my men, and I don't think I would trade jobs with any of you. Thank you."

INDEX

Achievement, satisfaction in, 69–70
American Federation of Labor, 136
American ideology, 47–50
  education, faith in, 48
  factualism, 49
  freedom of thought, 47
  initiative, individual, 48
  materialism, 49
  organization, faith in, 48
  popular government, 47
  religion, faith in, 48
  secularism, 50
  sensualism, 49
  social justice, passion for, 48
  speed, 49–50
Antidiscrimination provisions, 63–64, 66
Application form, 155
Assistant, 113–114
"Assistant to," 114
Attitudes, 17–19, 223–231
  changes in, 225–226
  definition of, 223–224
  learning, 17–19
  of management, 228–231
  and values, 224–226
  of workers, 228–231
Authority, 61, 81–88, 96, 109–116, 138–141
  "by-passing" of, 96, 109–113
  centralization of, 61
  delegation of, 113–114
  by esteem, 82–83
  formal, 81–85, 114–115
  of knowledge, 82–83
  limitation of, 85–86, 138–141
  and responsibility, 85–86
  and threat, 114–116
  and tradition, 87–88
  union invasion of, 140–141
  withholding of, 86–87

Balance in organization, 73–74
Bargaining as means of communication, 141–143

Bonus, 118–126
  of foremen, 124–126
  nonproduction, 123–124
  production, 118–123
    group, 121–123
    individual, 118–121
"Boss," multiple, 108–114
Brown, Alvin, 78–79
"By-passing" of authority, 96, 109–113

Centralization of authority, 61
Committee for Industrial Organization, 136
Communication, 93–104, 142–143
  through bargaining, 142–143
  blockage to, 102
  definition of, 93
  and foremen, 95–96, 103–104
  and language, 97–101
  methods of, 98–102
    audio, 101
    grapevine, 101–102
    oral, 99–100
    visual, 100
    written, 98–99
  and organization, 94–97
Communications, growth in, 66–68
Complaints, 163–170, 175–176
  and counseling, 175–176
  latent, 169–170
  manifest, 169–170
  nature of, 163–169
Conditioning, 15, 34–35
Congress of Industrial Organization, 137
Consultation, cooperation through, 209–211
Control by withholding authority, 86–87
Controls, social, breakdown of, 57
Cooperation, 78–79, 201–212
  motivation for, 201–212
  nature of, 78–79
Coordination, 73–80
  of functions, 73–77
  of people, 75–80

243

Coordination, of self, 75–76
Counseling, 163–176
    and complaints, 175–176
    development of, 163–168
    directive, 170
    and grievances, 175–176
    nondirective, 170–174
    permissive, 170–174
Counselor, role of, 174–175
Craft guild, 130
Craft skill, 131–138
Craft union, 131–134
Crime, social problem of, 56–57

Delegation, of authority, 113–114
    of responsibility, 113–114
Democracy, growth of, 65–66
Dependency, 51, 54–55, 136
    of non-craft-skilled worker, 136
    and old age, 54–55
    in urban life, 51
Disciplinary interview, 188–190
Discipline, 103, 178–188
    and feelings of supervisors, 187–188
    methods of, 184–187
        demotion, 186
        discharge, 186–187
        layoff, 186
        reprimand, 103, 185–186
    rules governing, 180–184
    theories of, 178–180
        reform and deterrence, 179–180
        retribution, 178–179
Disease, 55–56
    control of, 55–56
    mental, increase of, 55–56
Drucker, Peter, 138–140

Economic man, 22–24
Education, 48, 57–58, 66–67
    faith in, 48
    growth of, 66–67
    inadequacy of, 57–58
Efficiency rating, 159–162
Effort, voluntary, 79
Ego protection, 30–32, 197–198
Emotional appeals, effectiveness of, 9–12
Emotional thinking, 9, 12
Emotional words, 97–98
Evaluation of employees, 156–162
    merit rating, 159–162

Evaluation of employees, principles of, 156–159
    and promotion, 156–159

Factualism, 49
Family life, changes in, 52
Flattery, 103
Folkways, 40
Freedom, of thought, 47
    of worker, increase of, 63–70
Functions, 71–77
    balance in, 73–74
    coordination of, 73–77
    and objectives, 71–73
    organization of, 71–77

Government, 47–48
    popular, 47
    under the law, 47–48
Grapevine, 11, 101–102
Grievances, 141–142, 175–176
    counseling for, 175–176
    first step of, 141–142
Group, 36–44, 77–79, 119–122, 132–133
    belonging to, 39
    "code of," 119–121
    conformity to, 42–43, 119–121
    definition of, 36
    division of labor in, 37
    expectations of, 39–44
    experiences in, 38–39
    leaders of, 37–38
    nonconformity to, 42–43
    in organization, 77–79
    personality of, 37–38
    power of, 41–44
    role in, 38–39
    self-protection of, 119–122, 132–133
    unity of, 37–38
Guild, craft, 130

Hawthorne experiment, 163–166
Hedonism, 24–26
Human beings, conditioning of, 33–36
    interdependence of, 33–34
"Human nature," 59–60

Identification, 7–8, 25–26, 41–42
Ideology (see American ideology)
Immigration, control of, 65
Incentive plans, 118–124, 128
    failure of, 118–119, 122–123

Incentive plans, and nonproduction workers, 123–124
  and production workers, 118–123
    group, 121–123
    individual, 118–121
  profit-sharing, 128
  success of, 123
Industrialism, 50–51
Initiative, individual, 48
Insight, 14–16
Interdependence, 33–34
International tension, 52
Interview, 149–153, 188–190
  disciplinary, 188–190
  planning for, 188–190
  in selection, 149–153
Interviewer, training of, 150–151
I.Q., 154

Job significance, loss of, 60–63
Justice, social, 48

Labor, commodity concept of, 61–63
Labor unions (*see* Unions)
Language, 97, 168–169
  and feelings, 168–169
  nature of, 97
Leadership, union, 143–145
Learning, 14–16, 34–35
  by conditioning, 15, 34–35
  by thinking, 14–16
Letters of reference, 156
Lewis, John L., 38
"Line" relationship, 88–89, 108–113, 174–175
  and counseling, 174–175
  definition of, 88–89
  of foremen, 108–113

McGregor, Douglas, 119, 218
Mass production, 61
Materialism, 49
Mayo, Elton, 119
Mental illness, 55–56
Merit rating, methods of, 159–162
Morale, 39–41, 232–233
Mores, 40
Motivation, 22–26, 79, 126–127, 201–212
  for cooperation, 79, 201–212
  and incentive wage, 126–127
  theories of, 22–26
    economic, 22–24
    hedonistic, 24–26

Motives, 20–32
  economic, 22–24
  hedonistic, 24–26
  unconscious, 26–27
  of workers, 20–32
    management views of, 20–21

Needs, 26–32, 42, 69–70, 116, 137–138, 197–198
  for accomplishment, satisfaction of, 69–70, 137–138
  for recognition, 28, 42
  to be accepted, 28
  to be needed, 27–28
  to be respected, 28–30
  to be treated with dignity, 28–30
  to defend self, 30–32, 197–198
  to enhance self, 30–32
  unconscious, 26–27
Negroes, 43, 53
  discrimination and segregation against, 53
  misunderstanding of, 43
New Society, The, 138
Nondirective counseling, 170–174

Old age, 54–55
Organization, 48, 71–78, 94–97, 107–108
  and communication, 94–97
  faith in, 48
  functional, 107–108
  of functions, 71–77
    balance in, 73–74
    coordination of, 71–77
    interrelationship of, 73–75
  objectives of, 71–73
  of people, 76–78

Participation, 127–129
Paternalism, 196–198
Patterson, W. A., 214–215
Pavlov, Ivan, 15
Physical examination, 156
Praise, 103
Promotion, 156–159, 221–222
  by evaluation, 156–159
  policies of, 157–159
  principles of, 157–159
  and public relations, 221–222
Psychological testing, 153–155
Public relations, 213–222
  definition of, 213
  and human relations, 220–221

Public relations, methods of, 216–221
    extracurricular activities, 216–218
    speeches, 219
    writing, 218–219
    and personal conduct, 215–216
    policies, 214–215
    and promotion, 221–222
    and selection, 221–222
Punishment, 103, 114–115, 178–179,
    184–188
    and authority, 114–115
    and feelings of supervisors, 187–188
    methods of, 184–187
        demotion, 186
        discharge, 186–187
        layoff, 186
        reprimand, 103, 185–186
    theories of, 178–179

Race prejudice, 53
Rating, employee, methods of, 159–
    162
Rational behavior, 12
Rationalization, 77
Recognition, 28
Reference, letters of, 156
Religion, faith in, 13, 48
Responsibility, 81, 85–86, 113–114
    assignment of, 113–114
    and authority, 81, 85–86
    delegation of, 113–114
Roethlisberger, F. J., 119
Rules, changes in, 180–183
Rumors, 11

Satisfaction of needs, 116
"Scientific Management," 105–108
Seagoville, Federal Correctional Institu-
    tion, 179–180
Secularism, 50
Selection, 146–156, 221–222
    devices of, 149–156
        application form, 155
        interviewing, 149–153
        letters of reference, 156
        physical examination, 156
        testing, 153–155
    principles of, 146–149
    and public relations, 221–222
Self-coordination, 75–76
Self-interest, 79
Self-picture, 30–32
Self-respect, 102–103

Sensualism, 49
Service rating, 159–162
Sex mores, 52
Skill, 106–107, 131–138
    change of application of, 106–
        107
    craft, 131–138
    non-craft, 134–138
Social classes, 43–44
    folkways of, 43–44
    mores of, 43–44
Social problems, 50–57
    alcohol, 57
    crime, 56–57
    dependency, 54–55
    disease, 55–56
    family life, changes in, 52
    industrialism, 50–51
    international tension, 52
    old age, 54–55
    race prejudice, 53
    sex mores, 52
    statism, 53–54
    urbanization, 50–51
Specialization, 106–107
Speeches, 219
Speed, attitude toward, 49–50
Staff, functions of, 88–91
Staff relationship, 88–91, 114
Statism, 53–54
Status, 104, 226–227

Taylor, Frederick W., 88, 105–108, 118,
    134
Technological change, 133–134
Tension, international, 52
Testing, 153–155
Thinking, emotional, 9, 12
Threat and authority, 114–116

Unions, 21–22, 64, 130–145
    craft, 131–134
    growth of, 64, 136–137
    history of, 64, 136–137
    leadership of, 143–145
    management views of, 21–22, 143–
        144
    non-craft, 134–137
    political structure of, 140–141, 143
    trade, 131–134
Urbanization, 50–51

Values, 224–231
    and attitudes, 224–226
    of management, 228–231

Values, and status, 226–227
  of workers, 228–231
Voluntary effort, 79

Wages, 123–125
  of foremen, 124–125

Wages, inequities in, 123–124
Western Electric Company, 163
Work, 192–196, 198–200
  lost value of, 192–194
  significance of, 198–200
  traditional attitude toward, 194–196